W9-BUH-444

Mr Excel

ON EXCEL

Mr Excel ON EXCEL

Copyright© 2003 by Bill Jelen and Joseph Rubin

All rights reserved. No part of this book may be reproduced or transmitted in any form or by any means, electronic or mechanical, including photocopying, recording, or by any information storage or retrieval system without written permission from the publisher.

Written by:
Bill Jelen and Joseph Rubin

Edited by:
Marie Erb

Cover Design:
Design by Irubin Consulting (http://www.irubin.com)

Published by:
Holy Macro! Books
13386 Judy Avenue Northwest
Uniontown, Ohio, USA 44685

Distributed by:
Holy Macro! Books

First printing:
April 2003
Printed in Hong Kong

Library of Congress Data
Jelen, Bill and Joseph Rubin
Mr Excel ON EXCEL / Bill Jelen and Joseph Rubin
Library of Congress Control Number: 2002117108

ISBN: 0-9724258-3-7

Trademarks:
All brand names and product names used in this book are trade names, service marks, trademarks, or registered trade marks of their respective owners. Holy Macro! Books is not associated with any product or vendor mentioned in this book.

ABOUT THE AUTHORS

Bill Jelen is the principal behind the popular MrExcel.com website. With over 10 million annual pageviews, MrExcel.com is a leading Excel website. Along with a dedicated team of Excel gurus, Bill Jelen provides custom Excel and Access applications for hundreds of clients around the world. He is the author of "Guerilla Data Analysis Using Microsoft Excel" and offers an entertaining seminar on the power tips and tricks for Microsoft Excel.

Contact the Author - consult@MrExcel.com, http://www.MrExcel.com

Joseph Rubin, CPA has over 25 years of financial experience in the accounting industry. He has served as CFO, Controller and run his CPA practice for years. Joseph Rubin, CPA is an independent consultant specializing in the development of applications using Microsoft Excel for the financial industry and has instructed thousands of professionals on Microsoft Excel.

Contact the Author - jrubin@exceltip.com, http://www.exceltip.com

ACKNOWLEDGEMENTS

The authors would like to thank Marie Erb for excellent editing of the book. Jacquie Skrzypiec and Anne Troy for technical expertise with Microsoft Word. Sara Amihud for final layout. Roy Rubin of Irubin Consulting for cover design, Chank Diesel for font design, Cecilia Sveda for logo design.

The original galley proofs of this book were reviewed by several of the MVP's from the MrExcel.com message board. Thanks to Yogi Anand, Chris Davison, Paddy Davies, Juan Pablo Gonzalez, G. Russell Hauf, Ian MacConnell, Ivan Moala, Mark O'Brien, Nate Oliver, William Roe, Richie Sills, Tom Urtis and Joe Was.

Thanks to our families for patience and understanding.

Thanks to the Bill Jelen family, Mary Ellen Jelen, Josh & Zeke Jelen.

Thanks to Joseph Rubin family, Mati Rubin, Roy, Liron & Gil Rubin.

Table of Contents at a Glance

Table of Contents

Chapter 3: Formatting Numbers 43

Chapter 4: Date and Time...................................55

Chapter 8: Summing and Counting 125

Chapter 9: Security and Protection 139

Chapter 13: Customizing Excel 213

Chapter 14:
Opening, Closing and Saving Workbooks 231

Chapter 15: Data 239

Chapter 22: PivotTable 315

Chapter 23: Using Functions and Objects to Extract Data 355

Chapter 28: Other VBA Techniques 437

Foreword

If you are like me, you consider yourself a power user of Microsoft Excel. While we consider ourselves far more proficient than those who are more comfortable in Word than in a spreadsheet, almost everyone that I've met does not understand the full depth of features available in Excel.

In this book, Jelen and Rubin provide us with a wealth of rarely used tips and techniques for unleashing the power of Microsoft Excel. Because Excel was developed to accommodate former users of Microsoft Multiplan and Lotus 1-2-3, we all find that there are many ways to accomplish the same task in Excel. From the first chapter with simple but brilliant methods for saving time navigating the spreadsheet to the powerful & dynamic charts, you will find many new techniques that will take your usage of Excel to the next level.

You will find that the book is dense with tips. There are not long-winded explanations here – you need to stay alert and pay attention because you will learn something new in every paragraph. If you study and learn these tips, you will find that you are far more efficient with Excel, while at the same time, your range of techniques available in Excel will be greatly enhanced.

Best of all, the authors are living, breathing 24/7 resources for your Excel needs. Through their websites at www.MrExcel.com and http://www.exceltip.com, you can find an excellent community of Excel gurus who are ready to share their knowledge and expertise in order to help your Excel skills grow.

Ivana Taylor, Third Force Marketing

Introduction

Microsoft Excel is an incredibly feature-rich product. Far too many people are introduced to Excel through a trial-by-fire basis – they discover they need Excel for their job, learn the basics and then continue to do things the hard way without learning the tips which can cut hours and hours from their routine tasks.

It is very possible to use Excel for 40 hours a week and not be aware of many of the incredibly powerful techniques available to them in Excel. Both of the authors teach others these power tricks in Excel. My favorite experience is to be in front of a room full of accountants who believe they must know everything about Excel because it is their main tool at work. When I hear the first collective gasp from the room within the first two minutes of the seminar, I know that I have hit my stride and will provide an enriching class to these experienced Excel users.

This book is designed for the intermediate to advanced Excel user. It is for the person who can perform the basics with their eyes closed all day but has been too busy to really delve into the menus and learn all of the "new" techniques that were introduced since we all switched over from Lotus to Excel in the 1990's. You should be able to turn to any chapter and find that it is dripping with tips designed to make your use of Excel far more efficient. Dig in & enjoy!

Bill Jelen & Joseph Rubin
2003

Chapter 1

Time is Money
Give Your Mouse
a Break

Is your time valuable? If you are not sure that it is, do not bother reading this chapter – keep using the Excel menus and icons to perform common operations. But if you do value your time, this chapter will attempt to convince you to use the keyboard instead.

This chapter will teach you how to move and maneuver quickly and efficiently between cells in a worksheet and between worksheets and workbooks. You will also learn to select cells and the data they contain quickly. In short, you will learn to save time (if you have decided that it is valuable). The example above illustrates why it is important to work more efficiently.

	Running Number	Invoice Number	Date	Customer Name	Market	Quantity	Income
2	1	101	05/10/1996	MrExcel	USA	15	2,136.75
3	2	102	06/10/1996	Intel	USA	17	2,270.94
4	3	103	07/10/1996	Motorola	Asia	20	10,152.14
5	4	104	08/10/1996	Pacific Bell	Western Europe	50	11,111.11
6	5	105	09/10/1996	Motorola	Asia	100	8,717.95
7	6	107	11/10/1996	Amazon	Asia	15	29,280.00
8	7	108	12/10/1996	Microsoft	Asia	30	6,020.00
9	8	109	01/10/1997	AIG	Asia	40	8,040.00
10	9	110	02/10/1997	Cisco	Asia	50	37,065.81
11	10	111	03/10/1997	MrExcel	USA	67	15,452.00
12	11	112	04/10/1997	Pacific Bell	Asia	77	13,032.00
13	12	113	05/10/1997	Amazon	Africa	89	13,095.00
14	13	114	06/10/1997	Intel	USA	101	23,084.00
15	14	116	08/10/1997	Intel	USA	125	18,495.00
16	15	117	09/10/1997	Microsoft	Asia	138	23,506.50
17	16	118	10/10/1997	AIG	Africa	150	25,129.90
18	17	119	11/10/1997	Pacific Bell	Africa	162	26,753.30
19	18	120	12/10/1997	Microsoft	Asia	174	28,376.70
20	19	121	01/10/1998	Cisco	Asia	186	30,000.10
21	20	122	02/10/1998	Amazon	Africa	198	31,290.86
22	21	123	03/10/1998	AIG	Western Europe	210	32,850.02
23	22	124	10/04/1998	MrExcel	USA	222	34,409.18

When you open a workbook in Excel, you are bombarded with information. You see a worksheet that contains data in every cell.

At first glance, you can't tell what the current region is, if cells contain formulas, how to get to the end of a range of cells containing data, if there are totals beneath the columns, if there are comments in the cells that you ought to read to learn about the data in the worksheet, and more.

Cell, Cells, Move and Select

With scroll bars, you can control the part of the worksheet that appears in the window's frame. In a worksheet, you can scroll vertically, from top to bottom, or horizontally, from side to side. However, using the scroll bars is slow, inefficient and, most of the time, annoying as well. It is even more annoying to use the mouse to select large ranges for copying or printing because the screen flickers incessantly.

The solution is simple--just put your hands on the keyboard. (Kick the habit of using the mouse and give it a break from time to time.) Learn to use keyboard commands!

Tip – Lock the scroll bars

Press **Scroll Lock**, and you will see that the letters SCRL appear in the status bar. Locking the scroll bars lets you use the navigation keys (the four arrow keys and/or **Enter**) the way you would use the wheel on the mouse.

Moving to the last cell in a range

Select cell A1 in your worksheet. See the figure on the next page.

To move vertically from top to bottom, press **Ctrl+Down Arrow**.

To move vertically from bottom to top, press **Ctrl+Up Arrow**.

To move horizontally from left to right, press **Ctrl+Right Arrow**.

To move horizontally from right to left, press **Ctrl+Left Arrow**.

Example: See figure below.

Move from cell A1 to the last cell in a range of cells that contains data (before an empty cell).

Select cell A1 and press **Ctrl+Down Arrow**. The result: You moved to cell A14, the last cell in a range that contains data. (Note: You can also uoo **[End]**, and then Down Arrow, instead of Ctrl+Down **Arrow**.)

Continue and move to the next range of cells that contain data. Press **Ctrl+Down Arrow** again to move to cell A17. Press **Ctrl+Down Arrow** one more time to move to the last cell that contains data in the range that begins with cell A17, and so forth.

Selecting a horizontal or vertical range of adjacent cells

Add the **Shift** key to the combination of keys used above.

By pressing the **Shift** key along with **Ctrl** and one of the four arrow keys, you select a range of adjacent cells.

To select a vertical range of cells that contain data, from top to bottom, press **Ctrl+Shift+Down Arrow**.

To select a vertical range of cells that contain data, from bottom to top, press **Ctrl+Shift+Up Arrow**.

To select a horizontal range of cells that contain data, from left to right, press **Ctrl+Shift+Right Arrow**.

To select a horizontal range of cells that contain data, from right to left, press **Ctrl+Shift+Left Arrow**.

Example: Select a contiguous range from A1 to the end of the data range. In the example, this is A1 through A14. Select cell A1, and press **Ctrl+Shift+Down Arrow**.

To select the range A1 through D14, select cell A1, and press **Ctrl+Shift+Down Arrow**. Continue to hold down the **Ctrl+Shift** keys, and press **Right Arrow**.

 Note

The cells in the range of A1 through A14 and the cells from A1 through D1 contain data. The continuity of data in the vertical cells in column A and in the horizontal cells in row 1 enable the selection of the contiguous range. Delete the data in cell A5, and try this technique again.

Selecting a range of non-adjacent cells

Select cell A1. Press **Ctrl + Shift + Down Arrow**. Continue holding down **Ctrl**, and use the mouse to select another range. Release the mouse button, and select another range while continuing to press **Ctrl**.

Selecting a contiguous or non-contiguous range of cells without pressing Ctrl or Shift

For contiguous selection, press **F8**. The letters **EXT** appear in the status bar. Pressing **F8** extends the selected region. Select cell A1, and extend the selected region by pressing one of the arrow keys.

To toggle off the option of contiguous selection, press **F8** again.

For non-contiguous selection, press **Shift+F8**. The letters **ADD** appear in the status bar. Select a number of non-contiguous ranges by using the mouse to select one range after another.

To toggle off the option of non-contiguous selection, press **Shift+F8** again.

Selecting the current region

The current region is a contiguous range of cells that contain data. The current region is enclosed by blank rows and blank columns and/or the edge of the worksheet.

Ctrl+* (the star above the 9 in the numeric pad) is the keyboard shortcut for selecting the current region.

For those of you using laptops, the shortcut is **Ctrl+Shift+***.

	A	B	C	D	E	F	G	
1	Running Number	Invoice Number	Date	Customer Name		Market	Quantity	Inco
2	1	101	05/10/1996	MrExcel		USA	15	2,13
3	2	102	06/10/1996	Intel		USA	17	2,27
4	3	103	07/10/1996	Motorola		Asia	20	10,1
5	4	104	08/10/1996	Pacific Bell		Western Europe	50	11,1
6	5	105	09/10/1996	Motorola		Asia	100	8,71
7	6	107	11/10/1996	Amazon		Asia	15	29,2
8	7	108	12/10/1996	Microsoft		Asia	30	6,02
9	8	109	01/10/1997	AIG		Asia	40	8,04
10	9	110	02/10/1997	Cisco		Asia	50	37,0
11	10	111	03/10/1997	MrExcel		USA	67	15,4
12	11	112	04/10/1997	Pacific Bell		Asia	77	13,0
13	12	113	05/10/1997	Amazon		Africa	89	13,0
14	13	114	06/10/1997	Intel		USA	101	23,0
15								
16								
17		116	08/10/1997	Intel		USA	125	18,4
18	17	117	09/10/1997	Microsoft		Asia	138	23,5
19	18	118	10/10/1997	AIG		Africa	150	25,1
20	19	119	11/10/1997	Pacific Bell		Africa	162	26,7
21	20	120	12/10/1997	Microsoft		Asia	174	28,3
22	21	121	01/10/1998	Cisco		Asia	186	30,0
23	22	122	02/10/1998	Amazon		Africa	198	31,2

Moving the Cellpointer around a selected range

When you select a range of cells, the borders of the selected range are clearly defined.

To move vertically downward within the selected range, press **Enter**. To move vertically upward, press **Shift+Enter**.

To move horizontally to the right, press **Tab**. To move horizontally to the left, press **Shift+Tab**.

Would you like to move among cells at the corners of the selected range? Press **Ctrl+.** (**Ctrl**+period).

Selecting the first cell in a worksheet

A1 is the first cell in a worksheet.

To return to the first cell in the sheet from any other cell, press **Ctrl+Home**.

Selecting the last cell in the used range

In its memory, Excel stores the address of the last cell in the used range of every sheet in the workbook.

In the figure, the last cell in the used area in the active sheet is determined as the result of entering data into any one of the cells in row 40 and any one of the cells in column K.

The used range in the active sheet is the range of cells from A1 to K40. Therefore, the last active cell in the used area in the active sheet is K40.

To discover which cell is the last cell in the used area in the active sheet, press **Ctrl+End**.

Example: Select a worksheet, and then select cell F1000. Enter data into the cell, and clear the cell. Now press **Ctrl+Home** to move to the first cell. Move to the last cell in the used area by pressing **Ctrl+End**. The last cell in the used area is F1000.

Reducing the used area in a worksheet

Delete rows that do not contain data (rows 38-40 in the figure), and then press **Ctrl+S** to save the file. Press **Ctrl+End**. The address of the last cell in the new used area is K37. The address of the last cell in the used area is updated when the file is saved.

Why is it important to reduce the address of the last cell in the used area?

▣ **Vertical scroll bar** – it gets shorter as the used area of a worksheet grows larger, and this makes it inconvenient to use.

▣ **Print area** – the default print area is the used area in the worksheet. If you do not set a specific range as the print area, Excel will automatically print all of the cells from A1 through that last cell in the used area.

▣ **Display of the current region** – later in this chapter, in the section titled **View all data in the worksheet**, you will want to reduce the used area in order to use this option.

Tip – Easily delete data from cells in the worksheet

The shortcuts **Ctrl+Shift+End** and **Ctrl+Shift+Home** allow you to quickly select a cell that contains data and extend the selection to the beginning of the worksheet or the last used cell in the worksheet.

Select a cell in the worksheet. Press **Ctrl+Shift+End**, and your selection will include all of the cells from the selected cell through the last used cell in the worksheet.

Example: In the worksheet there are about 1,000 rows of data. In order to delete the data from row 21 through the last used cell in the worksheet, select cell A21, press **Ctrl+Shift+End**, and press **Del**.

Rows and Columns

Selecting a column or columns

Select a cell or several cells in a worksheet, and press **Ctrl+Spacebar**.

Selecting a row or rows

Select a cell or several cells in a worksheet, and press **Shift+Spacebar**.

Adding a cell, a row, a column

Press **Ctrl++** (**Ctrl** and the **+** key)

Deleting a cell, a row, a column

Press **Ctrl+-** (**Ctrl** and the **-** key)

Hiding or unhiding a column or columns

Hide – select a cell or cells and press **Ctrl+0**.

Unhide – select the cells to the left and right of the hidden column, and press **Ctrl+Shift+0**.

Hiding or unhiding a row or rows

Hide – select a cell or cells, and press **Ctrl+9**.

Unhide – select the cells above and below the hidden row, and press **Ctrl+Shift+9**.

View All Data in Worksheet

An Excel worksheet is packed with hundreds or thousands of cells containing data. You can either view the complete data region in the worksheet or magnify or reduce the selected data region to the size of the window using the following technique.

1. Select the current region, press **Ctrl+***.

2. Choose **View**, **Zoom**.

3. Select **Fit selection**.

4. Click **OK**.

Increase the amount of data that appears in the window by hiding window elements such as the sheet tabs, toolbars, formula bar and status bar.

1. Choose **Tools**, **Options**.

2. Select the **View tab**.

3. Clear the check boxes for Row & column headers, Horizontal scroll bar, Vertical scroll bar, Sheet tabs, Formula bar and Status bar.

4. Click **OK**.

5. Select **View** (from the Excel menu), and uncheck the selection of Formula Bar and Status Bar.

6. Select any one of the toolbars and right-click. From the shortcut menu, clear the check boxes beside each of the toolbars displayed.

Result

Only the title row is displayed, and more rows are visible.

Microsoft Excel - Chapter1						
File	Edit	View	Insert	Format	Tools	Data	Window	Help

	A	B	C	D	E	F	G
1	Running Number	Invoice Number	Date	Customer Name	Market	Quantity	Income
2	1	109	01/10/1997	AIG	Asia	40	8,040.00
3	2	118	10/10/1997	AIG	Africa	150	25,129.90
4	3	123	03/10/1998	AIG	Western Europe	210	32,050.02
5	4	133	01/10/1999	AIG	USA	331	48,441.63
6	5	138	06/10/1999	AIG	USA	392	56,237.43
7	6	104	08/10/1996	Pacific Bell	Western Europe	50	11,111.11
8	7	112	04/10/1997	Pacific Bell	Asia	77	13,032.00
9	8	119	11/10/1997	Pacific Bell	Africa	162	26,753.30
10	9	128	08/10/1998	Pacific Bell	USA	271	40,645.82
11	10	137	05/10/1999	Pacific Bell	USA	380	54,678.27
12	11	107	11/10/1996	Amazon	Asia	15	29,280.00
13	12	113	05/10/1997	Amazon	Africa	89	13,095.00
14	13	122	02/10/1998	Amazon	Africa	198	31,290.86
15	14	131	11/10/1998	Amazon	Africa	307	45,323.30
16	15	110	02/10/1997	Cisco	Asia	50	37,065.81
17	16	121	01/10/1998	Cisco	Asia	186	30,000.10
18	17	127	07/10/1998	Cisco	Africa	259	39,086.66
19	18	136	04/10/1999	Cisco	Africa	367	53,119.11
20	19	139	07/10/1999	Cisco	Africa	404	57,796.59
21	20	102	06/10/1996	Intel	USA	17	2,270.94
22	21	114	06/10/1997	Intel	USA	101	23,084.00
23	22	116	08/10/1997	Intel	USA	125	18,495.00
24	23	126	06/10/1998	Intel	USA	246	37,527.50
25	24	132	12/10/1998	Intel	USA	319	46,882.46
26	25	101	05/10/1996	MrExcel	USA	15	2,136.75
27	26	111	03/10/1997	MrExcel	USA	67	15,452.00
28	27	124	10/04/1998	MrExcel	USA	222	34,409.18
29	28	130	10/10/1998	MrExcel	USA	295	43,764.14
30	29	140	08/10/1999	MrExcel	USA	416	59,355.75
31	30	108	12/10/1996	Microsoft	Asia	30	6,020.00
32	31	117	09/10/1997	Microsoft	Asia	138	23,506.50
33	32	120	12/10/1997	Microsoft	Asia	174	28,376.70
34	33	129	09/10/1998	Microsoft	Asia	283	42,204.98
35	34	135	03/10/1999	Microsoft	USA	355	51,559.95
36	35	103	07/10/1996	Motorola	Asia	20	10,152.11
37	36	105	09/10/1996	Motorola	Asia	100	8,717.95
38							

Sheet1 / Sheet2 / Sheet3 /

Tip – Using a wheel mouse?

Quickly increase or decrease the percentage of the screen magnification. Select cell A1, press **Ctrl**, and roll the mouse wheel forward or backward.

Moving between Sheets in a Workbook

Each Excel workbook can contain a number of worksheets.

Switching between the sheets is difficult if you use a mouse to select a worksheet by name in the workbook. This is particularly true if the workbook has a large number of sheets and the names of the sheets are long.

There are a number of ways to select a worksheet, aside from the (annoying) method of using the mouse to search for and locate the name of the worksheet among the names of many worksheets.

Using keyboard shortcuts to move between sheets

To move to the next sheet in the workbook, press **Ctrl+Page Down**.

To move to the previous sheet in the workbook, press **Ctrl+Page Up**.

Selecting a sheet from the shortcut menu

To the left of the sheet tabs in the horizontal scroll bar row are several small arrow buttons. Place the mouse pointer over one of the arrows and right-click. From the shortcut menu, select a sheet from the list of sheet names.

Jumping Quickly between Cells in a Workbook

Merely selecting a sheet, no matter which method you use, will not bring you to your destination, which is the specific address you want to reach. The best way to move to the cell in a current sheet or to a cell in a different sheet in the workbook is by selecting the **name** of the cell or the **name** of the range from the **Name box**.

The **Name box** can be found to the left of the formula bar.

Using the Name box

Name box – an address box. Selecting a **name** is the same as selecting the address of the cell or range of cells in the active workbook.

Move to cell – type the cell address in the **Name box**. For example, type Z5000, and press **Enter**. As a result, you will move to cell Z5000 (similar to using **F5** or selecting **Go To...** in the **Edit** menu).

Selecting a large range of cells for copying, cutting or pasting

Example: Copy text from cell A1 to cells A2 through D1000.

1.   Select cell A1.

2.   In the **Name box**, type the cell reference D1000.

3.   Press **Shift+Enter**.

For more information about naming cells and ranges in a workbook, see **Chapter 6, Names**.

Copying, Cutting and Pasting

When using Excel on a regular basis, you repeatedly perform a large number of common operations. The most widely used of the common operations are **Copy**, **Cut** and **Paste**.

Keyboard shortcuts are the fastest way to perform these common operations.

Keyboard shortcuts

Copy	**Ctrl+C**
Cut	**Ctrl+X**
Paste, with the option of repeating the operation	**Ctrl+V**
Paste, without the option of repeating the operation	**Enter**

Paste copied selections to several locations

In Excel version 2000 and higher, you can paste areas that you saved on the Clipboard to several locations.

In Excel 2000, the Clipboard presents the various copied fields (up to 12). In Excel 2002, use the keyboard shortcut **Ctrl+C+C** to open the **Tasks** dialog box, which contains the copied areas that have been saved to memory.

Copying and pasting, using the mouse and keyboard

Press **Ctrl**, and click a cell at the same time. Now drag the cell to a new location. Release the mouse button and the **Ctrl** key.

Cutting and pasting, using the mouse and keyboard

Click and drag the cell a new location, and then release the mouse button.

This method of copying and/or cutting using the mouse with or without the **Ctrl** key is also a good method for copying/cutting rows, columns or an entire worksheet.

Copying a cell with text or a formula to thousands of cells easily

Example: Copy text from cell A1 to cells A2 through A5000.

1. In cell A1, type **Excel Book**.

2. Copy cell A1.

3. Select cell A2.

4. Click the arrow beside the **Name box**.

5. Type **A5000**.

6. Press **Shift+Enter** (select an adjacent range of cells).

7. Press **Enter** (paste).

Copying a cell by double-clicking

1. Select cell C2 (see figure at right).

2. Point to the handle on the bottom right-hand corner of the cell pointer.

3. Double-click when the mouse pointer changes its shape to a plus symbol.

    Excel copies the text or formula in the cell down the length of column B. The cell is pasted to the bottom of the data in the adjacent column.

Moving between Open Workbooks

From the **Window** menu, select a workbook from the list of open workbooks.

The keyboard shortcut for moving between open workbooks is **Ctrl+Tab** or **Ctrl+F6**.

Copying or Moving a Sheet

There is a difference between copying all the cells in a sheet and copying a complete sheet.

Copying cells from a sheet

Select all of the cells in the sheet by pressing **Ctrl+A**, or click the button to the left of the column heading for column A. Press **Ctrl+C**. Select another sheet and select cell A1. Then press **Enter**.

Copying a sheet

Copying a sheet means copying all of the cells, including the page setup and names.

1. **Option 1** – Move the mouse pointer to a sheet tab. Press **Ctrl**, and use the mouse to drag the worksheet to a different location. Release the mouse button and release the **Ctrl** key.

2. **Option 2** – Right-click the appropriate sheet tab. From the shortcut menu, select **Move or Copy**. The **Move or Copy** box lets you copy the worksheet to a different location in the current workbook or move the complete worksheet to a different workbook. Be sure to mark the checkbox beside **Create a copy**.

3. **Option 3** – From the **Window** menu, select **Arrange**, and check the first of the four options. When all of the open workbooks are tiled in the window, use **Option 1** (dragging the worksheet while pressing **Ctrl**) to copy or move a worksheet.

Caution

Moving a worksheet from a workbook with cell names or formulas that are linked to a different worksheet and/or a different workbook will create the links in the new workbook.

After you move the worksheet, from the **Edit** menu, select **Links**, and update or cancel them before you save the new workbook. For more information, see the sections pertaining to links in **Chapter 7, Formulas**.

Chapter 2

Text

Cells in an Excel worksheet can contain different types of characters, including text characters, numbers and dates.

Entering basic text into Excel cells is simple. It can seem complicated if you want to do any of these tasks:

- ▣ Enter a large amount of text, perhaps a few paragraphs in a cell.
- ▣ Edit text once it is entered.
- ▣ Mix formatting in a single cell, i.e., having bold and non-bold text in a single cell.
- ▣ Join multiple text entries into a single cell.
- ▣ Join text in a cell with the results of a formula.
- ▣ Create a header above columns and prevent text from overflowing into certain cells.

Many Excel users do not view Excel as a platform for editing text, but only as a pure spreadsheet. If you are still using Word to create financial statements, you should not be. Excel offers you all of the text editing tools needed to create financial statements, including efficient handling of text. This chapter will try to convince you to create those financial statements in Excel.

Text and Toolbars

Excel offers a large variety of **toolbars** with a wide range of formatting icons. **The following is a list of the toolbars available in Excel 97 and Excel 2000 that are helpful for dealing with text**:

- ▣ Formatting

◨ Drawing

◨ Picture

◨ Shadow Settings

◨ 3-D Settings

◨ WordArt

Excel 2002 includes 3 new toolbars: **NEW
                                                                        IN 2002**

◨ Borders

◨ Drawing Canvas

◨ Power Formatting

A significant addition to the set of toolbars is the Border Toolbar. The icons on the toolbar make it easy for you to draw borders, fill cells in different colors, and use different line styles to mark cell borders. You can also erase borders quickly by turning your mouse into a pencil, just like in graphics programs.

Entering Text in Cells

Excel offers a number of tools to help you enter text in cells:

Using AutoComplete

When you enter text in a cell, Excel searches the column to see if the characters you have entered match an existing entry in that column. If it finds matching text, it will automatically fill in the remaining characters for you. This saves you the trouble of typing in the entire entry (only if you want to take advantage of it).

Selecting from list of Previous Entries

This feature works after you have entered several entries in a column. You can right-click a cell and select **Pick from list** from the shortcut menu. The shortcut is to press **ALT + Down Arrow**. You can then select from a unique sorted list of text that has been entered in that column.

Validating data

By selecting validation criteria, you can prevent entry of incorrect data or data that does not meet the selected criteria. This technique is discussed in more detail later in the chapter.

Moving selection after Enter

Depending on the nature of your data entry, you may want the cellpointer to automatically move to the right or down after entering a value. This is easy to control.

1. Choose **Tools**, **Options** and click the **Edit** tab.

2. Be sure the box next to **Move selection after Enter Direction** is checked.

3. Change the direction of **Move selection after Enter** as desired.

Tips

Prevent moving to the next cell when you finish entering data

Press **Ctrl+Enter**.

To temporarily override the move selection after enter direction, use the **Down Arrow** key instead of **Enter** to move the cellpointer down one row. Use the **Right Arrow** key instead of **Enter** to move the cellpointer to the right.

Selecting a range

Selecting a range will help you enter data efficiently. Select a range of cells, and begin entering data. Use **Enter** to move from cell to cell. The data will be entered in the range of cells selected. When you have entered data into the last cell selected in a column, the cursor will automatically move to the first cell in the next column of the selected range.

Example: Select cells A1 through D5. Assuming the **Enter** direction is set to down, begin entering data. After you have entered data into cell A5, press **Enter**, and cell B1 will be selected automatically.

Using AutoCorrect

Choose **Tools**, **AutoCorrect Options** (in Excel 97, select **AutoCorrect**).

AutoCorrect allows you to correct common typos; exchange text shortcuts for full text, such as 'between' instead of 'betwen' (see figure); and to quickly insert frequently used text.

Example: You can save **The Best Excel Book** with the shortcut **Book**. When you type **Book**, AutoCorrect will automatically replace the entry with the full text, as defined in the AutoCorrect settings.

Tip – Use AutoCorrect to enter special symbols

Example – enter the euro sign in a cell

In the cell, enter the formula =CHAR(168), press **F2**, and then **F0** (**Paste Special**, **Values**). Copy the euro sign from the formula bar by using the **Ctrl+C** shortcut. From the **Tools** menu, select **AutoCorrect**. In the **Replace** box, type "**euro**", and in the **With** box, press **Ctrl+V** (Paste). Click **Add**, and click **OK**.

To check this – in any cell, type the word "euro." The text changes to the euro sign.

Note

AutoCorrect shortcuts for frequently used text defined in **Excel** can be used in **Word**. Likewise, AutoCorrect text you define in **Word** will be available in **Excel**.

Validating Data

When you enter data into a cell, Excel validates the data against validation criteria that you defined. If the data does not validate, it will not be entered into the cell.

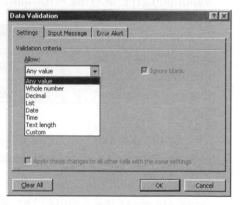

Example: You can set criteria for a range of cells to only allow dates for 2002.

1. Select cells A1:A15.

2. Choose **Data**, **Validation**.

3. Select the **Settings** tab, and in the **Allow** box, click **Date**.

4. In the **Start date** box, enter 1/1/2002.

5. In the **End date** box, enter 12/31/2002.

6. Select the **Input Message** tab.

7. In the **Title** box, enter **Date validation**.

8. In the **Input message** box, enter the criteria or any message you like.

9. **Error Alert** – Select the **Error Alert** tab, and in the **Title** box, enter the title of the alert. In the **Error message** box, enter the date validation criteria. This error alert will appear when the date entered into the cell is found to be invalid and cannot be validated against the validation criteria.

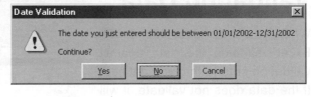

The Error Alert tab has three different options for alerts about errors – **Stop**, **Warning** and **Information**.

The **Stop** option prevents you from typing data into a cell if the data does not meet the criteria. The **Warning** option allows you to enter invalid data, after acknowledging the error in the warning box shown above. The **Information** option only presents information about the criterion, but allows the user to enter invalid data.

Caution

Validation is only performed when data is entered into a cell manually. The **validation** technique does not work on data that is pasted into cells.

In Excel 97, you cannot use **validation** in cells of the frozen titles section of the worksheet.

List

Validation by list allows you to attach lists to cells. By doing this, you can select text from a list or enter text manually. The text will be validated against the list, which actually serves as the validation criteria for the text.

You can create several types of **validation** lists, such as a list of company employees, customer list, account list, inventory list and others.

In the **Data Validation** dialog box, select the **Settings** tab. In the **Allow** box, select **List**.

See the customer list in the figure below.

1. Select the customer list in column A.

2. Press **Ctrl+F3** to define a **name** for the list. In the **Names in workbook** box, enter the name **CustomerList** and click **OK**.

3. Select cells D1:D10.

4. Choose **Data**, **Validation**.

5. Select the **Settings** tab, and in the **Allow** box, select **List**.

6. In the **Source** box, press **F3** and paste the name **CustomerList**.

7. Click **OK**.

8. Select cell D1 and open the customer list (click the small arrow on the right side of the cell). Select one of the customers.

Preventing duplicate data entry

Use **Validation** to enter a formula to catch entry of duplicate data.

1. Select cells A2:A20.

2. Choose **Data**, **Validation**.

3. Select the **Settings** tab.

4. In the **Allow** box, select **Custom**.

    Note – The title of the third box in the dialog box changed to **Formula**.

    Enter the following formula into the box: =COUNTIF($A$2:$A$20,A2)=1

5. Select the **Error Alert** tab.

6. In the **Title** box, enter **duplicate**.

7. In the **Error message** box, enter **The value you entered already appears in the list**.

Validating text entries

The **Allow** box in the **Settings** tab does not include criteria for validating text. You can validate a text entry, but you cannot check whether the entry is text or not.

Solution: Enter a formula that will check whether the data is text.

1. Choose **Data**, **Validation**.

2. Select the **Settings** tab.

3. In the **Allow** box, select **Custom**.

4. In the **Formula** box, enter =IsText(D4) (D4 is the first cell in the range).

5. Click **OK**.

Copying validation

When copying a cell that contains validation criteria to a different cell, the criteria are copied along with the text, formula and format.

If you want to copy only the validation criteria, use **Paste Special**.

To copy only the validation criteria, first copy the cell which contains the validation, and then select a different cell and right-click. From the shortcut menu, select **Paste Special**, click **Validation**, and click **OK**.

Deleting validation criteria

Locate, select and delete validation criteria defined for cells.

1. Press **F5**, and click **Special**. Select **Data validation**, and click **OK**.

2. Choose **Data**, **Validation**.

3. In the **Data Validation** dialog box, click **Clear All**.

Wrapping Text

Text wrapping allows you to display multiple lines of text within a single cell and prevents the text from spilling over into the neighboring cell.

Aside from the visual importance of keeping the text in a single cell, text wrapping is also important when working with data. See **Chapter 15, Data**.

Text wrapping techniques

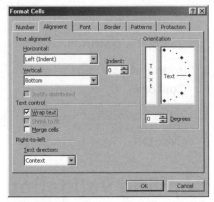

- Automatic text wrapping.

- Manual text wrapping.

- Text wrapping of text that extends beyond the selected range.

Wrapping text automatically

1. Type the following text into a cell A1: **This is the best Excel book ever published**.

2. Press **Enter**.

3. Select the cell.

4. Press **Ctrl+1** (Format Cells).

5. Select the **Alignment** tab.

6. Select **Wrap text**.

7. Click **OK**.

If you cannot see the full text, just resize the cell to make the row or column wider or smaller.

Canceling automatic text wrap

1. Select a cell that is formatted with text wrap.
2. Press **Ctrl+1**.
3. Select the **Alignment** tab.
4. Clear the **Wrap text** check box.
5. Click **OK**.

Wrapping text manually

1. In the **Formula** bar, place the cursor after the word "Excel."
2. Press **Alt+Enter**.

Canceling manual text wrap

1. In the **Formula bar**, place the cursor where you caused the text to wrap, that is, after the word "Excel."
2. Press **Delete**.

Wrapping text beyond the data range

When you enter a long string of text into cell A1, the text spills over into cells that are outside the area of the table (column E) or the print area. You do not want the text to extend into column E. See the example below.

	A	B	C	D	E	F	G
1	List of invoices issued to company customers for the last four years						
2							
3							
4	Invoice Number	Date	Customer Name	Quantity	Income		
5	101	05/10/1996	MrExcel	15	2,136.75		
6	102	06/10/1996	Intel	17	2,270.94		
7	103	07/10/1996	Motorola	20	10,152.14		
8	104	08/10/1996	Pacific Bell	50	11,111.11		
9	105	09/10/1996	Motorola	100	8,717.95		
10	107	11/10/1996	Amazon	15	29,280.00		
11	108	12/10/1996	Microsoft	30	6,020.00		
12	109	01/10/1997	AIG	40	8,040.00		
13	110	02/10/1997	Cisco	50	37,065.81		
14	111	03/10/1997	MrExcel	67	15,452.00		
15	112	04/10/1997	Pacific Bell	77	13,032.00		
16	113	05/10/1997	Amazon	89	13,095.00		
17	114	06/10/1997	Intel	101	23,084.00		
18	116	08/10/1997	Intel	125	18,495.00		
19	117	09/10/1997	Microsoft	138	23,506.50		
20	118	10/10/1997	AIG	150	25,129.90		

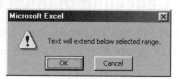

1. Be sure that the text you typed was only entered into cell A1.

2. Select cells A1:E1.

3. Choose **Edit**, **Fill**, **Justify** (**ALT+E+ I+J**).

4. Click **OK** and the following message will appear: **Text will extend below selected range**.

Caution

Before you click **OK**, check if there is data or text in the rows below. Allowing the text to extend below that will overwrite the existing data.

Adding a wrap text shortcut

Wrap text is a useful function that you will use frequently when working in Excel. You add the shortcut by adding a style in the **Style** box. For more information, see **Chapter 5, Styles**.

Adding the Style box to the Formatting toolbar

Right-click one of the toolbars, and select **Customize**. Select the **Commands** tab, and then select **Format**.

Drag the **Style** icon from the **Customize** dialog box to the **Formatting** toolbar, and drop it next to the **Font Size** box (or anywhere else you choose). Then click **Close**.

Adding wrap text to the Style box

Enter text or several words into a cell in the worksheet, and press **Ctrl+1**. Select the **Alignment** tab, check the **wrap text** check box, and click **OK**.

In the **Style** box, enter the text **wrap text**.

Changing the Indentation in a Cell

In the figure, note the text in Column A.

The cells contain a list of expenses for each department, with an indentation of a few characters.

1. Type the text in the cells.

2. Select the list of expenses below each division. For example, select cells A2:A6 (group of expenses for Department 1) and so forth for each group of expenses for each department.

3. Click the **Increase Indent** icon on the **Formatting** toolbar several times, until you reach the indentation you want. Alternatively, select A2:A6; press **Ctrl+1**; select the **Alignment** tab; and in the **Indent** box, change the number of characters to indent. Click **OK.**

Dividing a Title in a Cell

See cell A1 in the figure below.

1. In cell A1, enter the text **Title Number**

2. Select cell A1. In the **Formula** bar, place the cursor after the word **Title**.

3. Press **Alt+Enter** twice (text wrap and an additional row).

4. Press **Ctrl+1** (**Format Cells** dialog box).

5. Select the **Border** tab.

6. Select the **left diagonal border**.

7. Select the **Alignment** tab.

8. In the **Horizontal** box, select **Justify**.

9. In the **Vertical** box, select **Justify**.

10. Click **OK**.

Transposing Data

Transpose is used to change a vertical range of cells to a horizontal range or vice versa.

1. Copy a range of cells (see cells A1:C9 in the figure).

2. Select a cell in the current or any other worksheet and right-click.

3. From the shortcut menu, select **Paste Special**.

4. Check the **Transpose** check box.

The result:

	A	B	C	D	E	F	G	H	I
1	Invoice Number	101	102	103	104	105	106	107	108
2	Customer Name	MrExcel	Intel	Motorola	Pacific Bell	Motorola	Amazon	Microsoft	AIG
3	Income	2,136.75	2,270.94	10,152.14	11,111.11	8,717.95	29,280.00	6,020.00	8,040.00
4									
5									
6									

See the **Array Formula** section of **Chapter 7, Formulas** for a method of transposing using a formula.

Changing a Numeric Heading to Text

When editing reports, you occasionally use numerals in headings. For example, in reports that are organized according to year, you might enter the year 2001 in the heading cells as a number and so forth.

You will want to prevent these numbers from being calculated along with the other numeric data.

The solution: enter the ' (apostrophe) symbol before the number. The result: '2001 as a text entry.

Selecting Cells That Only Contain Text

By selecting cells that only contain text, you can distinguish between cells containing different types of data, which allows you to delete, fill or lock cells by type.

Technique 1

1. Press **F5**, or choose **Edit, Go To...**

2. In the **Go To** dialog box, click **Special**.

3. In the **Go To Special** dialog box, select **Constants**.

4. Click **OK**.

Technique 2 – Conditional Formatting

1. Select the data area.

2. From the **Format** menu, select **Conditional Formatting**.

3. In Condition 1, select **Formula Is**.

4. In the Formula Box, enter the formula =Istext(A1).

5. Click **Format...**, choose any format from the **Format Cells** dialog box, and click **OK**.

6. Click OK.

Searching and Replacing

To search for text, use the keyboard shortcut **Ctrl+F** or choose **Edit, Find**. To search and replace text, use the keyboard shortcut **Ctrl+H** or choose **Edit, Replace**.

Using wild cards in the Text Search

Use * as a wild card for any number of characters. The * may appear before or after text.

Example: Searching for *CO will find Cisco or Telco.

Use ? as a wild card for a single character.

Example: searching for R?N will find Ron or Ran but not Rain.

To search for an asterisk, enter ~* in the search box.

Searching All the Sheets in the Workbook

The shortcut **Ctrl+F** allows you to search only in the active sheet.

To search the entire workbook, you must activate a macro by attaching the macro to a button or icon, or to a keyboard shortcut. (See more **Chapter 26, Running a Macro**.)

```
Sub AllSheetFind()
    Dim i As Integer, sh As Worksheet
    Dim MyFind As Range
    Application.ScreenUpdating = False
    Set sh = ActiveSheet
    Dim Message, Title, MyValue
    Message = "Enter item number"
    Title = "Search Item"
    MyValue = InputBox(Message, Title, Default)
    For i = 1 To Sheets.Count
        Sheets(i).Select
        Set MyFind = Cells.Find(What:=MyValue)
        If Not MyFind Is Nothing Then
            Cells.Find(What:=MyValue).Activate
            Application.ScreenUpdating = True
            Exit Sub
        End If
    Next i
    MsgBox "Item not found, search again"
    sh.Activate
    Application.ScreenUpdating = True
End Sub
```

Using Text Formulas

In the figure below, you can see a list of **text formulas**, including explanation, details (Column E) and the results of the formula's calculation (Column C).

Joining Text

You can create new text by joining text from several cells, including a combination of linked and formatted numbers.

Joining text using a keyboard shortcut

A simple technique for combining, clearing and cutting text is using the keyboard shortcuts **Ctrl+C**, **Ctrl+V**, and **Ctrl+X**.

Example: Select a cell containing text. In the **Formula bar**, select characters or full words and press **Ctrl+C**. Select a different cell, and in the **Formula bar**, enter the location where you want to paste the text you copied. Press **Ctrl+V**.

Joining text using a manual formula

1.   In cell A1, enter the text **This is the**.

2.   In cell A2, enter the text **Best Excel book ever published**.

3.   In cell A3, enter the formula **=A1&" "&A2**.

Explanation

The ampersand symbol (&, Shift+7) joins text the same way the + symbol joins numbers. The quotation marks are used to add empty spaces between them.

In the example above, a space is added between the words combined. In cell A3, you can see the combined sentence. Combining text from different cells results in merged text.

Joining text using the concatenate function

Much like writing a formula to join text, as described, the **Concatenate** function allows you to merge values from multiple cells into a single cell.

In a formula, you create a space between words by pressing the **Spacebar**. In the second box in sample figure, pressing the **Spacebar** will automatically add the quotation marks when you move to the next box.

Joining text with a linked number

Example: Format a number without decimal places, with a thousands separator, and combine it with text.

1. In cell A1, enter the text **You still owe the sum of**.

2. In cell A2, enter the number **5434**.

3. In cell A3, enter the text **for invoice # 2232 from 6/15/2001**.

4. In cell A4, enter the formula =A1&""&TEXT(A2,"#,##0")&""&A3.

Formatting a number with the thousands sign – the letter K

The formula =A1&" "&TEXT(A2,"#,K")&" "&A3

The sentence appearing in the cell – You still owe the sum of 5K for invoice # 2232 from 6/15/2001.

For an explanation of formatting numbers, see **Chapter 3, Formatting Numbers.**

Formatting a date containing text

The formula =A1&" "&TEXT(A2,"mm/dd/yyyy")&" "&A3

The sentence appearing in the cell – On 10/22/2000 you had a cup of coffee…

For more information on the various formatting options, see **Chapter 3, Formatting Numbers**.

Extracting Characters from Text

Using formulas to extract characters from text

Microsoft Excel - Book1								
File Edit View Insert Format Tools Data Window Help					Type a question for help			
B2		*fx* =LEFT(A2,3)						
	A	B	C	D	E	F	G	H
1	Number	first 3 characters	3 characters from middle	2 last characters				
2	10120101	101	201	01				
3	20130102	201	301	02				
4	30140103	301	401	03				
5								
6	Functions in Row 2	=LEFT(A2,3)	=MID(A6,4,3)	=RIGHT(A6,2)				
7								

See figure – A budget item number or an index number in accounting is made up of three parts:

☐   a department number – the first three digits.

☐   the expense item number – the next three digits.

◉ and secondary description of the expense – the last two digits.

Use the formulas shown in Row 6 to extract these portions from the text. You can find the formulas for extracting characters in the **Text** category, under the **Paste function**.

Parsing characters from text without formulas

Use **Text to Columns** to parse text.

1. Select column A.

2. Choose **Data**, **Text to Columns**.

3. In step 1 of 3, select **Fixed width**.

4. Click **Next**.

5. In step 2 of 3, you parse the data in the column by clicking the mouse between columns you want to parse.

6. Click **Next**.

7. In step 3 of 3, in the **Destination** box, enter cell B1.

8. Click **Finish**.

Separating first name and last name

Formulas for separating first name and last name

Cell A1 contains a name – John Smith.

The formula for extracting the first name is =LEFT(A1,FIND(" ",A1)).

The formula for extracting the last name is =MID(A1,FIND(" ",A1)+1,LEN(A1)).

Separating first name and last name without using formulas

The cells in Column A contain a list of names, first name and last name.

1. Select Column A or the range of cells containing the list of names.

2. From the **Data** menu, select **Text to Columns**.

3. In Step 1 of 3, select **Delimited**.

4. In Step 2 of 3, select the **Space** option.

5. In Step 3 of 3, in the **Destination** box, select Cell B1, and click **Finish**.

	A	B	C	D	E	F	G	H
1	Henry Kissinger	Henry	Kissinger					
2	John Dark	John	Dark					
3	Elvis Presley	Elvis	Presley					
4	Bill Clinton	Bill	Clinton					
5								
6								
7								
8								
9								
10								

Chapter 3

Formatting Numbers

Excel offers a wide range of numeric formats, so you can choose the one that best suits your needs. Numeric formats are set on the number tab of the **Format Cells** dialog. To display this dialog, use any of these methods:

▣ Press **Ctrl+1**.

▣ Right click a cell and choose **Format Cells**.

▣ Press **Alt+O+E**.

▣ From the menu, select **Format Cells**.

Although Excel offers a wide variety of formats, the range is incomplete. Standard formats do not offer formats such as formatting negative numbers with parentheses, rounding a number to the thousands, adding characters to the number format (for example, characters that identify weight, like ton and pounds), adding characters like the euro sign in Excel 97, adding words and text to the format, coloring values according to criteria, and more.

With Excel, you can create custom number formats that suit your needs and save them for repeated use.

This chapter teaches you the structure of number formats and the special symbols Excel uses to create number formats.

Where Custom Formats Are Saved

Display the **Format Cells** dialog. Select the **Number** tab, and under **Category** select **Custom**. You will see a list of additional formats. The custom formats that you create are saved in the **Custom** dialog box in the workbook in which you created and saved them.

You can create and save custom number formats and use them in additional workbooks by saving the number format as a **style** in a workbook **template**.

See **Chapter 5, Styles**.

See the **Template** section of **Chapter 13, Customizing Excel**.

Symbols Used in Excel to Format Numbers

Get to know the special symbols you will use to create custom formats.

0 (zero) symbol – displays a digit in a cell, including the digit 0.

Example: The format 0.00 displays the number 0.987 as a number with two places after the decimal point, that is, 0.99 (without the 7). Places are omitted after the number is rounded. Any omitted insignificant digits cause the number to be rounded. In this case, 0.98 was rounded to 0.99.

 # (pound) sign – displays significant digits and does not display insignificant zeroes.

Example: A format with two places after the decimal point, with or without the digit 0:

The format code for 50 cents:

#.##	The cell displays .5
#.#0	The cell displays .50
0.00	The cell displays 0.50

, (comma) – separates thousands

Example: With the format #,##0 the number 4543 is displayed as 4,543.

The comma has a second use in the number format. If you place the comma at the end of the digits, then the displayed number will be divided by 1000 for each comma.

#,##0, will display numbers in thousands

#,##0,, will display numbers in millions

/ (forward slash) symbol – the division sign for displaying a fraction.

* (asterisk) symbol – fills in empty characters, up to the beginning of the number.

Example: The number 4543 is displayed as $ 4,543 with the format $ *#.##0. The $ sign is displayed on the left side of the cell, and the number is displayed on the right side.

"TEXT" – if text characters are enclosed in quotation marks and followed by a number format, the text is displayed and the digits are formatted.

Example: With the format "Balance" #,##0, the number 4543 is displayed as Balance 4,543. In the worksheet cell, you only need to enter the digits, not the text.

\<Any single character> - Use the backslash followed by a single text character to display that character. The following format will display a number in millions: #,##0.0,,\M. Using this format, 123,789,456 would be displayed as "123.8M". Excel will allow you to omit the backslash when displaying a capital letter K. This format will display a number in thousands: #,##0,K. Using this format, 123,789,456 would be displayed as 123,789K.

Special formats, rounding a number to the thousands, displaying in the thousands, displaying text and a number

The figure below shows examples of special formats. The format code is in column D, and the explanation is in column A.

	A	B	C	D
1	**Special Formats**	**Number**	**Result**	**Format**
2	Two decimal places	345345.345	345,345.35	#,##0.00
3	Zero decimal places	345345.345	345,345	#,##0
4	Round to Thousands	345345.345	345	#,###,
5	Round To Millions	23424442377	23,424	#,###,,
6	Round To Millions with hundreds and M letter	23424442377	23,424.4 M	#,##0.0,, \M
7	Round to Thousands with hundreds	345345.345	345.3	0.0,
8	Round to Thousands with hundreds with K letter	345345.345	345.3 K	#,##0.0, \K
9	Number & Text	345345.345	Balance: 345,345	"Balance:" #,##0
10	Number & Characters	345345.345	345,345 T	#,##0 T
11				
12				

The Four Sections of the Format

After you enter a number into a cell, Excel evaluates the number. The format of every number is divided into four sections. Excel uses the results of the evaluation to classify the number and display the correctly formatted number in the cell.

The four sections of the format are positive numbers, negative numbers, zero values, and number+text.

The sections of the format are separated from one another by a semicolon (;).

Formatting a negative number with parentheses, replacing 0 with a dash

The format: #,##0 ;[RED](#,##0) ;- ;

In the example, the format has three sections. Below are step-by-step instructions for formatting.

Formatting the positive section

In the **Type** box, enter #,##0

1. Press the **Spacebar**, and type ; to indicate the end of the section.

   Formatting the negative section

2. Type the color in brackets [RED].

3. Type ((open parentheses), enter the format just as you typed it for the positive number section, and type) (close parentheses).

4. Type ; to indicate the end of the second section.

   Formatting zero values

5. Type the symbol – (minus), use the **Spacebar** to enter five spaces, and type ; to indicate the end of the third section.

6. Click **OK** in the **Formatting Cells** dialog box.

Explanation

On the left hand side of the format (positive number), you left a space. This means that the positive number is entered into the cell with a space on the right side, since the format code for the negative number includes parentheses (see Cells A1 and A2 in the figure).

In the third section of the number format, display of zero values, the resulting 0 in the cell is replaced by a dash. The five spaces you entered position the dash in line with the hundreds place in the positive or negative number (see cell A3 in the figure).

Tip

Is the data in the cell formatted as a date instead of as a number?

Press **Ctrl+Shift+~**.

Special Formats – Examples

The examples in the figure below illustrate format codes for three sections of the number format.

	A	B	C	D
1	Special Formats	Number	Result	Format
2	No decimal places,Brackets,Negative numbers in red,0 replace by dash	-45646	(45,646)	#,##0 ;[Red](#,##0);- ;
3	Round to thousands,Brackets,Negative numbers in red, 0 replace by dash	-45646	(46)	#, ;[Red](#,);- ;
4	Text with special format	-45646	Credit:(45,646)	"Balance:"#,##0 ;[Red]"Credit:"(#,##0);"Zero:"- ;
5	Percentage, brackets for negative	-10.00%	(10.00%)	0.00% ;[Red](0.00%)
6				
7				

Microsoft Excel - Book1
O1
Sheet1 / Sheet2 / Sheet3 / Sheet4 / Sheet5 /

Adding special symbols to the number format

You can add special symbols to the number format, such as symbols that are not included in the currency or accounting formats.

The CHAR formula displays the symbol. To add a symbol to the new format you create, copy the symbol to the **Type** box.

Example: Create a format with the € symbol (euro)

(The symbol does not appear in the format list in Excel 97).

1. Enter the formula **=CHAR(128)** in the cell.

2. Press **F2** and then **F9** to delete the formula and leave the value in the cell.

	A	B
1	120	€
2	129	□
3	130	,
4	131	ƒ
5	132	„
6	133	…
7	134	†
8	135	‡
9	136	^
10	137	‰
11	138	□
12	139	‹
13	140	□
14	141	□
15	142	□
16	143	□
17	144	□
18	145	'
19	146	'
20	147	"
21	148	"
22	149	•
23		

3. In the **Formula** bar, select the € symbol, and press **Ctrl+C** (copy).

4. Select another cell. Press **Ctrl+1**.

5. Select the **Number** tab, and choose **Custom**.

6. In the **Type** box, press **Ctrl+V**.

7. Continue by typing the format code #,##0.

8. Press **Enter**.

The result: €#,##0.

Tip – Insert the Euro sign into AutoCorrect

Refer to **Chapter 2, Text**.

Returning characters specified by numbers

To display all symbols, letters and numbers, create a series of ascending numbers from 33 to 250 in Column A beginning with Cell A1. In Cell B1, type the formula CHAR with a reference to Cell A1. Copy the formula to all the cells in Column B, alongside the series in Column A.

Formatting Numbers According to Criteria

There are two ways to format numbers according to criteria:

▣   Custom formatting for a number with criteria

▣   Conditional formatting

Using custom formats for numbers with criteria

Your options for coloring a number are not limited to displaying negative numbers red. You can color positive and/or negative numbers in any color you wish (do not get excited – the number of colors is limited to eight, and most are difficult to read). Do this by adding the name of the color to the number format in brackets.

Example: [BLUE] #,##0 ;[RED](#,##0)

A positive number is displayed in blue; a negative number is displayed in red; and 0 is displayed in blue (since there is no third section, 0 receives the format of the positive number by default).

Add a condition to the formatting, and have each section be displayed in a different color:

[BLUE] [>5000]#,##0 ;[RED](#,##0); #,##0

Explanation:

A positive number that is greater than 5,000 will be displayed in blue; a negative number will be displayed in red; and positive numbers from 0 to 4,999 in black (the default is applied to the third section of the number format).

Other valid colors are [BLACK], [CYAN], [MAGENTA], [WHITE], [GREEN], and [YELLOW].

Conditional Formatting

With **Conditional formatting,** you can add up to three criteria. The number or text is evaluated according to these criteria, before the custom format for a conditional number is applied.

Select a cell or cells in the sheet. From the **Format** menu, select **Conditional Formatting**.

The figure illustrates three different format conditions, according to the calculated value in the cell(s) you selected.

Totaling Rounded Numbers

How Excel performs calculations

Excel does not take the number format into account when performing mathematical calculations. For example, a cell contains a number with 10 digits after the decimal. The chosen format is a whole number format, with no places after the decimal. When performing the calculation, Excel relates to the entire number, without considering the formatting, for a calculation of up to 15 significant digits.

When the amounts displayed in the cells and the amounts that Excel uses for calculations are different, there can be difference in the number totals.

Example:

In Cells B3 to B7, the numbers were rounded according to their number formats. The total in Cell B8 is not equal to total of the displayed numbers, which is 16.

	A	B	C	D
2				
3	1.11	1	1	
4	2.22	2	2	
5	3.33	3	3	
6	4.44	4	4	
7	5.55	6	6	
8	**16.65**	**17**	**16**	
9				
10	=SUM(A3:A7)	=SUM(B3:B7)	{=SUM(ROUND(C3:C7,0))}	
11				
12				
13				

Microsoft Excel - Book1
File Edit View Insert Format Tools Data Window Help   Type a question for help
Sheet1 Sheet2 **Sheet3** Sheet4 Sheet5

Permanent solution (no way back)

Choose **Tools, Options**.

Select the **Calculation** tab, and select the **Precision as displayed** option.

The result: all the places after the decimal are cut in the cells. The numbers displayed in the cells are whole numbers, and the total is the sum of these whole numbers.

The disadvantage – there is no way to undo this, as the numbers have been permanently cut.

Flexible solution, array formula

Use an **array formula** to total rounded numbers. See the **Array Formula** section of **Chapter 7, Formulas.**

1. In Cell C8 (see figure below), type =ROUND. Press **Ctrl+A**. In the first **Number** box of the ROUND formula, enter the range C3:C7. In the **Num_digits** box, type 0, which rounds the number to the nearest whole number.

2. After the = symbol, type SUM. Then, type ((open parentheses), press **End**, and type) (close parentheses). Press **Ctrl+Shift+Enter** at the same time, creating an **array formula**.

If the formula returns a **#VALUE** error, press **F2**, and then press **Ctrl+Shift+Enter**.

Enter this array formula in every intermediate total. This formula means you do not have to use many ROUND formulas, and the result assures that the totals match the precision that you used in the numeric formats.

Chapter 4

Date and Time

How Excel Calculates Date and Time

Excel handles dates and times numerically. The numbers for dates range from 1 to 2958465. The number 1 indicates the date January 1, 1900, and the number 2958465 indicates the date December 31, 9999.

Enter any number in a cell, press **Ctrl+Shift+#** and see the date for the number you entered.

Because of this numeric method, you can treat dates as values and perform calculations such as subtraction or totaling dates. The results of subtracting an earlier date from a later date are displayed as a number, which (as it happens) is also the number of days between the two dates.

Time, on the other hand, ranges from 0 to 1 and indicates precise time intervals of seconds:

Midnight = 0, noon = 0.5, and 14:09:03 = 0.589618.

Entering the Date in a Cell

Excel recognizes a number as a date by the date format, which uses a slash (/) as a separator.

An example of the date format in Excel: 7/25/2001.

Some users prefer to use a period (.) as a separator, instead of a slash (/).

If you are one of those people and would like to change the default setting for the date format, perform the following steps: From **Windows**, choose **Start, Settings, Control Panel, Regional Options**.

Select the **Date** tab. In the **Date separator** box, change the slash (/) to a period (.). Click **Apply** and **OK**.

Choose a Date Format with a Different Structure

New
In 2002

In the **Format Cells** dialog box (**Ctrl+1**), the **Number** tab shows date formats with a period as a separator instead of a slash.

Easily entering the date in a cell

Use the slash separator (/) on the right side of the keyboard above the number 8 to enter the date. Using this key ensures the correct date format.

Tip – Did you enter a date in a cell, but the cell is formatted as a number?

Press **Ctrl+Shift+#**, and change the formatting to a date format.

Shortcuts for entering current date and time

To enter the current date in a cell, press **Ctrl+;**.

To enter the current time in a cell, press **Ctrl+Shift+;**.

Typing dates in cells quickly

Typing a large amount of data in cells in the sheet can be tiring if it includes a series of dates. Minimize the work by typing the day of the current month and adding the following formula to insert the month and year.

=DATE(YEAR(TODAY()),MONTH(TODAY()),A1)

Type a full number in the cell and change it to a date by using the formula below. For example, type 10222002. The result is 10/22/2002.

=DATEVALUE(LEFT(A1,2)&"/"&MID(A1,3,2)&"/"&RIGHT(A1,4))

Date and time – displaying the number behind the format

Press **Ctrl+~**. This shortcut can also be used to display the syntax of formulas in cells.

Press **Ctrl+~** again to restore the sheet to its normal appearance.

To change a date or time to a number, press **Ctrl+Shift+~** (be careful, as this change is permanent).

Entering Dates Automatically

New In 2002

The **Smart Tag** lets you enter a series of dates automatically. You can enter an ascending series according to days, months and years.

1. Select Cell A1, and press **Ctrl+;**.

2. Click the **Fill handle** at the bottom right edge of Cell A1, and drag it to several cells in the column.

   Do not cancel the selection of the range of dates. Excel creates a series according to days.

3. Click the arrow in the **Smart Tag**.

4. Select **Fill Months**.

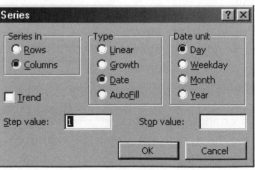

Using the series dialog box to enter a series of dates

1. Select Cell A1, and press **Ctrl+;**.

2. Select Cells A1 through A10.

3. From the **Edit** menu, select **Fill** and then **Series**.

4. In the **Series** dialog box, select **Date** and **Day**.

5. Click **OK**.

Using the shortcut menu to enter a series of dates

1. Select Cell A1, and press **Ctrl+;**.

2. Select the **Fill handle** in the bottom right corner of the cell. The cursor changes to a plus sign (+).

3. Right-click.

4. Drag vertically, and release the mouse.

5. From the shortcut menu, select the series you need.

Automatically Entering Time Data

Entering a time series in intervals of one minute

1. Select Cell A1, and press **Ctrl+Shift+;**.

2. Select Cells A1 through A10.

3. From the **Edit** menu, choose **Fill, Series**.

4. In the **Series** dialog box under **Type**, select **Linear**, and in the **Step value** box, enter 0.000694.

5. Click **OK**.

Entering a time series in intervals of one hour

1. Select Cell A1, and press **Ctrl+Shift+;**.

2. Click the **Fill handle** in the lower right-hand corner of Cell A1.

3. Drag and release the mouse button.

Custom Dates

Customizing the date

1. Select Cell A1 in the sheet, and press **Ctrl+;**.

2. Select Cell A1, and press **Ctrl+1**. Select the **Number** tab, and then select **Custom**.

3. Clear the **Type** box.

In the dialog box, note the sample that appears above the **Type** box. Enter the date format into the box, according to the list of symbols in the date format table.

Date format table

m	Month. The number of the month, without 0 if the number is lower than 10.
mm	Month. The number of the month, including 0 if the number is lower than 10.
mmm	Month. The first three letters of the name of the month are displayed.
mmmm	Month. The full name of the month is displayed.
d	Day. The number of the day of the month, without a 0 if the number is lower than 10.

dd	Day. The number of the day of the month, including 0 if the number is lower than 10.
ddd	Day, as three-character text. For example, Thursday is displayed as **Thu**.
dddd	Day, as complete text. For example, Thursday is displayed as **Thursday**.
yy or y	Year. Two digits. For example, 1997 is displayed as **97**.
yyy or yyyy	Year. The full number of the year is displayed. For example, 1997 is displayed as **1997**.

```
Microsoft Excel - Book 1
 File   Edit   View   Insert   Format   Tools   Data   Window   Help          Type a question for help
         A              B            C          D         E        F        G         H        I
 1  Date Format - Samples
 2
 3  Name            Date of Birth   Month     Format    Day     Format   Year     Format
 4  John            11/05/1971      11        M         5       D        71       YY
 5  Mark            01/01/1950      1         M         1       D        50       YY
 6  Nancy           08/25/1965      08        MM        25      DD       1965     YYYY
 7  Craig           09/18/1945      September MMM       18      DD       1945     YYYY
 8  Brian           03/15/1954      March     MMMM      Monday  DDDD     1954     YYYY
 9  Patrick         03/20/1990      March     MMMM      Tuesday DDDD     1990     YYYY
10  Lee             01/17/1962      January   MMMM      Wednesday DDDD   1962     YYYY
11
12
    Sheet1 / Sheet2 \ Sheet3 / Sheet4 / Sheet5 /
```

Date – Formulas and Calculations

To select a date formula, select **Insert** and then **Function**. In the **Paste Function** box, select **Date & Time**.

Note

It is important to install the add-in **Analysis ToolPak**. The add-in contains many formulas for calculating dates.

To install the Add-In, select **Add-Ins** from the **Tools** menu. Then select **Analysis ToolPak**, and click **OK**.

	A	B	C	D	E
	Microsoft Excel - Book1				
	File Edit View Insert Format Tools Data Window Help				
1	**Function**	**Date**	**Result**	**Syntax**	**Details**
2	TODAY		1/4/2003	=TODAY()	Returns the current date.
3	NOW		1/4/2003 7:51	=NOW()	Returns the current date & time.
4	DAY	1/23/2001	23	=DAY(B4)	Returns the day of a date (from 1 to 31).
5	MONTH	1/23/2001	1	=MONTH(B5)	Returns the month of a date (from 1 to 12).
6	YEAR	1/23/2001	2001	=YEAR(B6)	Returns the year of a date.
7	DATE		1/23/2001	=DATE(C6,C5,C4)	Returns the date for a particular year, month, day.
8	DATEVALUE	1/27/2001	1/27/2001	=DATEVALUE(B8)	Returns the date represented by text.
9	EDATE	1/15/2003	4/15/2003	=EDATE(B9,3)	Returns the date that is the indicated number of months before or after a specified date
10	EOMONTH	1/15/2003	4/30/2003	=EOMONTH(B10,3)	Returns the serial number for the last day of the month that is the indicated number of months before or after start_date.
11	DAYS360	1/15/2003	105	=DAYS360(B11,C10)	Returns the number of days between two dates based on a 360-day year
12	NETWORKDAYS	2/28/2003	33	=NETWORKDAYS(B11,B12)	Returns the number of whole working days between start_date and end_date. Working days exclude weekends and any dates identified in holidays.
13	WEEKDAY	2/2/2003	1	=WEEKDAY(B13)	Returns the day of the week corresponding to a date. The day is given as an integer, ranging from 1 (Sunday) to 7 (Saturday), by default.
14	YEARFRAC	6/17/2003	0.422222	=YEARFRAC(B14,B11)	Calculates the fraction of the year represented by the number of whole days between two dates

Calculating the difference between dates

Use the formula DATEDIF to calculate the difference between dates. The results of the calculation are displayed as days, full months, and full years. The formula is not located in **Paste Function** in the **Date & Time** category. You must enter the formula manually.

	A	B	C	D	E	F
	Microsoft Excel - Book 1					
	File Edit View Insert Format Tools Data Window Help				Type a question for help	
1	**DATEDIF**	**Start Date**	**End Date**	**Diffrence**	**Syntax Function**	
2	Days	3/10/95	12/31/98	1392	=DATEDIF(C4,D4,"d")	
3	Months	3/10/95	12/31/98	45	=DATEDIF(C5,D5,"m")	
4	Years	3/10/95	12/31/98	3	=DATEDIF(C6,D6,"y")	
5						
6	Number of Months above Years	3/10/95	12/31/98	9	=DATEDIF(B8,C8,"ym")	
7	Number of Days above Years	3/10/95	12/31/98	296	=DATEDIF(B9,C9,"yd")	
8						
9						

Sheet1 Sheet2 Sheet3 **Sheet4** Sheet20 Sheet

Calculating the number of the week

To calculate the number of a week, use the **Weeknum** function. This function is included in the **Analysis ToolPak** add-in.

Calculating a quarter number

This section, including the figure below, explains how to calculate the quarter of a calendar year and of fiscal years that begin in July or October.

To calculate a quarter for a calendar year, see the syntax of the formula for Cell B2 as shown in Cell B15.

To calculate a quarter for a fiscal year that begins in October, see the syntax of the formula for Cell B2 as shown in Cell B17.

To calculate a quarter for a fiscal year that begins in July, see the syntax of the formula for Cell D2 as shown in Cell B19.

The formula INT rounds the result of the calculation to a whole number, which represents the quarter.

	A	B	C	D	E
1	Date	Calculate Quarter Number	Calculate Quarter number- Fiscal year starting October	Calculate Quarter number- Fiscal year starting July	
2	01/01/2001	1	2	3	
3	02/01/2001	1	2	3	
4	03/01/2001	1	2	3	
5	04/01/2001	2	3	4	
6	05/01/2001	2	3	4	
7	06/01/2001	2	3	4	
8	07/01/2001	3	4	1	
9	08/01/2001	3	4	1	
10	09/01/2001	3	4	1	
11	10/01/2001	4	1	2	
12	11/01/2001	4	1	2	
13	12/01/2001	4	1	2	
14					
15	Formula Syntax Column B	=INT((MONTH(A2)-1)/3)+1			
16					
17	Formula Syntax Column C	=INT(IF(MONTH(A2)>=10,(MONTH(A2)-1)/3-2,(MONTH(A2)-1)/3+2))			
18					
19	Formula Syntax Column D	=INT(IF(MONTH(A2)>=7,(MONTH(A2)-1)/3-1,(MONTH(A2)-1)/3+3))			
20					

Inserting a function for calculating the number of a quarter in VBA

For an explanation of the technique for creating a customized function and inserting it into the Excel Paste Functions Wizard, see **Chapter 7, Formulas**.

Use the **DatePart VBA** function.

```
Function QuarterNum(Enter_Date)
    QuarterNum = DatePart("q", Enter_Date)
End Function
```

Custom Formatting for Time

Time values exceeding 24 hours

The serial value for time, as explained at the beginning of the chapter, is between 0 and 1.

The time format for a full 24-hour day is HH:MM:SS.

Example: the time 14 hours and 56 minutes is displayed as 14:56:00.

Problem

The default time format does not allow a time value to exceed 24 hours. In a cell, type a value larger than 24 hours, such as 28:56:00. The result is 04:56:00 (the number minus 24 hours).

Solution

Change the format of the cell, and place brackets around the hour. The format is displayed as [HH]:MM:SS, and the result is displayed as 28:56:00.

Time format table

h   Hour. The number of hours, without 0 if the number is lower than 10.

hh   Hour. The number of hours, including 0 if the number is lower than 10.

m   Minute. The number of minutes, without 0 if the number is lower than 10.

mm   Minute. The number of minutes, including 0 if the number is lower than 10.

s   Second. One digit per second, without 0 if the number of seconds is lower than 10.

ss   Second. The number of seconds, including 0 if the number is lower than 10.

[ ]   Brackets around the hour, to display a time value that exceeds 24 hours.

Time – Formulas and Calculations

See the formulas for calculating time in the **Date & Time** section of the **Paste Function** box.

	A	B	C	D	E
1	Function	Time	Result	Syntax	Details
2	NOW		09/29/02 11:02	=NOW()	Returns the serial number of the current date and time.
3	HOUR	23:50	23	=HOUR(B3)	Returns the hour of a time value.
4	MINUTE	13:52	52	=MINUTE(B4)	Returns the minutes of a time value.
5	SECOND	10:30:38	38	=SECOND(B5)	Returns the seconds of a time value.
6	TIME	02:50	11:52 PM	=TIME(C3,C4,C5)	Returns the decimal number for a particular time.
7	TIMEVALUE	3:50:00	03:50	=TIMEVALUE(B7)	Returns the decimal number of the time represented by a text string.

Converting hours to decimals

Use the formulas HOUR and MINUTE to convert a time value to a decimal.

	A	B	C	D	E	F
					Converting Time	
1			Summing Time		to Decimal	Syntax
2		15:10	15:10		15.17	=HOUR(C2)+(MINUTE(C2)/60)
3		20:50	20:50		20.83	
4		23:25	23:25		23.42	
5	Total	11:25	59:25		59.42	
6	Syntax	=SUM(B2:B4)	=SUM(C2:C4)		=SUM(F2:F4)	
7	Foramt Totals in line 5	h:mm	[h]:mm			

E2 = =HOUR(C2)+(MINUTE(C2)/60)

Calculating the difference between hours

Calculate an employee's working hours. In the figure below, notice the format in Cells E4:E8 is hh:mm. The number 1 in the formula IF represents a time value that exceeds 24 hours in a day.

See line 5 in the example. An employee named Mark arrived at work at 23:00 in the evening and finished work at 7:00 the next morning. The result is calculated as 8:00 working hours.

	A	B	C	D	E	F	G
1							
2		Employee Name	Start Time	End Time	Difference	Formula Syntax	
3							
4		John	03:00	11:00	08:00	=D4-C4+IF(C4>D4,1)	
5		Mark	23:00	07:00	08:00		
6		Nancy	19:00	05:00	10:00		
7		Craig	20:00	00:00	04:00		
8		Brian	22:00	03:30	05:30		
9							

Rounding hours up

In the figure below, note the use of the CEILING formula for rounding working hours up. The number 0.04167 is a decimal value of 1/24.

	A	B	C	D	E	F
1						
2		Name	Start Time	End Time	Round up	Formula Syntax
3						
4		John	08:22	12:00	4	=CEILING((+D4-C4)/0.04167,1)
5		Mark	09:43	13:24	4	
6		Nancy	07:25	13:58	7	
7		Craig	10:43	11:20	1	
8		Brian	12:38	13:50	2	
9						
10						

Converting a number to a time value

Excel's ability to convert numbers to time values means you can enter a time value quickly by typing four digits.

Example: Type 2330 for 23:30 in column A. Type the formula shown in row 9 below in column B. Format the cells in column B with the format hh:mm.

	A	B	C	D	E	F
1						
2	Number	Convert To Time				
3	2330	23:30				
4	1059	10:59				
5	622	6:22				
6	1428	14:28				
7						
8	Formula Syntax in Cell B3					
9	=IF(A3<1000,TIMEVALUE(LEFT(A3,1)&":"&RIGHT(A3,2)),TIMEVALUE(LEFT(A3,2)&":"&RIGHT(A3,2)))					
10						

Calculating time differences between regions of the world

The format in the formula cells is [hh]:mm:ss.

	A	B	C	D	E	F
1		NY	LA	London	Tokyo	
2	Hours Difference		5	-5	-14	
3	Local Time	20:00	1:00	15:00	6:00	
4	Formula Syntax in row 3		=$B$3+(C2/24)			
5						

Microsoft Excel - Book1

File Edit View Insert Format Tools Data Window Help

D6

Sheet1

Ready   NUM

Chapter 5

Styles

When you format a cell in a worksheet, you can define cell shading, font color, font, font size, borders, underlining, customized text or number formatting, cell locking, hidden text when protected, and much, much more. In short, there are many definitions that can be set for a single cell.

In **Chapter 2, Text**; **Chapter 3, Formatting Numbers**; and **Chapter 4, Date and Time**, you learned how to format and save special formats using the **Format Cells** dialog box, **Number** tab, and **Custom** in the active workbook.

In **Custom** formatting you save all the formatting you have customized. The main limitation is that all custom formatting is only saved in the current workbook. Without defining a name for the format, it will be difficult for you to find and reuse it. Furthermore, when using this method, you cannot save definitions such as font, patterns, borders and any of the wide variety of formatting options in the **Format Cells** dialog box.

From the **Format** menu, select **Style**. The **Style** dialog box allows you to save numerous styles with names. Each style saves the full range of options that appear in the tabs in the **Format Cells** dialog box.

 Note

The formatting you save as a **Style** is only saved in the current workbook. You can save styles for use in other workbooks by creating a **Template** (see the **Template** section of **Chapter 13, Customizing Excel**).

Copying Formatting

Copying the formatting of one cell to a different cell or to a range of cells, row and column, including row or column width, is an operation commonly performed by Excel users.

Copying formatting with the Format Painter

You can copy and apply formatting by using the **Format Painter** icon that appears on the **Standard** toolbar.

Painting a format repeatedly

Double-click the **Format Painter** or use the **F4** keyboard shortcut, see below.

Using F4 to copy formatting to adjacent and non-adjacent ranges

Select a cell in the sheet (or a range of cells, row or column), and apply the formatting you like. Select additional cells (the selection will include the cell with the formatting as the first active cell in the selected region) by using the **SHIFT** key to select adjacent cells or the **Ctrl** key to select non-adjacent cells. Now press **F4**. The formatting of the active cell will be copied to all of the selected cells.

The F4 key can be very useful when copying formatting such as borders, background color or font color.

Using Paste Special to copy formatting

Paste Special is very useful when you want to copy formatting from one sheet to another. Copy a cell or sheet and select a different cell, range of cells or sheet. Now right-click, and from the shortcut menu, select **Paste Special**. Select **Formats** and click **OK**.

Changing the Default Style in a Workbook

The name of the default style is **Normal**.

Changing the definitions of the style will modify the default format of text or numbers in the workbook.

Style	? X
S̲tyle name: `Normal` ▼	OK
Style includes	Cancel
☑ **N̲umber** General	
☑ **A̲lignment** General, Bottom Aligned, Context Reading Order	Modify...
☑ **F̲ont** Tahoma (Hebrew) 10	Add
☑ **B̲order** No Borders	Delete
☑ **Patterns** No Shading	Merge...
☑ **Pr̲otection** Locked	

1. Choose **Format**, **Style** or use the **Alt+'** shortcut.

2. In the **Style name** box, select **Normal**.

3. Click **Modify**.

4. Select the **Number** tab.

5. In the **Category** box, select **Custom**. In the **Type** box, enter the following format (recommendation only): **#,##0;[Red]-#,##0;0;@**

6. Select the **Font** tab.

7. Select the font and font size you want.

8. Click **OK**.

Explanation

The formatting suggested by default in the workbook allows you to enter both text and numbers into cells. Formatting a cell for text only by selecting the **Text** format from the list of standard formats appearing in the **Category** box in the **Number** tab of the **Format Cells** dialog box will allow *only* text and not numbers to be displayed in the cell. The opposite is also true. If you format a cell for numbers only, you will not be able to display text in the cell.

Number formatting is made up of four parts. See a more detailed explanation in **Chapter 3, Formatting Numbers**. The fourth part of the number format is designed to allow text to be displayed by the inclusion of the @ sign.

Preventing the display of 0

In the third part of the number formatting is the digit 0. You can leave this part empty (by not entering anything between the ;; signs). By doing this you prevent zeroes from being displayed in cells without data.

Creating and Saving Custom Styles

In the **Style** dialog box, you can create a wide range of complex styles and save each one separately with a unique name. These styles can then be applied repeatedly.

Example: Format a number so that a negative number displayed in brackets and zero (0) is replaced with a dash (-). Choose the font and font size.

1. Choose **Format, Style** or press **Alt+'**.

2. In the **Style name** box, enter **Negative Numbers with brackets, 0=-**.

3. Click **Modify**.

4. Select the **Number** tab, and in the **Category** box, select **Custom**.

5. In the **Type** box enter the following number format **#,##0 ;[Red](#,##0);- ;**

6. Select the **Font** tab.

7. In the **Font** box, select **Arial**. In the **Font style** box, select **Regular**, and in the **Size** box, select **10**.

8. Click **OK**.

9. In the **Style** dialog box, click **OK**.

Using the same technique, create many styles in which numbers are rounded to the nearest thousand, underlined with a single line, or underlined with a double line.

Copying (merging) styles from one workbook to another

Excel saves the styles you define in the workbook in which you created and saved them. To use the styles in a different workbook, you need to merge them, or copy them, from one workbook to another.

Open a new workbook.

1. Choose **Format**, **Style**.

2. Click **Merge**.

3. In the **Merge Styles** dialog box, select **Book1** (assuming that this is the workbook that contains the styles you created and want to copy).

4. Click **OK**.

5. If a dialog box appears asking if you want to **Merge Style with Same Format**, click **OK** (only click **OK** if you are sure that you have not created custom styles with the same names, because they will almost surely be overwritten in the update).

6. In the **Style** dialog box, click **OK**.

Note

You can only **merge** styles between open (active) workbooks. Before merging, be sure that the workbook containing the styles you want to merge is open.

Applying a style to a cell or cells in a worksheet

Add the **Style** icon to the **Formatting** toolbar.

1. Select a toolbar.

2. Right-click, and in the shortcut menu select **Customize**.

3. Select the **Commands** tab. In the **Categories** box, select **Format**.

4. From the **Commands** box, select **Style**. Drag the command to the

Customize   ? X

Toolbars | Commands | Options

To add a command to a toolbar: select a category and drag the command out of this dialog box to a toolbar.

Categories: Commands:
File   Cells...
Edit
View   Font:
Insert
Format   Font Size:
Tools
Data   Style...
Window and Help
Drawing   Style:
AutoShapes

Selected command:

Description   Modify Selection

Close

Formatting toolbar, and drop it near the **Font** icon.

See in the figure,

Microsoft Excel - Book1

File Edit View Insert Format Tools Data Window Help

| Arial | | Normal | | 10 | | **B** **U** | ≡ | ⊞ | ⋵ | ⊞ ▾ | ⚫ ▾ | **A** ▾ | Show All | » |

C3

Comma
Comma [0]
Currency
Currency [0]
Negative with Brackets
Normal
Percent
Round to Thousands

	A	B			E	F	G	H	
1									
2									
3									
4									
5									
6									
7									
8									
9									
10									
11									

Sheet1 / Sheet2 / Sheet3 /

The **Formatting** toolbar with the **Style** icon.

Tip – Create styles directly from cells

After you format a cell, you can quickly and easily save that format as a style by entering the name of the style in the **Style** box and then pressing **Enter**.

Note

After you have added the **Style** icon to the toolbar, using the **Alt+'** shortcut lets you select the font in the icon itself. It does not open the **Style** dialog box.

Displaying statements rounded to thousands

By changing the style you can quickly change data in financial statements or any report so that figures are displayed rounded to thousands of dollars in the worksheet, allowing you to print statements that are rounded to thousands.

Select the columns with the data that you want to round, using the technique for selecting non-adjacent columns.

The technique: select the first column, and continue selecting the other columns while pressing the **Ctrl** key.

After you have selected the columns, go to the **Style** box, and select **Round to Thousands**. Want to reapply the previous style so that the data is displayed with cents? Just select another style from the **Style** box.

Chapter 6

Name

What is a Name?

A **Name** can replace the reference of a cell or cells, a row, a column and/or a sheet. After you define it, a name is saved along with its reference in the **Name** box.

The **Name** box appears at the left end of the formula bar.

Why Define Names?

The definition of a **Name** for a cell or a range of cells is essential for efficient and professional work.

1. A **Name** reduces the length of a formula. For example, instead of typing the reference =Sheet2!A1, you can enter the Name that you defined as =David, where David is the name of Cell A1 in Sheet 2.

2. Use **Names** to move quickly to another reference in the workbook, regardless of the name of the sheet. This is an excellent technique to use when handling workbooks that have a large number of sheets.

3. A **Name** takes the place of an absolute reference. It makes copying and pasting formulas easy.

4. Updating a **Name's** reference allows you to dynamically update calculation ranges for formulas, update data ranges in a **PivotTable**, update **Validation** lists, or input ranges in a **Combo Box**.

Name syntax

▣ A **Name** must begin with a text character and not a number (after that, you can add numbers).

▣ A **Name** consists of adjacent characters. Join two words by using an underscore. For example, the name **Excel Book** is illegal. Type **Excel_Book**.

▣ You cannot use a **Name** that could otherwise be confused as a cell reference. For example, you cannot use A1 or IS2002 because these are already cell references.

▣ There is no limit on the number of names you can define.

▣ Be sure to define unique names for a specific workbook. Defining a **Name** that resembles names in other sheets only complicates your work.

Defining a Name

There are two ways to define a **Name**:

Type the text directly in the Name box

1. Select Cell A1.

2. In the **Name box**, type the text.

3. Press **Enter**.

Use the Define Name dialog box

1. Select cell B1.

2. Press **Ctrl+F3**, or from the **Insert** menu, select **Name**, **Define...**

3. Type the text in the **Names in workbook** box.

4. Click **OK**.

Saving names

A workbook saves only the **Names** defined in that workbook.

Deleting names

Press **Ctrl+F3**, select the **Name**, and click **Delete**.

Tip – Delete unnecessary Names

1. Make it easier to locate a **Name**. A large number of Names makes it more difficult to locate a specific **Name**.

2. Names create references. A reference is a link to an address in the active workbook or in another workbook. To delete unnecessary links, see the **Changing links/deleting unwanted links** section of **Chapter 7, Formulas, Links**.

Changing a reference

Press **Ctrl+F3**, and select the **Name**. In the **Refers to…** box at the bottom of the dialog box, change the reference manually, and then click **OK**.

Reviewing names

1. Select any cell in the sheet.

2. Press **F3**.

3. Click **Paste List**.

The list of **Names** in the workbook is pasted into the sheet. Check the list, locate unnecessary **Names** or those with incorrect references, and delete them. In the **Define Names** dialog box, press **Ctrl+F3**.

Automatically defining Names according to the text in the top row and the left column

1. Open a workbook with a data range. There is text in the top row and in the left column.

2. Select the current region and press **Ctrl+***.

3. Press **Ctrl+Shift+F3**, or from the **Insert** menu, select **Name**, **Create**.

4. Select the options **Top row** and **Left column**.

5. Click **OK**.

Open the **Name** box and check to see that the names have been defined.

Entering and Pasting a Name in a Formula

The most important reason for defining **Names** is so that you can paste them in formulas. See figure.

The default for a **Name's** definition is Absolute Reference. In the **Define Name** dialog box, notice that the **Refers to** box contains a $ sign in the NAME reference.

Plan your work and define **Names** before beginning to enter formulas in the sheet's cells.

Automatically entering a name in a formula

1. Type some numbers in Cells B1:B10.

2. Select Cells B1:B10, and define a **Name** for the selected range. Press **Ctrl+F3**, and type **Array** in the **Names in workbook** box.

3. Select Cell B11.

4. Press **Alt+=** or click the **AutoSum** icon, and press **Enter**.

The formula in cell B11: =SUM(Array). Excel recognizes that the cell range has a **Name** and enters it automatically in the formula instead of the ordinary reference.

Pasting a name in a formula

1. Select another cell in the sheet, such as E1.

2. Press **Alt+=** or click the **AutoSum** icon.

3. Press **F3**, or from the **Insert** menu, select **Name**, **Paste**.

4. Select the name **Array**, and click **OK**.

5. Press **Enter**.

The result – the formula for Cell E1 is: =SUM(Array).

 Note

If you define Names after entering formulas in the sheet's cells, the formula will not reflect the Names and you will not have a readable formula.

Example: Type some numbers in the cell range A1:A10.

Select the range A1:A10, and press **Alt+=** or click the **AutoSum** icon (sigma).

The result – the formula in cell A11 is =SUM(A1:A10).

In the example, no **Name** was defined for the cell range before entering the formula.

Pasting Names in a formula's argument boxes

In the sheet illustrated in the figure, define **Names** for the columns based on the text in the first row.

Press **Ctrl+***, and then press **Ctrl+Shift+F3**. In the **Create Names** dialog box, select the first option – **Top row**. Click **OK**.

Account Name	January 2002	February 2002	March 2002	April 2002	May 2002	June 2002
Income	100,000	200,000	300,000	400,000	500,000	600,000
Wages & Salary	-70,000	-71,000	-72,000	-73,000	-74,000	-75,000
Pension & Benefits	-10,000	-11,000	-12,000	-13,000	-14,000	-15,000
Commissions	-1,000	-2,000	-3,000	-4,000	-5,000	-6,000
Car Exp.	-3,000	-3,500	-4,000	-4,500	-5,000	-5,500
Travel	-5,000	-5,100	-5,200	-5,300	-5,400	-5,500
Postage	-1,000	-1,100	-1,200	-1,300	-1,400	-1,500
Training	-1,500	-1,600	-1,700	-1,800	-1,900	-2,000
Office Supplies	-4,000	-4,050	-4,100	-4,150	-4,200	-4,250
Materials	-2,000	-2,050	-2,100	-2,150	-2,200	-2,250

The result

Names were defined for the data ranges in each column. The reference range for the **Name January** is =Sheet1!$B$2:$B$11.

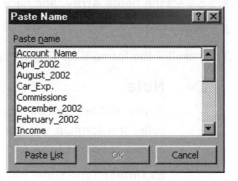

Enter a formula to total the data for the first quarter.

Function Arguments	? X

SUM

Number1	January_2002	= {100000;-70000;-10
Number2	February_2002	= {200000;-71000;-11
Number3	March_2002	= {300000;-72000;-12
Number4		= number

= 295800

Adds all the numbers in a range of cells.

Number3: number1,number2,... are 1 to 30 numbers to sum. Logical values and text
are ignored in cells, included if typed as arguments.

Formula result =   295800

Help on this function   OK   Cancel

1. Select another sheet in the workbook, and select a cell in it.

2. Type the formula =Sum.

3. Press **Ctrl+A**.

4. Select the first argument box and press **F3**.

5. Select the name **January_2002**, and click **OK**.

6. Paste the names **February_2002** and **March_2002** in the next two argument boxes.

7. Click **OK**.

You have entered the following formula into the cell:
=SUM(January_2002, February_2002, March_2002).

The advantages of working with names, as in the example, include:

1. You can enter a formula into a cell without selecting a range in the sheet. It is easy and prevents mistakes.

2. The formula is easy to read and understand.

3. It is easy to review – from the **Name** box, select one of the names that was entered into the formula. In the sheet where the **Name** is defined, the range containing that **Name** is quickly selected.

Replacing a reference in a formula with a newly defined name, after entering the formula into the cell

Now you understand the reason to define names and paste them into formulas, but there are no **Names** in the files in which you have already created reports and tables. Define **Names** and replace their references.

From the **Insert** menu, select **Name**, **Apply**. Select the **Name(s)** that you want to replace, and click **OK**.

Saving a Formula or Numeric Value for Reuse in the Name Box

When working in Excel, you use certain formulas over and over again. Instead, you can enter a formula and save it in the **Define Name** dialog box in the **Refers to** box.

Example: A formula for calculating the number of the previous year:

=Year(Today())-1

Explanation: The formula calculates and returns the number of the previous year – 2002.

1. Press **Ctrl+F3**.

2. In the **Names in workbook** box, type **LastYear**.

3. Type the formula =YEAR(TODAY())-1 in the **Refers to** box.

4. Click **OK**.

Enter the formula into a cell in the sheet.

1. Type the = sign. Press **F3**.

2. Select the name **LastYear**, and click **OK**.

Define Name   ? ×

Names in workbook:

LastYear		OK
		Close
		Add
		Delete

Refers to:

=Year(Today())-1|

Saving values in the Define Name dialog box

In the **Define Name** dialog box, you can save values in the **Refers to...** box, just as you saved the formula in the example above.

Example: The rate of exchange for the euro, defined with the **Name Euro**, is set at 0.88.

Type the amount in Cell A1.

In Cell B1, type the formula =A1/Euro. You do not have to type the text Euro. Instead, use the **F3** shortcut.

Updating a value that was saved as a Name

Press **Ctrl+F3**, select the name **Euro**, change the value of the rate of exchange in the **Refers to...** box, and click **OK**.

 Tip

Save values in the **Refers to...** box. You can save values such as rates of exchange, indexes, and so forth.

Automatically Updating a Name's Reference

One of the most important advantages of replacing a formula's reference with a **Name** is the ability to automatically update the references of the cells in formulas by updating the **Name's** reference.

Updating a **Name's** reference is not very efficient if you use many names in your workbook.

One solution is to use a macro that quickly updates all the Names in the workbook.

Another solution, which does not use a macro, is to define a **Name** with a formula that automatically updates the **Name's** reference.

Example: In the range B2:B11, the name **January_2002** is defined (income from sales).

The formula =SUM(January_2002) returns the total income from sales in January 2002.

	A	B	C	D	E	F	G
1	Account Name	January 2002	February 2002	March 2002	April 2002	May 2002	June 2002
2	Income	100,000	200,000	300,000	400,000	500,000	600,000
3	Wages & Salary	-70,000	-71,000	-72,000	-73,000	-74,000	-75,000
4	Pension & Benefits	-10,000	-11,000	-12,000	-13,000	-14,000	-15,000
5	Commissions	-1,000	-2,000	-3,000	-4,000	-5,000	-6,000
6	Car Exp.	-3,000	-3,500	-4,000	-4,500	-5,000	-5,500
7	Travel	-5,000	-5,100	-5,200	-5,300	-5,400	5,500
8	Postage	-1,000	-1,100	-1,200	-1,300	-1,400	-1,500
9	Training	-1,500	-1,600	-1,700	-1,800	-1,900	-2,000
10	Office Supplies	-4,000	-4,050	-4,100	-4,150	-4,200	-4,250
11	Materials	-2,000	-2,050	2,100	-2,150	-2,200	-2,250
12							
13		2,500					
14							
15							

Adding rows that contain data from additional sales receipts requires updating the reference of the **Name January_2002**.

Solution: In the **Define Name** dialog box, type a formula in the **Refers to...** box and save the formula with the **Name** you defined.

Formula for updating an automatic reference, with a vertical range of cells

The formula =OFFSET('1'!$A$2,0,0,COUNTA('1'!$A:$A))

Explanation: The syntax of the formula OFFSET – (Reference,Rows,Cols,Height,Width)

Offset Reference – the reference of the first cell in the range (in the example, A2).

Rows,Cols – the number of rows and columns, moving from the initial cell (for example, 0 rows and 0 columns).

Height,Width – the height and width, moving from the initial cell.

Define Name   `?` `X`

Names in workbook:

Data

Data

OK

Close

Add

Delete

Refers to:

`=OFFSET(Sh1!$A$1,0,0,COUNTA(Sh1!$A:$A),COUNTA(Sh1!$1:$1))`

In the example, height is calculated by the formula CountA (a formula that returns the number of cells that are not empty in the range). Width has been omitted; in the example, there is no need to determine the width.

Formula for updating an automatic reference, for the name of the current region (data table)

`=OFFSET('1'!$A$1,0,0,COUNTA('1'!$A:$A),COUNTA('1'!$1:$1))`

Explanation

Width (columns) and height (rows) of the data table are calculated by the formula CountA, in which the digit '1' is the name of the sheet containing the formula.

Note

Type an absolute reference carefully (add the $ sign before the row and column reference)

Defining a Name and Updating a Range Reference with a Macro

You can **define a Name** and update a range reference for the **Name** with the same line of code.

After selecting a cell/range of cells, insert the following line:

```
ActiveWorkbook.Names.Add Name:="Table", _
    RefersToR1C1:=Selection
```

Example:

Define a Name and/or update the Name of the cell range A1:A10:

The second line of code is parallel to the shortcut **Ctrl+Shift+Down Arrow**.

```
Sub NameToSelectRange()
    Range("A1").Select
    Range(ActiveCell, ActiveCell.End(xlDown)).Select
    ActiveWorkbook.Names.Add _
        Name:="List", RefersToR1C1:=Selection
End Sub
```

Define a Name and/or update the Name in the active region:

The second line of code is parallel to the shortcut, **Ctrl+***.

```
Sub NameToSelectTable()
    Range("B2").Select
    Selection.CurrentRegion.Select
    ActiveWorkbook.Names.Add Name:="Table", _
        RefersToR1C1:=Selection
End Sub
```

Note

An easier syntax for adding or updating a name to a workbook is

```
Selection.Name = "Table"
```

Chapter 7

Formulas

Entering a Formula into a Cell

Excel offers two options for entering a formula into a cell.

☑ **Typing a formula**

Experienced Excel users prefer to type formulas directly into a cell, in the formula bar. This is a good technique for skilled users who are familiar with the syntax of formulas (where to place commas and parentheses, the order of arguments, and more). If you are not sure of the syntax of the formula, type = and the name of the function, and then press **Ctrl+Shift+A**. You will now see the syntax of the function.

When typing a function in the formula bar, a yellow **Tip** box pops up, which contains the function's syntactic structure.

New In 2002

☑ **Entering data into the function's edit boxes**

The edit boxes guide you in handling the syntax of functions.

Shortcuts for opening the Formula Palette

Ctrl+A – opens the Formula Palette immediately after typing the name of the function. For example, type **=SUM**, and press **Ctrl+A** to open the Formula Palette.

Shift +F3 – opens the **Paste Function** dialog box. Alternatively, use the **Paste Function** icon (*fx*) on the toolbar.

Tip – Enter a formula more quickly by changing the names of the sheets

When you enter a formula that links cells in different sheets in the workbook and you do not use names for the references, the formulas are long and often take up several rows. They are also difficult to enter and edit.

If you rename the sheets with shorter names, such as 1, 2 or 3, the formulas will be shorter. When you are done entering/editing, change the names of the sheets back to meaningful names.

Copying a Formula, Relative and Absolute Reference

Relative reference

When a formula is copied, the relative reference is used. Relative reference is the distance, in rows and columns, between the reference and the cell containing the formula. For example, in Cell A1, type the number 100. In Cell B1, type the formula =A1. Cell B1 is one column to the right of Cell A1. When the formula is copied from Cell B1 to Cell B10, the distance between the reference and the cell containing the formula remains one column. The formula in Cell B10 is =A10.

Absolute reference

Use the previous example, and select Cell B1. In the formula bar, select the reference A1, and press **F4**. The result is =$A$1.

Copy the contents of Cell B1 to Cell B10. Notice that the formula does not change; the formula reference remains constant as =$A$1.

The F4 key

This is an important shortcut. The **F4** shortcut, which deals with relative and absolute references, has four states. Select Cell B1, and then select the formula bar after the = sign. Press **F4** several times. Notice how the formula changes each time you press **F4**.

State 1 – absolute reference to the column and row, =$A$1.

State 2 – relative reference (column) and absolute reference (row), =A$1.

State 3 – absolute reference (column) and relative reference (row), =$A1.

State 4 – relative reference to the column and row, =A1.

Maintaining a relative reference when pasting a formula

In many cases, you copy a formula from cell to cell when you want to avoid changing the reference of the cell containing the formula. In this case, use **F4** to change the formula to absolute, copy it and paste it; then use **F4** to change the original formula back to relative.

Using **F4** twice is annoying, but there is a way to avoid this repetitive task. Copy and paste the formula from the formula bar back to the formula bar, instead of from cell to cell.

For example: Cell A1 contains the formula =A$1. Select the text from the formula bar (that is, select the formula) and press **Ctrl+C** (copy). Leave the formula bar by hitting **Esc** or by clicking **Enter** or **Cancel** (click the √ or the X to the left of *fx* on the formula bar). Select another cell in the sheet and press **Ctrl+V**.

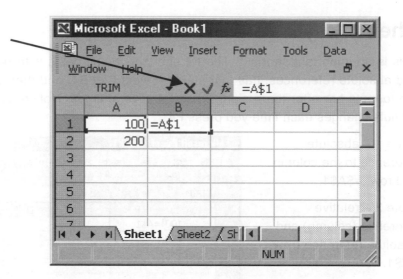

Tip – Copy and paste a range of cells containing formulas without changing the relative reference

Select a range of cells containing formulas. Press **Ctrl+H** to replace the = sign with the # sign. After pasting the cells in a different location, replace the # sign with the = sign.

Nesting Formulas

Nesting is the term for a formula within a formula.

For example:

In Cell A1, type the number 100. In Cell A2, type the number 200.

In Cell B1, enter the formula =SUM(A1:A2) (the result = 300).

In Cell B2, enter the formula =A2-B1 (the result = -100).

In Cell C1, enter the formula =IF(A1>A2,B1,B2).

When the formula in Cell C1 is calculated, the result depends on the values in Cells A1:B2.

In this case, the result in Cell C1 is −100.

In the figure above, note the formula in Cell D1. The IF formula links two formulas.

Excel's method of nesting formulas is not particularly easy if you are interested in using complex formulas.

For example: For Cell E1, type =IF in the formula bar, and press **Ctrl+A**.

In the first edit box for the IF formula, select the relevant cells to enter the formula A1>A2.

Notice the **Name box** to the left of the formula bar. The **Name box** has changed to **Paste Function**. Click the little arrow on the right to open the list of formulas, and select the formula SUM. In the first line of the SUM formula, select Cell A1. In the second line of the SUM formula, select Cell A2. Click **OK**.

The IF box has disappeared. In the formula bar, click between the two right-hand parentheses and type a comma (,); this brings back the IF formula palette. Then type the formula A2-B1, and click **OK**.

This is clearly a tedious process. Chances are you will not manage to nest complex formulas by this method without lots of practice.

Copying and pasting a formula within a formula

This technique is easy. Copy and paste one formula into another by copying the first formula from the formula bar. Then select a new cell, click on the formula bar, and paste using **Ctrl+V**. See **Copying a Formula, Relative and Absolute Reference**; the technique is similar.

For example:

In Cell D1, enter the formula   =SUM(A:A)

In Cell E1, enter the formula   =SUM(B:B)

In Cell F1, enter the formula   =SUM(D1+E1)

Copy and paste all the formulas into a single formula in a single cell, instead of three formulas in three cells. For Cell D1, select in the formula bar SUM(A:A) without the = sign. Press **Ctrl+C** and click the X to exit edit mode for the cell. In the formula bar for Cell F1, select the reference D1, and press **Ctrl+V**

Perform the operation again to copy the formula (without the = sign) from Cell E1 to Cell F1, and paste over the reference E1. The result is a single formula: =SUM(SUM(A:A)+SUM(B:B)).

Adding Statistical Formulas

Analysis ToolPak, Analysis ToolPak-VBA

When Excel is installed on your computer, not all functions are automatically installed. The Analysis ToolPak contains about 100 functions. You must install this add-in if you want to use any of its functions.

You should also install the Analysis ToolPak-VBA add-in. This add-in includes VBA functions that are useful in developing applications in the VBA programming language.

Install both add-ins before beginning to work in Excel.

Installing the add-ins

1. From the **Tools** menu, select **Add-ins**.

2. Select both add-ins, Analysis ToolPak and Analysis ToolPak-VBA.

3. Click **OK**.

Now check to see if the functions included in Analysis ToolPak have been installed. Press **Shift+F3** (**Paste Function**) and select **All**. In **Select Function**, notice the functions whose names are printed in lower-case letters. You have installed these functions by installing the Analysis ToolPak.

Array Formula

Use an **array formula** to create a formula that performs complex calculations.

For example: there are names defined for three ranges:

Range A4:A12	Part_Number
Range B4:B12	Quantity
Range C4:C12	Price

In Cell D16 is the **array formula** ={(SUM(Quantity*Price)}.

The formula returns the result of the Quantity range times the Price range.

Tip – To enter an array formula, you must hold down Ctrl+Shift while hitting enter.

For example:

Cell D19 contains the formula ={SUM(IF(Part_Number=C19,Price*Quantity,0)}.

The formula returns the result of the Quantity times the Price for part number A663.

Use the following technique to enter an **array formula**:

1. In any cell, enter the formula =SUM(Price*Quantity). Define Names before beginning to enter the formula.

2. Press these three keys simultaneously: **Ctrl+Shift+Enter**.

3. The **array formula** is created when these three keys are pressed simultaneously. In order to identify the **array formula**, brackets ({}) are inserted around the formula.

4. If you forget to hold down **Ctrl+Shift** while pressing **Enter**, the formula will evaluate to the **VALUE! ERROR**. If this happens, then press **F2** (Edit Cell), or use the mouse to select any character in the formula bar.

The technical side of array formulas

An **array** saves calculations in the temporary memory, which are used later in the calculation of the total. The ability to save results in the temporary memory allows you to perform complex calculations such as the one displayed.

Using array formulas to create links with a change of direction

Select a range of cells in the sheet, and press **Ctrl+C**. Select the last cell in the sheet, right-click, and select **Paste Special**.

In the **Paste Special** dialog box, there is a **Paste link** option. This option allows you to paste link formulas into cells. The **Paste Special** dialog box also has a **Transpose** option, which pastes the data in the opposite direction (that is, horizontally to vertically, or vice versa).

Problem

You cannot select the **Transpose** option together with the **Paste link** option. In other words, you cannot create a link while changing the direction of the paste operation.

Solution

Use the TRANSPOSE function together with the **array formula** technique to create links that change direction.

First, measure the number of cells in the selected columns and rows. When selecting the range, notice the **Name box**.

Select range A2:B6, which has the name **Range** defined for it. The size of the range is 4Rx2C – that is, four columns by two rows.

Starting with Cell A8, select a range whose size is 2Rx4C – that is, the same size in the opposite direction.

1. Enter the formula =TRANSPOSE, and press **Ctrl+A**.

2. Press **F3**, paste the name **RANGE**, and press **Ctrl+Shift+Enter**.

Creating a link between cells in a workbook

Create a link between two workbooks. In Cell A1 in one workbook, enter a formula that links to Cell A1 in another open workbook.

There are two ways to create links between cells. The first method is between sheets in an active workbook, and the second is between a sheet in one workbook and a sheet in another workbook. Here are two methods for setting up a link between workbooks. The second method is rarely used, but easier.

Method 1 Starting in the destination workbook:

In Cell A1, type the = sign. From the **Window** menu, select another workbook, select Cell B1 in one of its sheets, and press **Enter**.

Method 2 Starting in the source workbook:

Go to the source workbook. Copy Cell B1, and press **Ctrl+Tab** (to move between open workbooks). Select Cell A1, right-click, and from the shortcut menu, select **Paste Special**. Click **Paste link**.

Auditing

Auditing and tracing precedents (cells that contain formulas) or dependent cells (cells that are referenced by formulas) can be a big headache for the Excel user.

Using Names (see **Relative reference** and **Absolute reference**) is very helpful in reducing the time spent auditing and evaluating precedent cells. This section will show you ways to audit and evaluate formulas.

In Excel 2002, the relevant toolbar is called **Auditing formulas**. In Excel 97 and 2000, the toolbar is called **Auditing**.

Auditing formulas toolbar

Select one of the toolbars, and right-click. From the shortcut menu, select **Auditing formulas**.

In Excel 97 and 2000, the **Auditing** toolbar does not appear in the list of toolbars. Select one of the toolbars, right-click, and from the shortcut menu, select **Customize**. Select the **Toolbars** tab, and select the **Auditing** toolbar (or from the Excel menu, select **Tools, Auditing formulas**).

Moving to a precedent cell / moving to a dependent cell

Moving to a precedent cell

Select Cell A1 and click the **Trace precedents** icon on the **Auditing Formulas** toolbar. Double-click the dotted arrow, and in the **Go to** dialog box, select the reference to which Cell A1 is linked. Click **OK**. See the figure below.

Moving to a dependent cell

Select Cell A1 (without a formula), and click the **Trace dependents** icon on the **Auditing formulas** toolbar. Double-click the dotted arrow, and select the cell being referenced. Click **OK**.

Moving between linked cells in a sheet

Select a cell with a formula that is linked in the same sheet (for example, =B10). Click the **Trace precedents** icon on the **Auditing formulas** toolbar. Double-click the blue arrow between the linked cells to move between the precedent cell and the dependent cell.

Keyboard shortcuts to precedent and dependent cells

Precedent cell – **Ctrl+[**

Select all precedent cells – **Ctrl+Shift+{**

Press **F2** or double-click a cell that contains links within the sheet. The precedent cells are indicated in blue.

 ### Tip – Double-click a cell that contains links to mark all precedent cells in the current worksheet

From **Tools**, select **Options**, **Edit**.

Clear the **Edit directly in cell** option, and click **OK**.

Stepping into the Formula

New In 2002

Step into the formula's calculations, one step at a time.

From the **Tools** menu, select **Audit formulas, Evaluate formula**, or from the **Audit formulas** toolbar, click **Evaluate formula**.

Evaluate Formula	? X
Reference:	Evaluation:
Sheet3!$B$1	= IF(A1>A2,A1,A2)

To show the result of the underlined expression, click Evaluate. The most recent result appears italicized.

[Evaluate]   [Step In]   [Step Out]   [Close]

The **Evaluate formula** dialog box allows you to move between the calculations in a formula. Click **Step In** to view a calculation that is part of this formula.

Handling Errors

Entering formulas into cells in Excel sheets is not foolproof. It is impossible to completely avoid mistakes, but there are ways to keep them to a minimum.

The method described in **Nesting Formulas** (see above) will help you to create formulas inside other formulas. Combining the IF formula with the ISERROR formula returns a calculation whose result is TRUE, if the result of a calculation returns an error.

For example:

In Cell A1, type the number 100.

In Cell B1, type the formula =A1/A2. The calculation returns an error - #DIV/0!

The error is created when you try to divide a number in a cell by 0 (A2).

To avoid displaying an error in a cell:

1.   In Cell C1, enter the formula =ISERROR(B1). The formula returns the result TRUE. That is, Cell B1 contains an error in the calculation of the formula (the formula ISERROR is located in the category **Information** in the **Paste Function** dialog box).

2.   In Cell D1, enter an IF formula =IF(C1,0,B1).

3.   Combine the formulas into one nested formula. From Cell C1, copy the formula (without the = sign), and paste it into Cell D1 instead of C1.

4.   From Cell B1, copy the formula (without the = sign), and paste it twice – instead of the digit 0 and instead of B1.

The result – one nested formula: =IF(ISERROR(A1/A2),0,A1/A2).

Function Arguments   ? ×

IF

Logical_test	ISERROR(A1/A2)	= TRUE
Value_if_true	0	= 0
Value_if_false	A1/A2	= #DIV/0!

= 0

Checks whether a condition is met, and returns one value if TRUE, and another value if FALSE.

Value_if_false is the value that is returned if Logical_test is FALSE. If omitted, FALSE is returned.

Formula result =   0

Help on this function   OK   Cancel

Marking Cells Containing Errors

Mark cells containing errors so that they can appear in color, be easily identified, or be deleted.

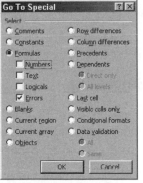

Technique 1

1. Press F5, or from the **Edit** menu, select **Go To...**

2. In the **Go To** dialog box, click **Special...**

3. Select **Formulas**, **Errors**.

4. Click **OK**.

Technique 2

Use conditional formatting to mark and/or color cells containing errors.

1. Make A1 be the active cell. Press **Ctrl+A** to select the sheet.

2. From the **Format** menu, select **Conditional Formatting**.

3. In **Condition 1**, select **Formula Is**.

4. In the formula box, type the formula **=IsError(A1)**. Now click **Format**, and select the desired properties.

5. Click **OK**.

Tracing errors

New
In 2002

In Cell A1, type the number **100**.

In Cell B1, type the formula =A1/A2. The result of the calculation returns the error #!DIV/0!.

Select Cell B1 with the error, and click the **Error checking** icon (the first icon on the left on the **Auditing formulas** toolbar.

Smart tag

New
In 2002

The smart tag for handling errors is created automatically in the cell whose calculation returned an error. Open the shortcut menu by clicking the small **Smart tag** arrow.

Through the shortcut menu, you can get an explanation of the type of error in the formula, edit the formula, ignore errors, and view the evaluation steps by selecting **Show Calculation Steps...**

Circular References

A **circular reference** is created if you enter a formula into a cell and the cell is its own precedent.

The **Circular Reference** toolbar (shown on next page) indicates the reference of the cell containing the circular reference. If you glance at the formula or the Status bar (at the bottom of the sheet), you can pinpoint the source of the error and correct it.

Iteration

You can use a **circular reference** intentionally by using the **Iteration** box. **Iteration** enables circular calculation and offers a method to control it.

For   example: Value-added tax (VAT) gross-up formula

1. In Cell B1, type the formula =B3-B2 (the result of this calculation is a total without VAT).

2. In Cell A2, type the VAT percent (%) 0.17.

3. In Cell B2, type the formula =A2*B1 (calculates the VAT amount). Click **OK** to dismiss the circular reference warning.

4. In Cell B3, type the amount 100.

A **circular reference** is created in Cell B1. The calculation of the amount without VAT is conditioned upon the calculation of VAT in Cell B2.

Select the **Iteration** box to perform a circular calculation.

From the **Tools** menu, select **Options**. In the **Calculation** tab, select the **Iteration** box and click **OK**.

Excel allows you to define the number of iterations (number of times the formula is calculated) until the exact calculation is performed.

Links Between Workbooks

Creating links between workbook sheets

▣ Links are created by formulas.

▣ Links are created by moving sheets with Names from one workbook to another. When you move or copy a sheet by selecting its tab, right-clicking, and then selecting **Move or copy** from the shortcut menu, the sheet with Names that you defined is moved from the active workbook to a new workbook. This results in the creation of unwanted links in the new workbook.

▣ Broken links are created when the location of the precedent workbook is changed on the hard disk. When you save a workbook that is linked to another workbook and then move or copy the linked workbook to another folder on the hard disk, the first workbook still saves the original reference on the hard disk.

Tip – quick creation of link formulas

Use **Paste special** to create links automatically. Copy a range of cells with data, select a cell in another sheet or workbook, right-click, and select **Paste special**. Then click **Paste links**.

Canceling the message about creating links when opening a workbook

1. From the **Tools** menu, select **Options**, and then select the **Edit** tab.

2. On the **Edit** tab, clear the selection of the **Ask to update automatic links** box.

The Edit Links Dialog box

From the **Edit** menu, select **Links**.

Excel 2002 offers new solutions for handling the problem of links between files.

New
In 2002

Source	Type	Update	Status	
Book1.xls	Worksheet	A	Source is open	**Update Values**
Book3	Worksheet	A	Source is open	**Change Source...**
Book4	Worksheet	A	Source is open	**Open Source**
Book5	Worksheet	A	Source is open	**Break Link**
				Check Status

Location: E:\ExcelBookEnglish\Chapter 7

Item:

Update: ⦿ Automatic   ○ Manual

Startup Prompt...   Close

Startup Prompt

New In 2002

Click the **Startup Prompt** button, and define the method of opening linked fil

Startup Prompt [?][×]

When this workbook is opened, Excel can ask whether or not to update links to other workbooks.

○ Let users choose to display the alert or not

○ Don't display the alert and don't update automatic links

○ Don't display the alert and update links

[OK] [Cancel]

Break Links

Select the type of link you want to break, and click **Break links**. The links between workbooks are broken, and the linked formulas are deleted.

Caution

Double-check and make a backup copy of the workbook before breaking the links.

Changing a source

Changing a source allows you to change the location of the workbook on the hard disk or to exchange the location of one workbook for another.

1. Select the workbook in the old location.

2. Click **Change source**.

3. Select the workbook that should be linked in the folder you have opened.

4. Click **OK**. The location of all linked formulas will change.

Changing links and deleting unwanted links

Stage 1 – Check to see if there are any links that were created by Names

1. Select a cell in the sheet.

2. Press **F3**, and click **Paste list**.

3. Check the list, and identify the Names you want to delete.

4. Press **Ctrl+F3**.

5. Select the Name to be deleted, and click **Delete**.

Stage 2 – Check the link in the sheet and find the links that can be deleted

1. Press **Ctrl+F**.

2. In the Find box, type a square bracket ([). Every externally linked formula has a square bracket.

3. Start the search for formulas one cell at a time.

4. Delete unwanted and unnecessary formulas (do this with care).

Stage 3 – Check the data consolidate dialog

1. From the data menu, select **Consolidate**. This dialog remembers the last consolidation.

2. If any items in the **All References** box point to the undesired link, highlight them and click **Delete**.

Stage 4 – Check the link box

1. From the **Edit** menu, select **Links**.

2. Select the name of the workbook whose links you want to delete.

3. Click **Change source**.

4. In the folder, select the workbook you are currently working in (that is, link the workbook to itself).

5. Click **OK**.

Stage 5 – Save the workbook under a new name

If a linked workbook exists and it is not mentioned in the **Links** box, there is a solution. Save the workbook that has links under the name of the workbook to which it is linked (according to the **Links** box). The links are automatically deleted (the new workbook is linked to itself). Save the workbook again under whatever name you wish

Deleting Formulas, Saving Calculation Results

Using formulas does not mean you must keep them after performing calculations with them. Saving a large number of formulas has several disadvantages: It requires a large amount of memory; workbooks have a large file size; links are problematic; and more.

It is vital to delete formulas without deleting the necessary calculated values, whether to solve some of the problems mentioned above or to send reports to other people who should not see the calculation methods that were used.

Deleting formulas, maintaining calculated values

1. Copy the cells with the formulas.

2. Right-click, and from the shortcut menu, select **Paste special**.

3. In **Paste**, select **Values** and click **OK**.

 Tip – Quickly delete the formula without deleting the calculation result

Select a cell containing a formula, press **F2** and then press **F9**.

Deleting formulas and pasting values using a single line of code and a keyboard shortcut

Record a macro adding a Shortcut Key and save the macro in a Personal workbook. Enter the following code to the macro you created:

Selection.Formulas=Selection.Value

Selecting Cells with Formulas

Use the **Go To** dialog box to select formulas in a sheet to delete, to protect (see below), or to color.

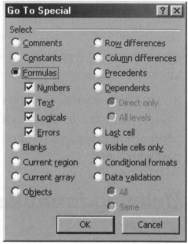

1. Press **F5**, or from the **Edit** menu, select **Go to**.

2. In the **Go to** dialog box, click **Special**.

3. Select **Formulas**.

4. Click **OK**.

Only cells that contain formulas are selected in the sheet.

Identifying and Formatting Cells with Formulas

Excel does not provide a formula that identifies formulas. VBA has a function called HasFormula. The solution is to create a custom function (see explanation at end of chapter) to identify a cell containing a formula.

```
Function FormulaInCell(Cell) As Boolean
FormulaInCell = Cell.HasFormula
End Function
```

Use the technique described below to combine the Get.Cell formula with conditional formatting to format cells containing formulas. After creating the formula FormulaInCell, combine it with Conditional Formatting.

Combining the Get.Cell formula and conditional formatting to format a cell with a formula

Excel includes the macro language XLM. This macro language has a function called Get.Cell. Use this function to identify a formula in a cell by combining it with conditional formatting. The technique is described below.

1. Select a cell in the sheet, and press **Ctrl+F3**.

2. In the **Define Name** dialog box, type the name FormulaInCell.

3. Type the formula =GET.CELL(48,INDIRECT("rc",FALSE)) in the **Reference** field.

4. Select all the cells in the sheet by pressing **Ctrl+A**.

5. From the **Format** menu, select **Conditional formatting**.

6. In **Condition 1**, select **Formula is**.

7. In the formula box, type =FormulaInCell.

8. Click **Format**.

9. From the **Font** tab, select the color **yellow**, and click **OK**.

10. Click **OK**.

Protecting Formulas in Cells

Protecting a cell or a group of cells prevents writing, editing or deleting the cell, or damaging the formula. Two conditions must be met to protect a cell: the cell must be **locked**, and the sheet must be **protected**.

Locking, the first condition

Select a cell in the sheet and press **Ctrl+1**. In the **Format Cells** dialog box, select **Protection**. Select the **Locked** option.

Protecting a sheet, the second condition

From the **Tools** menu, select **Protection**, **Protect sheet**, and click **OK** (password is optional).

Protecting formulas

Protecting formulas requires isolating cells with formulas from the rest of the cells in the sheet, locking them, and then protecting the sheet.

Stage 1 – Canceling the locked format of all the cells in the sheet

1. Select all the cells in the sheet by pressing **Ctrl+A**.
2. Press **Ctrl+1**.
3. Select the **Protection** tab.
4. Clear the selection of the **locked** option.
5. Click **OK**.

Stage 2 – Selecting cells with formulas

1. Press **F5**.
2. Click **Special**.
3. Select the **Formulas** option.
4. Click **OK**.

Stage 3 – Locking cells with formulas

1. Press **Ctrl+1**.
2. Select the **Protection** tab.
3. Select the **Locked** option.
4. Click **OK**.

Stage 4 – Protecting the sheet

1. From the **Tools** menu, select **Protection**, **Protect sheet**.
2. Click **OK** (password is optional).

The **Protect Sheet** dialog box in Excel 2002 allows you to select various topics for protection.

In **Allow all users of this worksheet to...** in the **Protect Sheet** dialog box, select the desired options.

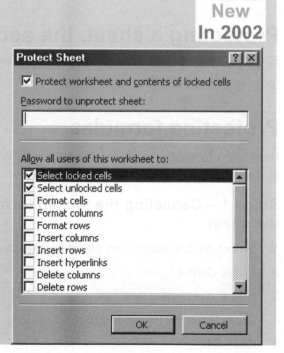

Displaying a Formula in a Cell and Printing Formulas

Displaying formula syntax

The result of calculating a formula (value) appears on the screen and can be printed by clicking the **Print** icon. However, you can usually view the syntax of a formula only by selecting the cell. To see all formulas on the sheet, press **Ctrl+~** (the ~ sign is located to the left of the number 1 on the keyboard), or from the **Tools** menu, select **Options**. Then select the **View** tab, and select the **Formulas** option.

To return to the normal view, press **Ctrl+~** again.

Printing the formula syntax

Use the usual method of printing in Excel to print from the sheet while formulas are displayed using **Ctrl+~**.

Using VBA to Create and Add Functions to the Function Wizard

When you work in Excel, there will be times when you need to create a complex custom formula.

Take, for example, a formula to calculate the net salary from a gross salary. This is a very complex calculation, as this type of formula is made up of fixed pieces of data, including income tax schedule, social security laws, tax credits and additional credits and deductions.

Another example would be a formula for calculating sales commission that varies depending on the level of sales, formulas for converting currency, conversion of weights and measures (a Convert function already exists in Excel), or a conversion of text. See **Chapter 16, Importing Text Files**.

VBA formulas can be used for several reasons, one of which is to create custom functions for your personal use. You can add these functions to the **Function Wizard**.

Custom functions, example and explanation

Create a function called Add to total two numbers in different cells. The function has two argument boxes.

```
Function Add(Number1, Number2) As Integer
    Add = Number1 + Number2
End Function
```

Formula structure:

▣ Function name = Add

▣ The function arguments are placed in parentheses. The above example has two argument boxes.

▣ The last piece of the formula, As Integer, defines the value of the variables as a whole number. See the explanation in the **Variables** section of **Chapter 28, Other VBA Techniques.**

▣ Function calculation – where the function receives the results of the calculation and returns the result.

Location to write and save function:

We advise saving the functions in an active workbook or personal workbook. See the **Storing a macro in a personal workbook section** of **Chapter 26, Running a Macro**.

Activation of function:

1. Type numbers into cells A1:A2.

2. Select cell A3 in the same sheet.

3. Press **Shift+F3** (opens the **Paste Function** dialog box).

4. Select the **User Defined** category.

5. Select the **Add** function.

6. In the first argument box, select cell A1.

7. In the second argument box, select cell A2.

8. Click **OK**.

Using a function to calculate accrued income tax from gross salary

This function will calculate the tax payable based on gross salary, marginal tax schedule and credit point schedule.

The function has a single edit box – gross salary (income).

Schedules – the values are defined using a constant variable, Const, which cannot be changed when the function is operating. The constant variables are loaded into memory cells when the function is operated.

Case – like IF, the function allows you to check a large number of instances.

```
Function IncomeTax(Income) As Single

    Const D1 As Double = 1940
    Const D2 As Double = 3890
    Const D4 As Double = 18560

    Const P1 As Double = 0.1
    Const P2 As Double = 0.2
    Const P3 As Double = 0.3
    Const P4 As Double = 0.45
    Const P5 As Double = 0.5

    Case1 = D1 * P1
    Case2 = (D2 - D1) * P2 + Case1
    Case3 = (D3 - D2) * P3 + Case2
    Case4 = (D4 - D3) * P4 + Case3
    Case5 = (D5 - D4) * P5 + Case4

    Select Case Income
        Case 0 To D1
            IncomeTax = Income * P1
        Case (D1 + 1) To D2
            IncomeTax = (Income - D1) * P2 + Case1
        Case (D2 + 1) To D3
            IncomeTax = (Income - D2) * P3 + Case2
        Case (D3 + 1) To D4
            IncomeTax = (Income - D3) * P4 + Case3
        Case Is > D4
            IncomeTax = (Income - D4) * P5 + Case4
        End Select
End Function
```

Marginal Tax Schedule

% Marginal Tax

Calculation of Accrued Tax

Amount to be returned according to gross income

Function Arguments   ? ✕

┌ IncomeTax ─────────────────────────────────────

   Income B4   = 7500

                                          = 1667

No help available.

   Income

Formula result =   1,667.00

Help on this function   OK   Cancel

Chapter 8

Summing and Counting

If you work in Excel, you are a heavy user of formulas that perform calculations such as summing or counting data. Excel provides you with a number of ways to quickly perform simple mathematical calculations, along with complex techniques for adding data according to criteria, by using formulas such as COUNTIF and SUMIF, and array formulas.

Summing Data Easily

To illustrate several techniques for summing numerical data, create a multiplication table in an Excel sheet.

1. In cells A1:A2, enter the digits 1 and 2, respectively.

2. In cells B1:B2, enter the digits 2 and 4, respectively.

3. Select cells A1:B2. Click the **Fill handle** and copy the cells by dragging down to row 10. Click the Fill handle again drag and across to column J.

4. Select the multiplication table (current region) by selecting cell A1 and pressing **Ctrl+***.

5.   Right-click the **Status bar**. From the shortcut menu, select **Sum**.

The result: As displayed in the Status bar, the resulting total is 3025.

Summing values in a vertical range

Select the multiplication table, and press **Alt+=** or click the **AutoSum** icon (sigma) in the Standard toolbar.

The result: The SUM formula is displayed automatically at the bottom of each column.

Summing values in vertical and horizontal ranges

Delete the row displaying the totals you just created in **Adding values in a vertical range** (click **Ctrl+Z** to Undo). Select the range of data, including the empty rows and columns surrounding the data A1:K11.

 Tip – A quick technique for selecting data without using the mouse: select cell A1, press **Shift**, and select cell K11.

Now press **Alt+=** or click the **AutoSum** icon.

Result: The SUM formula is added to the end of each row and the bottom of each column.

	A	B	C	D	E	F	G	H	I	J	K
1	1	2	3	4	5	6	7	8	9	10	55
2	2	4	6	8	10	12	14	16	18	20	110
3	3	6	9	12	15	18	21	24	27	30	165
4	4	8	12	16	20	24	28	32	36	40	220
5	5	10	15	20	25	30	35	40	45	50	275
6	6	12	18	24	30	36	42	48	54	60	330
7	7	14	21	28	35	42	49	56	63	70	385
8	8	16	24	32	40	48	56	64	72	80	440
9	9	18	27	36	45	54	63	72	81	90	495
10	10	20	30	40	50	60	70	80	90	100	550
11	55	110	165	220	275	330	385	440	495	550	3025

Cell K11: =SUM(A11:J11)

Summing data by selecting cells

Delete the horizontal and vertical totals by pressing **Ctrl+Z** or clicking the **Undo** icon.

To sum the data in cells G1 through J1: select the cells G1:K1 (the selection includes an empty cell), and press **Alt+=** The resulting total is displayed in Cell K1.

Sum subtotals

Delete the total you created by clicking **Undo**.

1. Right-click Row 5. From the shortcut menu, select **Insert**.

2. Select Cell A1, select the current region, press **Ctrl+***, and press **Alt+=** or click the **AutoSum** icon.

3. Select the range A6:J11, and press **Alt+=** or click **AutoSum**.

Result

Row 5 contains the formulas for summing the data in Rows 1:4.

Row 12 contains the formulas for summing the data in Rows 6:11.

Select Cell A1, select the current region, press **Ctrl+***, and press **Alt+=** or click the **AutoSum** icon.

Notice the formula in Cell A13 is =SUM(A12,A5). Excel recognized the subtotals in Rows 5 and 12 and "understood" that these are indeed subtotals.

 Note

Do not leave empty spaces between rows. Excel handles them as borders and creates formulas for summing the data only up to those rows.

Extending the range of sums for the SUM formula

In Cell E15, insert the SUM formula with the total for the data range A1:C5, =SUM(A1:C5). Now, say that we want to extend the range of cells included in the total so that it includes Cell C10.

The technique: Select Cell E1, and press **F2** (to edit the cell). Alternatively, select the formula in the Formula bar. Notice the cell references in the formula.

Click the handle of the range. The handle is located in the bottom right corner of the range, Cell C5. Drag the handle to extend the range. Press **Enter** after you have made your selection.

AutoSum, additional functions

New
In 2002

Excel 2002 has a new icon that offers new **AutoSum** options. Click the small arrow to the right of the **AutoSum** icon to select another function for calculating sums.

To insert the **AutoSum** icon, right-click one of the toolbars. From the shortcut menu, select **Customize**. Select the **Commands** tab, and from the **Insert** category, click and drag the **AutoSum** icon onto the toolbar.

Adding, subtracting, multiplying and dividing without using formulas

In the **Operation** area of the **Paste Special** dialog box, you can perform the four mathematical operations without using formulas. For example, a data range has data in Columns E and F.

1. Copy the cell range E1:E13.

2. Select the range F1:F13.

3. Right-click, and from the shortcut menu, select **Paste Special**.

4. In **Operation**, select **Add**, and click **OK**.

Tip – Multiplying by -1

Use **Paste Special** to multiply a range of numbers by -1.

1. In any cell, type -1.

2. Select the cell and press **Ctrl+C** (copy).

3. Select the range to be multiplied by -1.

4. Right-click, and from the shortcut menu, select **Paste Special**.

5. Select the **Multiply** option.

6. Click **OK**.

If one of the cells contains a formula, *-1 and parentheses are added to the formula.

Tip – Use the Formula Bar to perform quick calculations without a formula

In the Formula Bar, type the = sign, and then multiply two numbers (for example, 8*5). Press **F9**, then press **Enter**.

Summing data in the intersection of two ranges

Cells A1:D10 and Cells A5:E7 contain data. The two areas include some shared cells. Cells A5:D7 are shared.

Sum the data in only the shared area by using the SUM formula.

The formula is =SUM(A1:D10 A5:E7).

The technique is to leave a space between the two ranges.

Summing data from a cell in a number of sheets

Sum a single cell from a number of sheets.

For example: A workbook has four successive sheets. The names of the sheets are January, February, March and April. The formula: =SUM(January:April!B2).

1. Select the sheet in which you want to enter the formula.

2. Type **=SUM(**.

3. Select the tab for the first sheet, **January**.

4. Press **Shift**, and select the tab for the last sheet, **April**.

5. Select Cell B2.

6. Press **Enter**.

Summing According to Criteria, the SUMIF Formula

The SUMIF formula is one of the best and most useful formulas in Excel. The formula allows you to sum data according to various criteria. There is a wide range of criteria available to the SUMIF formula. In the figure below, notice that the total has been calculated according to two different types of criteria: one Is textual, and the other is numeric. The main advantage to the SUMIF formula is that you can sum data in an unsorted range.

The SUMIF formula, arguments

The first argument, Range

Select the range for the criterion.

The second argument, Criteria

Type the criterion (in quotes), or select the cell with the criterion.

The third argument, Sum_Range

Select the range that contains the data to be totaled.

The formula in Cell H4 is =SUMIF(B:B,G4,D:D)

Note

The cell ranges for the first and third arguments must be the same size.

Using two arguments of the SumIf formula

The third argument, Sum_Range, is colored gray in the argument box. This indicates that it is optional to use this argument. This means that you can use the SumIf formula with only the first two arguments.

In other words, sum the data range that you selected in the first argument according to the criteria in the second argument.

Using comparison operators (< >) as criteria

Use the < or > comparison operators as criteria to sum data.

For example:

In Cell G4 (in the figure), type >100. The result is a total of the amounts in Column D of invoice numbers that are greater than 100. You can enter a criterion into a formula (not recommended). If you choose to do so, be sure to place quotation marks before and after the criterion.

The syntax of the formula with criteria in the second argument is =SUMIF(C:C,">100",D:D).

Using SUMIF to sum two ranges according to criteria

The SUMIF formula sums data from a single range only. If you want to use the SUMIF formula to sum or subtract data from different ranges, then you have to create two SUMIF formulas and combine them into a single formula.

The combined formula is =SUMIF(B:B,G4,D:D)-SUMIF(B:B,G4,E:E).

In two cells, enter two SUMIF formulas.

1. In the formula bar, select the formula that is to be copied, without the = sign.

2. Press **Ctrl+C** (Copy).

3. Click **Cancel** (the X sign to the left of the formula in the formula bar).

4. Select the second formula in the formula bar, and at the end of the formula, add a − sign (or + sign).

5. Press **Ctrl+V**.

6. Press **Enter**.

Summing totals with text characters as criteria

With the SUMIF formula, you can find totals according to complex criteria, such as the characters at the beginning of text, in the center of text, and/or special symbols.

In the figure below, notice the wide range of possibilities available for finding totals according to complex criteria.

The COUNT Formula

The COUNT formula comes in several forms. In the figure below, notice the various uses of the COUNT function.

In the **Database** category of **Paste Function**, there are two additional versions of the COUNT formula, the DCOUNT formula and the DCOUNTA formula. **See Chapter 15, Data**.

Counting the number of cells in a range that includes numbers

Example:

A data range that is 10 lines by 10 columns includes 100 cells with numeric data.

The formula is =COUNT(Table) (the **Name** Table was defined for the table of data).

Counting the number of cells in a range that includes text

Add a header row with text to the previous example.

The formula is =COUNTA(Table)-COUNT(Table). The COUNTA formula returns the number of cells in a range that includes any type of data. The COUNT formula returns the number of cells that include only numeric data.

Counting the cells with data according to criteria

The data sheet in the figure below includes **Names** that have been defined for the columns, according to the column headers.

To create **Names** according to headers, select a cell in the data table, press **Ctrl+***, and press **Ctrl+Shift+F3**. Select **Top Row**, and click **OK**.

The AND formula

Count the number of cells in the column **Customer Name = Intel** with the criterion **USA** in the **Market** column. The result of the calculation is 2. The formula is ={SUM((Market="USA")*(Customer_Name="Intel"))}.

The * symbol in the **array formula** returns a result equal to the AND formula. Here is a shortcut for inserting an **array formula** after entering the formula into the cell: select the cell, press **F2** (Edit), and press **Ctrl+Shift+Enter**.

The OR formula

Replace the * sign with the + sign in the formula. The result of the calculation is 18, five cells in the column named **Customer Name**, and thirteen cells in the column named **Market**. The + sign in the **array formula** returns a result equal to the OR formula.

You can use the COUNTIF formula instead of the array formula:

=COUNTIF (Market, "USA")+COUNTIF(Customer_Name, "Intel").

Comparing and Merging Lists, the COUNTIF Formula

The ability to compare two lists helps you to pinpoint the similarities and the differences between the lists. You can identify a name or item that appears in one list and not the other, and names or items that appear in both lists.

See more about comparing lists in **Chapter 21, Consolidating Data**.

A sample list: employees, inventory items, clients, suppliers and/or list of account names in the accounting system, and more. In the example, compare two lists of employees. In the figure below, notice that Column A contains one list of employees and Column E contains the other.

Stage 1 – check each list

In Cell B2, enter the formula =IF(COUNTIF(E:E,A2)>0,3,1).

In Cell F2, enter the formula =IF(COUNTIF(A:A,E2)>0,3,2).

Explanation

The COUNTIF formula returns the total number of times that a particular criterion appears in a range of cells or a column. When the result of the calculation is 3, the name of the employee appears in both lists. When the result of the calculation is 1, the name of the employee appears in the first list. When the result of the calculation is 2, the name of the employee appears only in the second list.

	A	B	C	D	E	F	G
1	List 1	Result	Function syntax		List 2	Result	Function syntax
2	Merrill	1	=IF(COUNTIF(E:E,A2)>0,3,1)		Neil	3	=IF(COUNTIF(A:A,E2)>0,3,2)
3	Neil	3			John	3	
4	Karen	1			Patrick	3	
5	Julie	1			Fred	3	
6	Bonnie	3			Joseph	2	
7	John	3			Bonnie	3	
8	Trudy	1			Bill	2	
9	Woody	1			lee	3	
10	lee	3			Mark	3	
11	Patrick	3					
12	Mark	3					
13	Craig	1					
14	Fred	3					
15							

Stage 2 – merging the lists

Select Cell B2, and click the **Sort Ascending** icon on the standard toolbar.

Select Cell F2, and click the **Sort Ascending** icon on the standard toolbar.

In Column E, beginning with Cell E2, copy the names of those employees for whom the digit 2 appears in Column F. Paste the names at the bottom of the first list.

In the figure below, the second list of employees now includes only those employees whose names do not appear in the first list.

	A	B	C	D	E	F	G
1	List 1	Result	Function syntax		List 2	Result	Function syntax
2	Merrill	1	=IF(COUNTIF(E:E,A2)>0,3,1)		Joseph	2	=IF(COUNTIF(A:A,E2)>0,3,2)
3	Karen	1			Bill	2	
4	Julie	1			Neil	3	
5	Trudy	1			John	3	
6	Woody	1			Patrick	3	
7	Craig	1			Fred	3	
8	Neil	3			Bonnie	3	
9	Bonnie	3			lee	3	
10	John	3			Mark	3	
11	lee	3					
12	Patrick	3					
13	Mark	3					
14	Fred	3					
15							

Cell reference: B2 = =IF(COUNTIF(E:E,A2)>0,3,1)

Sheet1 / Sheet2 / Sheet3

Chapter 9

Security and Protection

Data security is a critical issue in all organizations, as they need to ensure that data is kept confidential both internally and externally. Consequently, it is essential that you are able to prevent intentional or inadvertent deletion of data by other users and that you be able to protect data, formulas and calculations that you worked hard to prepare. These are only some of the reasons why there is a real need for securing and protecting data.

This chapter reviews all of the various options you can use to protect your files and the data they contain.

Security

New In 2002

In **Excel 2002**, a **Security** tab has been added to the **Options** dialog box. It contains a range of options that will help you secure and protect workbooks and the data they contain.

From the **Tools** menu, select **Options**, and then select the **Security** tab.

Security Tab Options

Password to open

By assigning a password to a workbook, you can prevent it from being opened by unauthorized users.

Advanced

Click **Advanced**, and select **Office 97/2000 Compatible**. This option allows you to send a password-protected Excel 2002 file to users of earlier Excel versions.

Digital signature

Adding a digital signature ensures a higher level of security when working with Excel files on a network.

Macro security

The **Macro security** option allows you to adjust the security level for scanning of files that might contain macro viruses.

Using a password to prevent opening a workbook

In Excel 2002, you can prevent the opening of a workbook by adding a password in the **Security** tab, as explained below. In all Excel versions, you can still use a password to prevent opening a workbook.

1. From the **File** menu, select **Save as**.

2. In Excel 97, select **Options**. In Excel versions 2000 and 2002, select **Tools**, **Options**.

3. Type the password twice, and click **OK**.

Protecting Workbooks

Protecting a workbook prevents the structure from being changed. By assigning a password to a workbook, you prevent sheets from being deleted, new sheets from being inserted, and hidden sheets from being opened.

From the **Tools** menu, select **Protection**, **Protect Workbook**. Type a password in the Password box, and click **OK**. Now confirm the password, and click **OK** again.

Unprotecting a workbook

From the **Tools** menu, select **Protection**, **Unprotect Workbook**. Type the password in the Password box, and click **OK**.

Hiding sheets

Excel allows you to hide sheets (one sheet must remain visible). Hiding a sheet or sheets lets you to prevent others from viewing and/or changing data or formulas.

Select the sheet you want to hide. Then, from the **Format** menu, select **Sheet**, **Hide**.

Unhiding sheets

If a workbook is protected, you need to unprotect it before you can unhide a sheet. From the **Format** menu, select **Sheet**, **Unhide**. Now select the sheet you want to unhide, and click **OK**.

Protecting Sheets/Cells

You can protect the content of cells from being changed and/or hide the formulas of cells from being viewed.

Conditions for protecting cells

- The cell must be locked (in the **Format Cells** dialog box).
- The sheet must be protected.

Conditions for hiding text/formula in the Formula bar

- The cell must be hidden (in the **Format Cells** dialog box).
- The sheet must be protected.

Locking/hiding a cell

Select a cell in the sheet, and press **Ctrl+1**. Select the **Protection** tab. By default, Excel automatically checks the **Locked** box and does not check the **Hidden** box.   If you will be protecting your worksheet, remember to unlock cells that you wish to be unprotected.

Protecting a sheet

From the **Tools** menu, select **Protection**, **Protect Sheet**.

In **Excel 2002**, the **Protect Sheet** dialog box allows you to select the operations you want users to be able to perform.

Under **Allow all users of this worksheet to**, select the checkboxes for the operations you want to leave unprotected.

New
In 2002

Protect Sheet   ? X

☑ Protect worksheet and contents of locked cells

Password to unprotect sheet:

Allow all users of this worksheet to:

☑ Select locked cells
☑ Select unlocked cells
☐ Format cells
☐ Format columns
☐ Format rows
☐ Insert columns
☐ Insert rows
☐ Insert hyperlinks
☐ Delete columns
☐ Delete rows

OK   Cancel

In previous versions of Excel, all of the operations appearing in the **Protect Sheet** dialog box were automatically protected, and you could not select them individually.

Moving between unprotected cells in a protected sheet

Move between unprotected cells in a protected sheet by pressing the **Tab** key.

Protecting Data by Hiding Rows and Columns

The range of movement in the sheet displayed in the picture below is A1:E14.

The columns from F forward and the rows from 15 downward are hidden. Consequently, the area that you can move in is restricted to A1:E14.

1. Select Column F.

2. Press **Ctrl+Shift+Right Arrow**.

3. Right-click, and from the shortcut menu, select **Hide**.

4. Select Row 15.

5. Press **Ctrl+Shift+Down Arrow**.

6. Right-click, and from the shortcut menu, select **Hide**.

Unhiding rows and columns

1. Select Row 14, and while pointing the cursor at the row number, click and drag it slightly downward.

2. Right-click, and from the shortcut menu, select **Unhide**.

3. Repeat this technique and unhide columns, as required.

Preventing Movement in Protected Areas

You can divide the area of a sheet containing data into two parts: an area where movement is unrestricted (scroll area) and an area where movement is restricted, meaning that it is protected.

You can set the scroll area in a sheet either by using the Scroll Area macro or by making a change in the sheet's **Properties** dialog box.

Changing properties in the Properties dialog box

To change the sheet's properties, you need to open the macro editor, **VBE**.

1. Press **Alt+F11**.

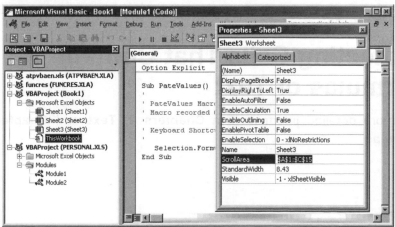

2. Under **VBA Project**, select the sheet for which you want to change the Scroll Area property (You may need to hit **Ctrl+R** to display **VBA Project**).

3. Under **Properties**, select the **Scroll Area** cell (see the picture), and type the reference of the range you want to set as the scroll area. In the figure, note that the reference given is $A$1:$C$15.

4. To close the **VBE** or return to Excel, press **Alt+Q**.

Note

If you can't see the **Properties** dialog box, hit **F4** in the **VBE**.

The result: in the range A1:C15, you can perform any action in the cells. In all the other cells in the sheet, you are restricted to viewing the cells and cannot move or scroll between them.

Using the VBA macro statements

The statement below, for example, sets the scroll area so that the user cannot activate any cells outside it:

```
Sheets(1).ScrollArea = "A1:C15"
```

To set scrolling back to normal, use a statement like the one below:

```
Sheets(1).ScrollArea = ""
```

Protecting Cells That Contain Formulas or Text

See more detailed information in **Chapters 2, Text and Chapter 7, Formulas**.

| Allowing Multiple Users to Edit Ranges | New In 2002 |

From the **Tools** menu, select **Protection**, **Allow Users to Edit Ranges**.

This advanced option allows multiple users (when working on a network for example) to update data in a well-defined and private area. Each user of the workbook is allotted a range in the sheet with a unique password.

Forgotten the Password? There's a Solution

Even if you have forgotten your password, do not despair. In exchange for a fee, software manufacturers will be happy to provide you with a password identification program that will also cancel password protection.

Go to the Internet, and type the words **Excel password** into any search engine. LostPasswords.com provides such a utility. For more information, point your browser to http://ref.lostpassword.com/?118812.

Chapter 10

Information

Excel is more than just an electronic spreadsheet for calculating, editing and printing data.

Excel lets you display and save information in cells by using formulas and lets you add comments to the cell. It also lets you download information from Web sites and view remote results of data and results of calculations through pictures and through a new tool in Excel 2002, the **Watch Window**.

Furthermore, you can link information in cells to objects such as text boxes and use an Excel VBA macro to calculate data and retrieve information from cells.

Viewing Worksheet Name, Workbook Name and Path

The full path of the folder where the active workbook is saved is the type of information you need in order to open or save the workbook.

You can use the **CELL** worksheet function to call information, or alternatively, you can add macros to your workbook that will present the information in the title bar.

Using the CELL worksheet function

The **CELL** worksheet function returns information about a cell, including its formatting, contents and location.

Type the **CELL** worksheet function in a cell (the function can be found in the **Information** category in the **Paste Function** dialog box) with the text filename in quotation marks: =CELL("filename"). The function returns the full path and file name.

Worksheet function that returns the full path:

=MID(CELL("filename"),1,FIND("[",CELL("filename"))-1)

Worksheet function that returns the workbook name:

=MID(CELL("filename"),1,FIND("[",CELL("filename"))+1,
FIND("]",(CELL("filename"))-FIND("[",CELL("filename"))-1)

Worksheet function that returns the sheet name:

=MID(CELL("filename"),FIND("]",CELL("filename"))+1,255)

Adding the path to the title bar or status bar

You can show the full path in the title bar or status bar using a VBA Macro. See **Chapter 14, Opening, Closing and Saving Workbooks**.

Viewing data and information in cells

Watch Window

New
In 2002

In the **Watch Window**, you can view a cell in an active or open workbook. You can view the results of a calculation, see the formula and links, and define the name of the cell.

This is a new and exciting feature that solves a well-known, difficult problem. You can view the resulting change in a distant cell. For example, you can see how changing one parameter affects the results when calculating profit and loss in a budget or when writing a business plan.

Use **Tools**, **Formula Auditing**, **Show Watch Window**.

Picture

Before the Watch Window in Excel 2002, you could use **Paste picture** or the camera icon to see the results of a distant cell.

Creating links for viewing through a picture

1. Select the relevant cells in the sheet, and press **Ctrl+C** (copy).

2. Select a different cell in any worksheet.

3. Press **Shift**. From the **Edit** menu, select **Paste picture**.

 Note

The sub-menu **Paste picture** is added to the **Edit** menu when you press **Shift**. The picture will show the value of the original cell as it changes.

Adding the camera icon to the toolbar

Select one of the toolbars and right-click. Select **Customize**, and then select the **Commands** tab. From **Tools**, select **Camera**, and drag the icon to the toolbar. Click **Close**.

Select a cell or range in the sheet. Click the **Camera** icon, and select a cell in a different sheet or open workbook. Click the cell to create the object.

Use of the **Camera** is limited. You can only view calculation results or the data in a defined range of cells.

Linking Cells to a Textbox or Object

1. From the **Drawing** toolbar, select **Text Box**. Add a text box to the worksheet.

2. Select the **Text Box**, and press **F2**.

3. In the **Formula** bar, create a link to a cell by typing **=** and then selecting the cell. The contents of the cell are displayed in the **Text Box**.

Using a MsgBox to Display Information from Cells

When working in a workbook with many sheets and information, as is the case with a budget or business plan, you need to call up information from various cells with the results of calculations in different cells from different sheets.

If you work in Excel 97 or Excel 2000, you do not have access to the **Watch Window** and using a picture will not solve the problem because it only captures a single range.

The solution is to use a macro to create a **MsgBox**(see **Chapter 27, Write Your First Program**).

Record a macro using a shortcut, such as **Ctrl+Shift+Q**, and type the following code into the macro you are recording:

```
Sub Results()
    Dim A As Long, B As Long, C As Long
    A = Range("CashFlow").Value
    B = Range("NetIncome").Value
    C = Range("IncomeTax").Value

    MsgBox "Cash Flow= " & Format(A, "$#,##0") & vbCr & _
           "Net Income= " & Format(B, "$#,##0") & vbCr & _
           "Income Tax= " & Format(C, "$#,##0"), _
           Title:="ABC Company Business Plan Results"

End Sub
```

Press **Ctrl+Shift+Q**.

The result:

Explanations and Comments:

1. **Define cell names in the workbook** – Before starting to enter the code for the model, define cell names for the cells containing results. In the example, we defined names for three cells – IncomeTax, NetIncome, and CashFlow.

2. **Add new lines in the MsgBox** – Enter the line of code for the **MsgBox** in a single line. It is divided into another line through the letters vbCr.

3. **Number formats** – See the **Format** formula with the variable and how to format it.

4. **Change the text in the message title** – Specify the title in the title parameter.

For more information about **MsgBox** syntax, use the Help function in **VBA**.

Adding Comments to a Formula

Use this trick to add a comment to a formula: at the end of the formula, add a + (plus) sign, the N function, and an open parentheses; then type your comment in quotation marks, and close the parentheses. You can view the comment in the formula bar when you select the cell.

Example:

=A1+A2*4.71+N("Total Sales for January and February * Rate of Exchange")

Saving Information in Comments

Excel lets you add comments to cells. A **Comment** is a box in which you can enter free text. Each comment is limited in length to approximately 32,000 characters.

Adding Comments

1. Select a cell.

2. Press **Shift+F2** or right-click, and from the shortcut menu, select **Insert Comment**.

3. In the Comment box, type the text you want.

By default, Excel does not display comments. The comment is displayed when you have the mouse pointer over the **small red triangle** in the upper right corner of any cell with a comment.

Changing the Name of the Comment Author

By default, each comment includes the author's name. To change or cancel the name of the comment author, perform the following steps: From the **Tools** menu, select **Options**, **General**, and **User name**. Change or delete the user name as desired. The change will only apply to new comments that you insert.

Changing the Default Comment Format

Changes to the default format of **Comments** are done from the **Display Properties** dialog box in **Windows**.

1. Minimize Excel and any other open programs.

2. Right-click. From the desktop shortcut menu, select **Properties**.

3. Select the **Appearance** tab.

4. In the **Item** box, select **ToolTip**, and change the color.

5. In the **Font** box, change the font as desired, and select the font size and color.

6. Click **OK** to the new selection.

7. Click **OK** again at the bottom of the dialog box.

Note

Changing the **ToolTip** impacts all of the **ToolTips** in Excel, including those that appear below the toolbar icons.

Viewing Comments

From the **Tools** menu, select **Options**, **View** or use the **Reviewing** toolbar. Excel offers three display options:

- ▣ **None** – The comment indicator (red triangle) does not appear, and comments are not displayed.

- ▣ **Comment indicator only** – A small red triangle in the upper-right corner of the cell indicates a comment. The comment is displayed when the cell is selected.

- ▣ **Comment & indicator** – All comments inserted in the sheet are displayed.

Displaying a single comment

Select a cell with a comment. Right click, and from the shortcut menu, select **Show Comment**.

Change the location of the comment by dragging it to a location where it does not hide data. You can only change the location of a comment when the comment is displayed.

Copying Comments to Different Cells

1. Select a cell with a comment, and press **Ctrl+C** (copy).

2. Select a different cell, and right-click. From the shortcut menu, select **Paste Special**.

3. Select **Comments**, and click **OK**.

Deleting Comments

Select a cell with a comment, and right-click. From the shortcut menu, select **Delete Comment**.

Deleting all comments in a sheet

1. Press **F5** (**Go To** dialog box), and click **Special**.

2. In the **Go To Special** dialog box, select **Comments**.

3. Click **OK**.

4. Right-click, and from the shortcut menu, select **Delete Comment**.

Printing Comments

From the **File** menu, select **Page Setup**, **Sheet**, and click the **Sheet** tab. Before printing, select one of the following options in the **Comments** box:

☑ **None** – Will not print comments.

☑ **At end of sheet** – Will print the comments on a separate page after printing the sheet.

☑ **As displayed on sheet** – Will only print the comments that are displayed.

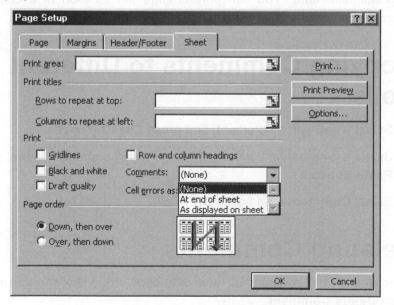

Tip – Print a Single Comment

Select a cell containing a comment. From the **File** menu, select **Page Setup, Sheet**. In the **Comments** box, select **At end of sheet**. Now click **OK,** and then click the **Print** icon.

Adding Pictures to Comments

Want to send your photo inside a comment? Your incredible picture can be included in a comment and surprise whoever opens the workbook. Or maybe you want to display pictures of your colleagues near the cells that contain their contact information?

Select a cell that contains a comment, right-click, and from the shortcut menu, select **Show Comment**. Select the edge of the comment so that the comment is surrounded by dots, not by slashes. Right-click, and from the shortcut menu, select **Format Comment**, **Colors and Lines**, **Fill**. Open the **Color** box. Choose **Fill Effects**. Click the **Picture** tab, and click **Select Picture**. Select a picture and click **OK**. Resize the comment as appropriate.

Send Information to Comments

In Excel, you cannot link a comment to a cell. In other words, you cannot make things easier by typing text or numerical data into a cell and have it be displayed in a comment.

The solution is to use VBA.

The code that will let you add and update text in comments appears below.

To add text to a comment:

```
Range("A1").AddComment Text:="Reviewed on " & Date
```

To update or change text in a comment:

```
Range("A1").Comment Text:="Change On " & Date
```

Importing and Refreshing Information from the Internet

An incredible amount of information is available on the Internet. Excel users can have access to updated information such as stock quotes, exchange rates, indexes, and so forth.

This book includes the technique for importing the information from the Internet and refreshing it within the three versions of Excel.

Excel 97

In Excel 97, you must save the site address (URL) for every new query in a text file with the extension .iqy.

To save an address in a text file as a query, perform the following steps:

1. Open the Internet site from which you want to import information to an Excel sheet. For example, open the site www.bloomberg.com. The site includes a table of various currency exchange rates. The address of the page containing the table of currency exchange rates is http://www.bloomberg.com/markets/fxc.html. Copy the address by selecting it and pressing **Ctrl+C**.

2. In **Windows**, select **Start, Programs, Accessories, Notepad**.

3. Press **Ctrl+V** to paste the address into the text file. Save the file under a name with the extension .iqy (be sure to use lower case letters). For example, save the file under the name CrossCurrencyRates.iqy.

4. Open Excel 97. From the Data menu, select **Get External Data, Run Web Query**.

5. In the **Run Query** dialog box, search for and select the File CrossCurrencyRates.iqy.

6. In the **Returning External Data to Microsoft Excel** dialog box, click **OK**.

7. Wait a few seconds, and the data is transferred from the Internet page to the Excel sheet.

Excel 2000

1. From the **Data** menu, select **Get External Data, New Web Query**.

2. In the **Enter the address** box, paste the full address of the Web site. For example, in order to import and refresh information from the Internet in the Excel 97 section, enter:
    http://www.bloomberb.com/markets/fxc.html.
    Click **Save Query**, type a name for the query, and click **Save.**

3. Click **OK**.

4. In the **Returning External Data to Microsoft Excel** dialog box, click **OK**.

Excel 2002

Excel 2002 lets you select the exact data table on the Web page to import and refresh only the data table.

New In 2002

1. From the **Data** menu, select **Import External Data, New Web Query**.

2. In the **New Web Query** dialog box, in the **Address** box, type or paste the address of the Internet site.

3. In the dialog box, notice the Web page. Click the small arrow in the upper left-hand corner of the table to select only the data table.

4. Click **Import**.

5. In the **Returning External Data to Microsoft Excel** dialog box, click **OK**.

Refreshing the Internet Data
(Excel versions 97, 2000, 2002)

 ## Note

The Internet site does not have to be open.

Select the cell in the sheet containing the data. From the **Data** menu, select **Refresh Data**, or display the **External Data** toolbar and click the **Refresh Data** icon.

To display the **External Data** toolbar, select one of the toolbars. Right-click, select the **External Data** toolbar, and click **OK**.

Refreshing the Internet Data Automatically

On the **External Data** toolbar, click the **Data Range Properties** icon.

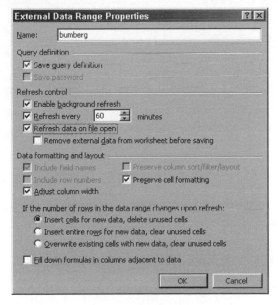

Select the **Refresh every** option, and set the number of minutes between each refresh action. Select the **Refresh data on file open** box to refresh the data automatically whenever the file is opened.

Running a Saved Query

In Excel 97, from the **Data** menu, select **Get External Data, Run Web Query.**

In Excel 2000, from the **Data** menu, select **Get External Data, Run Saved Query.**

In Excel 2002, from the **Data** menu, select **Import External Data, Import Data**.

Select the query you saved, and click **Get Data** (in Excel 2002, click **Open**).

Chapter 11

Printing

For most Excel users, printing is one of their least favorite features of Excel – to put it mildly. This chapter discusses all the issues, large and small, most of which are annoying. A thorough understanding of these issues will dramatically reduce the time you spend on printing.

Adding Icons to Toolbars

The **Standard** toolbar includes two icons that are related to printing, the **Print** icon and the **Print Preview** icon.

Other important icons that are not on the toolbar include the following:

- ▣ **Page Setup**

- ▣ **Set Print Area**

- ▣ **Custom Views**

Add these important additional icons as follows:

1. Use the mouse to right-click one of the toolbars.

2. From the shortcut menu, select **Customize**.

3. From the **Commands** tab, select the **File** category.

4. In the **Commands** dialog box, click and drag the **Page Setup** icon onto the Standard toolbar.

5. In the **Commands** dialog box, click and drag the **Set Print Area** icon onto the **Standard** toolbar.

6. Select the **View** category, and in the **Commands** dialog box, click and drag the **Custom Views** icon onto the menu bar. (You can add icons to the menu bar, and it is worth using it to add wide icons.)

Because of the first two icons you added, you will not need to use the **File** menu to access **Print** and **Set Print Area**.

For an explanation of the importance of the **Custom Views** icon, see the **Custom Views** section later in the chapter.

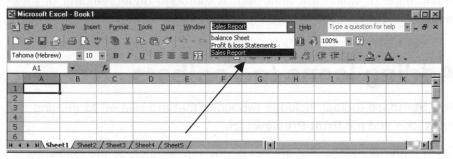

Changing and Customizing the Default Settings in a Workbook

Below are the default print-related settings for a standard Excel workbook that can be changed to suit your needs. (See also **Chapter 13, Customizing Excel** for customizing a workbook template.)

▣ **Headers and Footers** – the default settings do not include printing the name of the workbook, the name of the sheet, or the date and time of printing.

▣ **Black and White**, in the **Sheet** tab – most printers still print in black and white, but the default setting for printing a workbook is not black and white.

▣ **First Page Number**, in the **Page** tab – the default setting for the first page number is automatic. Change the default to 1. The reason – there is a bug in the automatic numbering for printing reports from the **Report Manager**. See below for details.

▣ **Scaling**, in the **Page** tab – generally, you print a single page or a collection of single pages (see **Customize Views** later in this chapter). Change **Scaling** to **Fit to: 1 page(s) wide by 1 tall**.

▣ **Inserting a logo into the header during printing** – see the explanation below.

Changed default settings are saved as a workbook **template** (see **Chapter 13, Customizing Excel**). Using a **template** lets you save the changes to the default settings for repeated use.

Changing the default settings for all sheets

1. In the workbook, select the tab for one of the sheets.
2. Right-click, and choose **Select All Sheets**.
3. From the **File** menu, select **Page Setup**.
4. Change the default settings as described below.
5. When you have finished changing the defaults, select the active sheet again. Right-click, and from the shortcut menu, select **Ungroup Sheets**.

Adding information to headers and footers on all printed pages

1. From the **File** menu, select **Page Setup**.
2. Select the **Header/Footer** tab.
3. Select **Custom Footer**.
4. Select **Left section**.
5. Click the icons **Date, Time, File, Tab**.
6. Click **OK**.

Adding the full path of the saved file

Excel 2002 lets you add the full path for where you saved the file on your computer or network. At step 5, click the **Add Path** icon. See the figure of the **Footer** dialog box.

New In 2002

Footer

To format text: select the text, then choose the font button.
To insert a page number, date, time, file path, filename, or tab name: position the insertion point in the edit box, then choose the appropriate button.
To insert picture: press the Insert Picture button. To format your picture, place the cursor in the edit box and press the Format Picture button.

Left section:
`&[Tab]&[File]&[Path]&[File]&[Time]&[Date]`

Center section:

Right section:

Using a macro to add data to each sheet printed from the workbook

Add a macro command that will automatically cause information, including the path, to appear on each sheet you print from the workbook. When using this technique, the full path for where you saved the workbook will be printed in Excel 97 and 2000.

1.   Open the VBE macro editor, and press **Alt+F11**.

2.   In the **Project Explorer**, double-click the **ThisWorkbook** module.

3.   Add an event called **Workbook_BeforePrint**.

4.   In the event, type code as follows:

```
Private Sub Workbook_BeforePrint(Cancel As Boolean)
    ActiveSheet.PageSetup.LeftFooter = _
        "&A&F&T&D " & ActiveWorkbook.Path
End Sub
```

The letters A, F, T, D = the name of the sheet, name of the workbook, time and date.

5. In Excel 2002, the middle line of code will be shorter:

```
.LeftFooter "&A&F&Z&F&T&D"
```

6. Save the file.

Inserting a picture (company logo) in the header

New
In 2002

1. Select the **Header/Footer** tab.

2. Click **Custom Header**.

3. Select **Left area**.

4. Click the **Picture** icon (second from right). In the **Insert Picture** dialog box, search for and select the logo or picture you want to add.

5. Click **Insert**.

6. Click **OK**.

Inserting a picture (company logo) in Excel 97 and 2000

1. Select Cell A1.

2. From the **Insert** menu, select **Picture**, **From File**.

3. Select the picture you want, and then copy and paste it into Cell A1.

4. Adjust the picture to the height and width of the row.

5. From the **File** menu, select **Page Setup**.

6. Select the **Sheet** tab.

7. Select **Rows to repeat at top**.

8. Select Row 1.

9. Click **OK**.

10. Repeat these steps for each sheet in the workbook.

Black and white printing

From the **Sheet** tab in the **Page Setup** dialog box, select **Black and white**.

First page number

From the **Page** tab in the **Page Setup** dialog box, change **First page number** to 1 or whatever number is appropriate.

Scaling

From the **Page** tab in the **Page Setup** dialog box, select and adjust the option **Fit to: 1 page(s) wide by 1 tall**.

For long reports where you wish to constrain the report to 1 page wide but allow it to span many pages in height, change this to 1 page wide by ___ (blank) pages tall.

Important Printing Techniques

Printing the page number and the running page number

Excel offers a number of options for printing a running page number.

▣ **Page Setup** using the **Page** tab.

▣ Manually inserting the page number in **Custom Footer**.

▣ Printing a page number in portrait layout on a page in landscape layout (see page 176).

▣ Utilizing Report Manager (see page 186).

Selecting the print area

An Excel sheet can have one continuous print area or a number of non-continuous print areas.

Defining a contiguous print area

Select a print area in the sheet, and click the **Set Print Area** icon (if you added it to the toolbar), or from the **File** menu, select **Print Area, Select Print Area**.

Defining a non-contiguous print area

Select a range of cells in the sheet, press **Ctrl**, and select another range of cells while holding the **Ctrl** key down. Click the **Set Print Area** icon, or from the **File** menu, select **Print Area, Set Print Area**. Each print area will be printed on a separate sheet.

Tip – Adding non-contiguous ranges to a single contiguous range for printing

In Excel 2000 and 2002, you can join non-continuous ranges to form a single contiguous range in order to print them as a single print area.

The **Paste All** icon is new addition to Excel 2000 and 2002.

Copy two or more separate ranges of cells separately. In Excel 2000 the **Paste All** icon appears on the **Clipboard** toolbar. In Excel 2002, press **Ctrl+C+C** to open the **Clipboard** pane, or from **Edit**, select **Clipboard**.

Select a cell and click the **Paste All** icon. The ranges that you copied are pasted in order. Now, define these continuous ranges as a single print area and print.

Unprinted blank pages

New
In 2002

Blank pages in the defined print area will not be printed.

Tip – Identifying and selecting the print area in a sheet

Each sheet has only one print area. When you select the print area, Excel creates a name for it – **Print_Area**. If you do not know what the print area is, select **Print_Area** from the **Name** box (to the left of the Formula bar).

Repeating rows and columns at the top of each page (Sheet tab)

Repeat a row at the top of each page to repeat the printing of data in the cells of a row, or series of rows, that you select.

Sound complicated? Below is an example to demonstrate the technique.

Example:

An Excel sheet contains a list of a company's customers. In the cells of the first row, you listed the headings customer name, contact person, address, telephone number and fax number. The list has 1,000 rows, and the print area that you defined is A1:E1000.

Select the **Sheet** tab, and in **Rows to repeat at top**, select Row 1 of the sheet.

The result – the top of each printed sheet will have a header row. After the header row, the text rows of the sheet are displayed.

Row and column headings (Sheet tab)

Select **Row and column headings** to print the sheet's headers, number of rows, and the letters A, B and C as the column headers.

Printing comments (Sheet tab)

Select **Comments, At end of sheet** to print the comments on an extra page with references to the cells containing the **comments**. If you select the **As displayed on sheet** option, the **comments** will be printed as they appear in the sheet. See the **Adding Comments to a Formula** section of **Chapter 10, Information**.

Hiding data before printing

Generally, you print the relevant data in a report. To print only the relevant data, you have to hide the irrelevant data.

Methods for hiding data

▣ Hide columns or rows before printing. See the explanation below of automatically hiding rows and/or columns by using **Custom Views**.

▣ For cells whose data should not be printed, change the font color to white.

▣ Hide parts of sheets by using a white text box that does not have a border. You can find the **Text Box** icon on the **Drawing** toolbar.

Hiding errors in formulas before printing

1. Select the print area, and from **Format**, select **Conditional Formatting**.

2. In **Condition 1**, select **Formula Is**. In the Formula box, type =IsError(A1).

3. Click **Format** and select the **Font** tab. Under **Color**, select white and click **OK**. In the **Conditional *Formatting*** dialog box, click **OK** again.

Hiding cell errors while printing

New
In 2002

In **Cell errors as**, select one of the four options for hiding errors or printing cell errors, and the type of error to be printed.

Page Setup	? X

Page | Margins | Header/Footer | **Sheet**

Print area: [   ]

Print...

Print titles

Rows to repeat at top: [   ]

Print Preview

Columns to repeat at left: [   ]

Options...

Print

- ☐ Gridlines   ☐ Row and column headings
- ☐ Black and white   Comments: (None) ▼
- ☐ Draft quality   Cell errors as: displayed ▼

displayed
\<blank\>
--
#N/A

Page order

- ◉ Down, then over
- ○ Over, then down

OK | Cancel

Scaling (Page tab)

Use **Scaling** for precise printing, without blank extra pages and without a column or row wrapping onto an extra page. Scaling to 1 page wide by 1 page tall is necessary to avoid printing a blank page in addition to the page you printed.

Problem: A common problem during printing is a column being wrapped onto an extra page. For example, you selected a print area that includes Columns A to F; you printed the data; and Column F is printed on an extra page.

Solution: Type 1 for **Number of pages wide**. Clear the box for **Number of pages tall**.

Continuous numbering of pages, first page number

If you want to print two pages from Sheet1 and three pages from Sheet2 and have them consecutively numbered from page 1 through page 5, be sure to print the entire workbook at one time. Use **File**, **Print** and select **Entire Workbook** in the **Print what** section of the **Print** dialog.

If you absolutely need to print individual worksheets and keep consecutive page numbering, then you can go to the **Page Setup** for Sheet2 and on the **Page** tab, change **First page number** from Auto to 3.

Note that if you are using Report Manager, you will want to change **First page number** from Auto to 1 to overcome a bug in the Report Manager.

Copying page settings to other sheets

Changing and updating the page settings takes a lot of time, so you certainly will want to copy page settings from one sheet to another, even if you still need to change some of the parameters you have defined in the new sheet. You will still save a lot of time by copying the page settings from one sheet to another sheet or sheets.

1. Select the sheet whose print settings you want to copy.

2. To select all the sheets in the workbook, select the sheet's tab, right-click, and choose **Select All Sheets**.

3. From the **File** menu, select **Page Setup**, and click **OK**. This will cause the page settings from the sheet selected in step 1 to be copied to all of the selected sheets.

4. To cancel the selection of the sheets, select the active sheet's tab, right-click and select **Ungroup Sheets**.

Printing page numbers in a report containing both portrait and landscape layouts

Problem

What do you do if one of the pages in a report is set up in landscape layout, while all the other pages are set up in portrait layout? When all the pages are combined into a single report, the page number that should be at the bottom of the landscape page will not be printed at the bottom, but at the right side (the footer of a page that is printed in landscape layout).

Solution

Print the page number from a cell in the sheet, not in the footer.

Example: A Profit and Loss Statement has 13 columns (A:M). The Profit and Loss Statement is part of a report with a large number of pages in portrait layout, but the Profit and Loss Statement is in landscape layout.

B	C	G	H	K	L	O	P
1							
2	April 2001 ▼						
3	ABC Company Limited						
4	Profit & Loss Statement for April 2001						
5							
6		YTD		Previous Year		Budget YTD	
7		$	%	$	%	$	%
8	Income						
9	Sales	1,015,016	98.77%	1,003,004	98.88%	901,016	98.91%
10	Interest	11,616	1.13%	10,404	1.03%	9,016	0.99%
11	Other	1,016	0.10%	1,004	0.10%	916	0.10%
12	**Total Income**	1,027,648	100.00%	1,014,412	100.00%	910,948	100.00%
13							
14	Cost of goods sold	24,992	2.43%	24,848	2.45%	26,678	2.93%
15	Gross income	1,002,656	97.57%	989,564	97.55%	884,270	97.07%
16							
17	General & Administrative	282,138	27.45%	281,922	27.79%	280,248	30.76%
18	Selling Exp.	164,792	16.04%	164,648	16.23%	190,772	20.94%
19	**Total G&A & selling Exp.**	446,930	43.49%	446,570	44.02%	471,020	51.71%
20							
21	Net Earnings	555,726	54.08%	542,994	53.53%	413,250	45.36%
24	Interest	5,332	0.52%	(5,308)	(0.52%)	(7,158)	(0.79%)
25	Net Earnings before income taxes	550,710	53.59%	547,998	54.02%	419,154	46.01%
26	Income taxes	198,256	19.29%	197,279	19.45%	150,896	16.56%
27	Net Earnings	352,454	34.30%	350,719	34.57%	268,259	29.45%
28							

P&L / Details / Totals / Parametrs / Data / Budget

1. Select Column A (see the figure at the end of the explanation).

2. Right-click, and from the shortcut menu, select **Insert**.

3. In Cell A1, type the number 5 (assuming that 5 is the number of the page in the report).

4. Select the range A1:A29.

5. Press **Ctrl+1** (Format Cells).

6. Select the **Alignment** tab.

7. In **Text Alignment, Horizontal**, select **Left** (in Excel 97, select **Right**). In **Text Alignment, Vertical**, select **Center.**

8. In **Text Control**, select **Merge cells**.

9. In **Orientation**, change the text orientation to -90 degrees (if the sheet direction is right to left, text orientation should be 90 degrees).

10. Click **OK**.

11. Update the print area – from the **File** menu, select **Page Setup**.

12. Select the **Sheet** tab.

13. In Print Area, change B1 to A1. The new print area is A1:N29 (the print area includes the new column).

14. Select the **Margins** tab.

15. Reduce the right margin to 0 (so that the page number will appear at the bottom of the printed page).

16. Select the **Header/Footer** tab.

17. Select **Custom footer**.

18. Delete Page (if it appears in one of the sections).

19. Click **OK**.

The result - the page number, 5, is displayed horizontally and centered in Column A.

			YTD		Previous Year		Budget YTD	
			$	%	$	%	$	%
	Income							
	Sales		1,015,016	98.77%	1,003,004	98.88%	901,016	98.91%
	Interest		11,616	1.13%	10,404	1.03%	9,016	0.99%
	Other		1,016	0.10%	1,004	0.10%	916	0.10%
	Total Income		1,027,648	100.00%	1,014,412	100.00%	910,948	100.00%
	Cost of goods sold		24,992	2.43%	24,848	2.45%	26,678	2.93%
	Gross income		1,002,656	97.57%	989,564	97.55%	884,270	97.07%
	General & Administrative		282,138	27.45%	281,922	27.79%	280,248	30.76%
	Selling Exp.		164,792	16.04%	164,648	16.23%	190,772	20.94%
	Total G&A & selling Exp.		446,930	43.49%	446,570	44.02%	471,020	51.71%
	Net Earnings		555,726	54.08%	542,994	53.53%	413,250	45.36%
	Interest		5,332	0.52%	(5,308)	(0.52%)	(7,158)	(0.79%)
	Net Earnings before income taxes		550,710	53.59%	547,998	54.02%	419,154	46.01%
	Income taxes		198,256	19.29%	197,279	19.45%	150,896	16.56%
	Net Earnings		352,454	34.30%	350,719	34.57%	268,259	29.45%

Page break

When you set the print area in a sheet that has more than one page to be printed, Excel divides the print area over individual pages. This division is done according to the **Page Setup** definitions, including margins, scaling, width and height of columns and rows, and also according to the size of the printing paper. It is best for you to manually insert a page break between the columns that will be printed, according to the subjects of the columns.

Look at the automatic page breaks. From the **View** menu, select **Page Break Preview**. In the figure below, the report is divided into two parts, a Profit and Loss Statement (C3:P27) and an appendix (C32:P37) that details general and administrative expenses.

In the example, the print area (C3:P37), which includes all the data in the appendix, is divided over two pages. Each printed page will include the appropriate header (repeated rows at the top of the page) and a page break at the appropriate place to separate the Profit and Loss Statement from its appendix.

Microsoft Excel - Profit & Loss Statemnets								
File	Edit	View	Insert	Format	Tools	Data	Window	Help

	C	G	H	K	L	O	P	Q
2	April 2001							
3	ABC Company Limited							
4	Profit & Loss Statement for April 2001							
5								
6			YTD		Previous Year		Budget YTD	
7			$	%	$	%	$	%
8	**Income**							
9	Sales		1,015,016	98.77%	1,003,004	98.88%	901,016	98.91%
10	Interest		11,616	1.13%	10,404	1.03%	9,016	0.99%
11	Other		1,016	0.10%	1,004	0.10%	916	0.10%
12	**Total Income**		1,027,648	100.00%	1,014,412	100.00%	910,948	100.00%
13								
14	Cost of goods sold		24,992	2.43%	24,848	2.45%	26,678	2.93%
15	**Gross income**		1,002,656	97.57%	989,564	97.55%	884,270	97.07%
16								
17	General & Administrative		282,138	27.45%	281,922	27.79%	280,248	30.76%
18	Selling Exp.		164,792	16.04%	164,648	16.23%	190,772	20.94%
19	**Total G&A & selling Exp.**		446,930	43.49%	446,570	44.02%	471,020	51.71%
20								
21	Net Earnings		555,726	54.08%	542,994	53.53%	413,250	45.36%
24	Interest		5,332	0.52%	(5,308)	(0.52%)	(7,158)	(0.79%)
25	Net Earnings before income taxe		550,710	53.59%	547,998	54.02%	419,154	46.01%
26	Income taxes		198,256	19.29%	197,279	19.45%	150,896	16.56%
27	Net Earnings		**352,454**	**34.30%**	**350,719**	**34.57%**	**268,259**	**29.45%**
28								
29								
30								
31								
32	**General & Administrative**							
33	Salary & Wages		45,212	16.02%	40,856	14.49%	42,532	15.18%
34	Employee Benefits		10,652	3.78%	9,856	3.50%	10,123	3.61%
35	Rent		19,523	6.92%	17,985	6.38%	18,962	6.76%
36	Office supplies		30,175	10.70%	25,652	9.10%	27,586	9.84%
37	Telephone		34,560	12.25%	29,562	10.49%	32,409	11.56%

P&L / Details / Totals / Parametrs / Data / Budget /

1. From the **File** menu, select **Page Setup**.

2. In the **Sheet** tab, enter the **Print Area** as C3:P37.

3. In the **Rows to repeat at top** box, select Rows 3:7.

4. In the **Page** tab, set the **Scaling** to **Fit to: 1 page(s) wide by 2 tall**.

5. From the **View** menu, select **Page Break Preview**.

6. Select Cell C28. This cell actually marks the separation between the Profit and Loss Statement and its appendix.

7. From the **Insert** menu, select **Page Break**.

8. From the **View** menu, select **Normal** to return to the normal view.

Removing or changing a page break

To manually change a page break, in **Page Break Preview**, drag the blue line (either solid or dotted) to another location. To remove the page break that you created by selecting Cell C28, select Cell C28 again, and from the **Insert** menu, select **Remove Page Break**.

Removing page breaks from the sheet

To remove all page breaks from a sheet, select all the cells in the sheet (use the keyboard shortcut **Ctrl+A**, or click the **Select All** button at the corner of the sheet's headings). From the **Insert** menu, select **Reset All Page Breaks**.

Inserting a watermark behind the text

Reports such as a company's financial statements are, by their very nature, confidential. Insert the text "Confidential" behind the data in the report in such a way that it does not interfere with reading the report.

	Microsoft Excel - Profit & Loss Statemnets								
	File Edit View Insert Format Tools Data Window Help						Type a question for help		

	B	C	G	H	K	L	O	P
1								
2	April 2001							
3	ABC Company Limited							
4	Profit & Loss Statement for April 2001							
5								
6			YTD		Previous Year		Budget YTD	
7			$	%	$	%	$	%
8	Income							
9	Sales		1,015,016	98.77%	1,003,004	98.88%	901,016	98.91%
10	Interest		11,616	1.13%	10,404	1.03%	9,016	0.99%
11	Other		1,016	0.10%	1,004	0.10%	916	0.10%
12	Total Income		1,027,548	100.00%	1,014,412	100.00%	910,948	100.00%
13								
14	Cost of goods sold		24,992	2.43%	24,848	2.45%	26,678	2.93%
15	Gross income		1,002,656	97.57%	989,564	97.55%	884,270	97.07%
16								
17	General & Administrative		282,138	27.45%	281,922	27.79%	280,248	30.76%
18	Selling Exp.		164,792	16.04%	164,648	16.23%	190,772	20.94%
19	Total G&A & selling Exp.		446,930	43.49%	446,570	44.02%	471,020	51.71%
20								
21	Net Earnings		555,726	54.00%	542,994	53.53%	413,250	45.36%
24	Interest		5,332	0.52%	(5,308)	(0.52%)	(7,158)	(0.79%)
25	Net Earnings before income taxes		550,710	53.59%	547,998	54.02%	419,154	46.01%
26	Income taxes		198,256	19.29%	197,279	19.45%	150,896	16.56%
27	Net Earnings		352,454	34.30%	350,719	34.57%	268,259	29.45%
28								

P&L / Details / Totals / Parametrs / Data / Budget /

Inserting a watermark

1. Display the **WordArt** toolbar. Select one of the toolbars, right-click, and select the **WordArt** toolbar.

2. On the **WordArt** toolbar, click the **Insert WordArt** Icon (A).

3. From the **WordArt Gallery**, select any example, and click OK.

4. In the **WordArt Edit Text** dialog box, type **Confidential** (or any other text), and select the font and the font size.

5. Right-click the **WordArt**, and from the shortcut menu, select the **Colors and Lines** tab.

6. In **Fill**, select **Color**, **No Fill**.

7. In **Line**, **Color**, select a color that is not too light.

8. Click **OK**.

9. Right-click, and from the shortcut menu, select **Order**, **Send to Back**.

10. Adjust the object's size and location to suit the sheet.

Printing objects

Excel allows you to include objects (dropdown menus, buttons, text boxes, arrows and more) in a sheet for a variety of purposes. It also allows you to decide if you want them to be hidden when you print or not.

There are a number of ways to prevent objects from being printed. Select **File**, **Page Setup**, **Sheet**. Select the **Draft quality** checkbox, and click **OK**.

Right-click the object, and select **Format Object** type. Select the **Properties** tab, and select the **Print object** checkbox if you want to print it.

Tip – Make printing faster

Objects make printing go slower, so you may want to temporarily delete them before printing by pressing **Ctrl+6+6**. After printing, press **Ctrl+6** to reinsert the objects into the sheet.

Selecting print options

With Excel, you can print whatever print areas you choose. From the **File** menu, select **Print**. In the **Print** dialog box, you can print whatever area you want, without changing the **Print_Area** of the sheet, by using the **Selection** option (remember, **Print_Area** is the last print area that was defined).

Select the **Entire workbook** option to print the print areas of all the sheets in the workbook.

To print a number of reports regularly, use the **Report Manager** (see below).

Custom Views

A full report consists of a combination of individual sheets. Different print options are defined for each sheet. It is a waste of time to begin redefining print options. It is much more effective and efficient to save print options for repeated use.

Custom Views allows you to save a set of print options that is unique for each print area in the sheet and create a menu of views that let you print any page at any time without redefining the **Page Setup** options for the page.

Inserting a custom view

1. Before defining the print area, hide the rows and columns that you do not want to print.

2. Define the **Page Setup** options for the page to be printed.

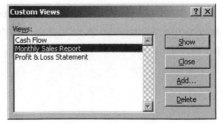

3. From the **View** menu, select **Custom Views**.

4. Click **Add**.

5. In the **Add View** dialog box, type the name of the view in the **Name** box.

6. Click **OK**.

When you save the view, the defined print options, rows, columns, and hidden filter options are saved. See **Chapter 18, Filtering**.

Tip – Unhide rows and columns by using Custom Views

To quickly unhide hidden rows and columns, insert a **Custom View** for the sheet with the rows and columns unhidden.

Printing a custom view

1. Select the view you want to print from the **Custom Views** dialog box.

2. Click **Show**.

3. Click the **Print** icon.

Adding a custom views icon

At the beginning of the chapter, see **Adding Icons to Toolbars**.

Adding a custom view quickly

You can type the name of the view you created directly into the drop-down list in the icon. Press **Enter** after typing the name of the view.

Deleting a custom view

From the **View** menu, select **Custom Views**, select the name of the view, and click **Delete**.

Custom views are saved at the workbook level

Custom views are saved in the active workbook. You are not supposed to remember which sheet has the view you want to print. When you select the view, you will select it in the sheet in which it is saved, and that sheet's page setup will change in accordance with the page setup that was saved in the view.

Caution

The custom view you saved is inflexible, and cannot be edited easily. Every little change requires deleting the view, making the change, and resaving the view.

Report Manager

Excel lets you save pages or views that are connected to entire reports and print them any time you choose. Use the **Report Manager** add-in to create and save the reports.

Installing the Report Manager add-in

The Office XP (2002) CD does not include the **Report Manager** add-in. To install it in your computer, you must download the add-in from the Microsoft Web site.

The site's address is: http://office.microsoft.com/downloads/2002.

Excel 97 and 2000 include the add-in. The name of the file is Reports.xla. If you have an earlier version of Excel, you can install the add-in in Excel 2002 without downloading the file from the Microsoft Web site. The add-in is the same for all versions of Excel.

Installing the add-in

1. From the **Tools** menu, select **Add-ins**.

2. If the add-in appears in the list of available add-ins, there is no need to install it. Go to Step 6

3. Click **Browse**.

4. Locate and select a file called Reports.xla.

5. Click **OK**.

6. In **Add-ins Available**, select **Report Manager**.

7. Click **OK**.

Adding a report and saving in Report Manager

1. From the **View** menu, select **Report Manager**.

2. Click **Add**.

3. In the **Report Name** box, type the name of the report.

4. From **Section to Add**, open **View** or **Sheet**.

5. Select the first view to add to the report Profit and Loss Statement.

6. Click **Add**. The view Profit and Loss Statement moves to the white list box at the bottom of the **Sections in this Report** box.

7. Use this method to add other views as necessary.

8. Select the **Use Continuous Page Number** box if you want to print continuous numbers at the bottom of the page.

Problem

There is no way to set the first page number or to number additional pages (for example, a page added from the Word program) so that it will print in the report. The first page that is printed will be numbered 1.

Solution

Insert additional views into the report (for example, reinsert the Profit and Loss Statement view), and use the report with the correct number in the footer (you may destroy the extra pages with the incorrect numbers).

Note

You can use **Report Manager** to control automatic numbering if you change the default setting of **First page number** from **Auto** to a number.

From the **File** menu, select **Page Setup**, **Page** tab, and change **First page number** from **Auto** to a number. Make this change in all the sheets you want to print.

Using custom views to add pages to reports

Using **Custom Views** to add a report is like buying an insurance policy for safe printing. The pages are printed according to the print options that were defined and saved earlier.

Add Report   ? ☒

Report Name: Full Balance Sheet report   [OK]

To create a section, select a sheet. You may also choose   [Cancel]
a View and/or Scenario. Then, choose the Add button.
                                                    [Help]

┌─ Section to Add ──────────────────────────┐   [Add]
│   │
│ Sheet: P&L   ▼ │
│   │
│ ☑ View: Profit & Loss Statement   ▼ │
│   │
│ ☑ Scenario: (None)   ▼ │
│   │
└──┘

Sections in this Report:

P&L, Balance Sheet, (None)   ▲   [Move Up]
P&L, Cash Flow report, (None)
P&L, Profit & Loss Statement, (None)   [Move Down]

                                    ▼   [Delete]

☑ Use Continuous Page Numbers

Printing, editing or deleting a report

1. From the **View** menu, select **Report Manager**.

2. Select the report you want to print.

3. Click **Print**.

To change a report, or add, close, or arrange printing the pages of a report, click **Edit**.

To delete a report, select the report and click **Delete**.

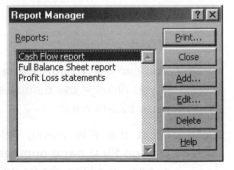

Report Manager   ? ☒

Reports: [Print...]

Cash Flow report   ▲   [Close]
Full Balance Sheet report
Profit Loss statements   [Add...]

                                  [Edit...]

                                  [Delete]

                          ▼   [Help]

Creating a custom Report Manager by writing a small program in VBA

Using the **Report Manager** to print reports is not a good solution for printing reports from single or multiple workbooks and does not provide an automatic solution for custom numbering of pages.

You can create a print manager by using a macro (this works for Excel 97, 2000 and 2002).

Column A – This column contains numbers between 1 and 3: print from sheet, print by range name, or print from custom view (recommended).

Column B – Type the name of the sheet, range name (be sure to type the exact name of the range including the underscore. To make this simpler, paste the list of names by creating a shortcut with **F3** and copying the name) and name of custom view.

Column C – Type the page number to be printed in the footer.

The macro will print from a sheet and automatically add the necessary information into the footer, including page number, workbook name, path, sheet name, date and time of printing.

```
Sub PrintReports()
    Dim NumberPages As Integer
    Dim PageNumber As Integer
    Dim i As Integer
    Dim ActiveSh As Worksheet
    Dim ChooseShNameView As String
    Dim ShNameView As String

    Application.ScreenUpdating = False
    Set ActiveSh = ActiveSheet

    For Each Cell In Range(Range("A2"), _
        Range("A2").End(xlDown))
        ShNameView = Cell.Offset(0, 1).Value
        PageNumber = Cell.Offset(0, 2).Value
        Select Case Cell.Value
            Case 1
                Sheets(ShNameView).Select
            Case 2
                Application.Goto Reference:=ShNameView
            Case 3
                ActiveWorkbook.CustomViews(ShNameView).Show
        End Select

        With ActiveSheet.PageSetup
            .CenterFooter = PageNumber
            .LeftFooter = ActiveWorkbook.FullName & _
                "&A &T &D"
        End With
        ActiveWindow.SelectedSheets.PrintOut Copies:=1
    Next Cell
    ActiveSh.Select
End Sub
```

Explanation and Comments:

1. The loop in the macro causes a separate print for each cell in column A starting at A2.

2. In the loop, the print area is selected using the Select Case technique.

3. The information printed on the left side of the footer: &08 = 8 point font, &D = Date, &T = Time.

4. The macro provided here only prints pages in the current workbook. You can add the option to print from other workbooks, even closed workbooks. Add two new columns, one for path and one for file name. See **Chapter 28, Other VBA Techniques** to see how to open a closed workbook and how to use the function to determine if the workbook is open or closed.

5. To run the macro, add a button to the sheet and attach the macro to it.

6. You can use this technique to add an unlimited number of reports.

Chapter 12

Charts

Each new version of Excel comes packed with numerous improvements over previous versions, and this is particularly true in terms of graphics, formatting tools and toolbars (see **Chapter 2, Text**). Microsoft has added a wide and diverse range of graphics and formatting tools, which gives Excel the impressive ability to display data graphically.

The improvements in Excel's graphics functionality allow you to use design tools such as WordArt, insert pictures or Clip Art images, add lines and AutoShapes, and more. Excel supports over 100 types of graphs and allows you to change virtually every element in any chart you create.

The chapter assumes that you already know how to create charts. Here you will find tips and additions to charts, and discussion on the various types of charts.

Creating Charts with F11

To illustrate, see the figure below, which shows sales data broken down by zone. Select a cell in the table, and press **F11**.

Zone	1999	2000	2001
N. America	10,000	5,000	1,500
W.Europe	15,000	6,000	2,500
E.Europe	7,500	7,000	3,500
Asia	2,000	8,000	4,500
Africa	2,500	9,000	5,500
S.America	3,000	10,000	6,500

The result: Excel opens a chart sheet, a sheet in your workbook that contains a new chart.

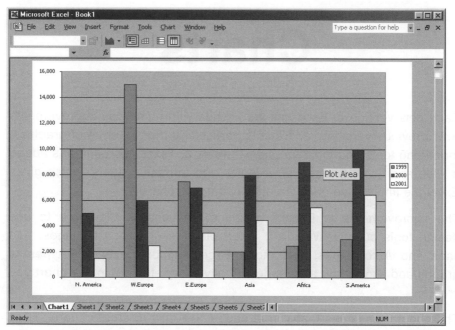

Creating Charts Quickly Using the Chart Toolbar

Select a cell in the data table, and in the **Chart** toolbar, click the **Chart Type** icon to display the different types of charts. Select the desired chart type.

The result: A chart is added quickly.

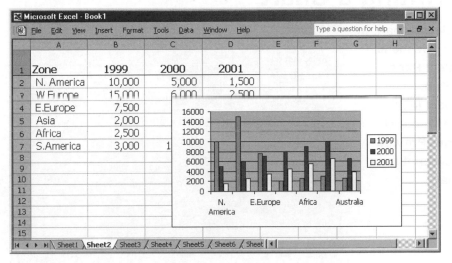

Sizing Charts with the Window

Select a chart sheet (if you do not have a chart sheet in your workbook, press **F11**), or select a chart that is embedded in a worksheet. From the **View** menu, select **Sized with Window**. The chart will automatically adjust to the size of the window.

Setting the Default Chart Type

You can change the default chart type by pressing **F11** or by selecting a different chart type from the **Chart** toolbar.

Select a chart sheet or select an embedded chart, and right-click. From the **Chart** menu, select the chart type you want from the list, and click **Set as default chart**. Click **OK**.

Printing a Chart

Select a chart. In
the **File** menu,
select **Page
Setup**. Then,
select the **Chart**
tab, and click
Print Preview.
Now print the
chart.

Page Setup `[?] [X]`

| Page | Margins | Header/Footer | Chart |

Printed chart size
- ● Use full page
- ○ Scale to fit page
- ○ Custom

Printing quality
- ☐ Draft quality
- ☐ Print in black and white

Print...
Print Preview
Options...

OK   Cancel

Saving chart printing definitions separately from data

Use **Custom Views** (see **Chapter 11**, **Printing**) to save different printing definitions for charts and data tables.

Preventing charts from being printed

Select a chart, and right-click. From the shortcut menu, select **Format Chart Area**. Select the **Properties** tab, and clear the checkbox beside **Print Object**. Click **OK**.

Format Chart Area   ? ☒

| Patterns | Font | Properties |

Object positioning
- ⦿ Move and size with cells
- ○ Move but don't size with cells
- ○ Don't move or size with cells

☐ Print object
☑ Locked

Locking objects has no effect unless the sheet is
protected. To protect the sheet, choose
Protection from the Tools menu, and then choose
Protect Sheet. A password is optional.

| OK | Cancel |

Using the Keyboard to Select Chart Items

Using the mouse, it is not easy to select the different chart items when you want to modify or update the definitions. Use the keyboard to move between different chart items by pressing one of the four arrow keys. When a range of data has been selected in a chart (the chart indicates columns), press the right or left arrow to move and select columns in the chart.

Changing the Layout of the Chart from Rows to Columns and Vice Versa

When you create a chart, Excel checks the number of rows and columns. In the example below, there are six rows (in Column A, Zone) and three columns (years). In a chart created automatically by pressing **F11**, rows from the data table are created on the category axis. To switch from rows to columns in the category axis, select the chart, and from the **Chart** menu, select **Source Data**. In **Series in**, select **Columns**.

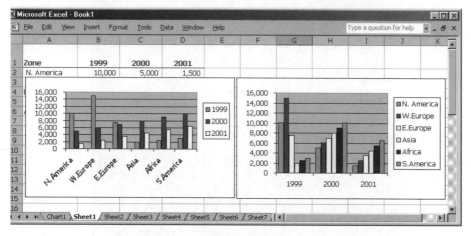

Using the Formatting Tools

Use Excel's formatting tools when you want to color a chart item that you have selected using the keyboard. From the **Formatting** toolbar, select a color by clicking the **Fill Color** icon. Continue formatting without using the chart shortcut menu that appears when you right-click the chart.

Nudge the Chart to a Different Place in the Sheet

Press **Ctrl** and select the chart. Now, nudge the chart in any direction by pressing **Ctrl** and one of the four arrow keys at the same time.

Adding a Linked Picture to a Chart

It would be an understatement to say that it is simple to update text in an object. Let's say, for example, that you add a title to the chart to indicate the period of the statement. A month later, the period of the financial statements changes, and you find yourself fighting to change the text in the object you have pasted into the chart. When you link an object to a cell in the sheet, any change to the text in the cell will automatically update the text in the object.

Creating a picture of cells that is linked to the source data

In the sheet, copy a cell or cells that contain text or data, and paste it into the chart. Hold down **Shift**, and click **Paste Picture Link** on the **Edit** menu.

-OR-

Select a cell or cells, click the **Camera** icon, and then click where you want to paste the upper-left corner of the picture.

Adding the camera icon to the toolbar

Right-click any toolbar. From the shortcut menu, select **Customize**. Select the **Commands** tab, and from the **Tools** category, click and drag the **Camera** icon onto the toolbar.

Guidelines for working with linked pictures

Formatting – The linked text in the picture is formatted according to the formatting in the cell. Any changes to the formatting must be done in the source cell. You can change the formatting of the text; add text wrapping; change the width of a column or cell; omit gridlines (From the **Tools** menu, select **Options**, select the **View** tab, and then clear the **Gridlines** checkbox); and change the font color and cell shading (background color).

 Note

Be sure to resize the column containing text you want in the picture *before* creating the link. Only the visible information in the cell will be included in the picture.

In the figure, two pictures have been pasted into a chart: a picture of the data table and a picture of the chart title.

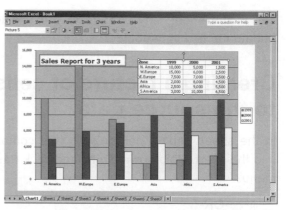

The text, **Sales Report for 3 years**, was typed and formatted in a single cell in a different sheet.

Updating Charts by Dragging and Dropping

If you have a chart with data for 1999 through 2001 and then enter a new column for 2002, you can drag and drop the new data on the chart.

🔲   Highlight the cells with the new data E1:E7.

🔲   Using the mouse, click the black border around the range and begin dragging the range towards the chart.

🔲   When the mouse pointer is over the chart, release the mouse button.

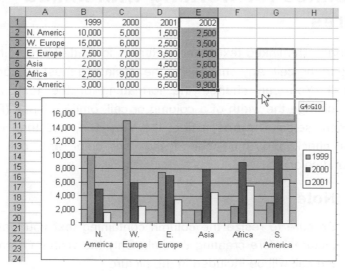

Result: the new data is added to the chart:

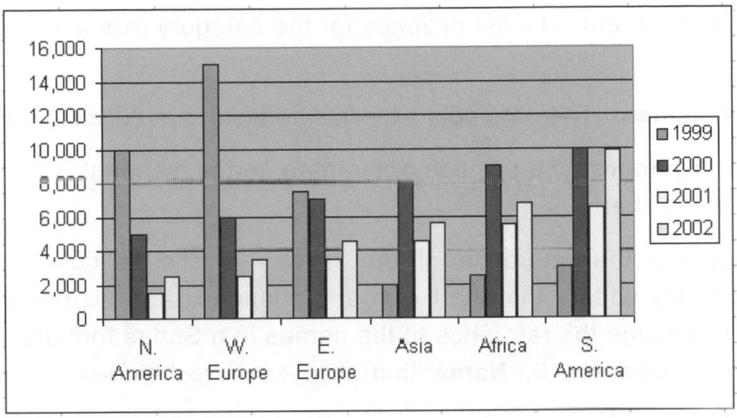
16,000
14,000
12,000
10,000
8,000
6,000
4,000
2,000
0
N. America
W. Europe
E. Europe
Asia
Africa
S. America
1999
2000
2001
2002

Automatically Updating Charts with New Data

Like formulas, a chart is automatically linked to a data table. Data series in a chart are linked to the data table using a Series formula. Click any of the series in a chart, and you will see a Series formula in the Formula bar.

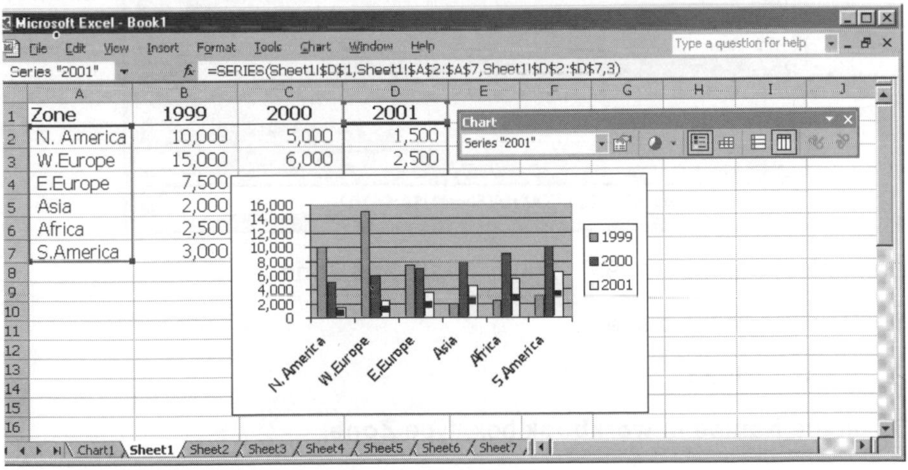
Microsoft Excel - Book1
File Edit View Insert Format Tools Chart Window Help
Type a question for help
Series "2001"
=SERIES(Sheet1!$D$1,Sheet1!$A$2:$A$7,Sheet1!$D$2:$D$7,3)
Zone 1999 2000 2001
N. America 10,000 5,000 1,500
W.Europe 15,000 6,000 2,500
E.Europe 7,500
Asia 2,000
Africa 2,500
S.America 3,000
Chart
Series "2001"
16,000
14,000
12,000
10,000
8,000
6,000
4,000
2,000
0
N.America
W.Europe
E.Europe
Asia
Africa
S.America
1999
2000
2001
Chart1 Sheet1 Sheet2 Sheet3 Sheet4 Sheet5 Sheet6 Sheet7

Look at the formula in the picture above to see the arguments in the Series formula.

First argument: The column title is cell D1.

Second argument: The list of zones for the category axis is in the range A2:A7.

Third argument: The data points for this series are in cells D2:D7.

Fourth argument: The position of the data series means this is the third series in the chart.

By changing the reference of the names in the formula, you can automatically update the chart with any change to the size of the data table. To change the reference of the names in a Series formula, see the section in **Chapter 6, Name** that discusses techniques for defining names.

Define names in the **Define Name** dialog box. In the **Refers to** box, type the formula. It will automatically update the reference to the name in the Series formula.

Define four names: _1999, _2000, _2001 and Zone.

1.   Select a cell in a sheet.

2.   Press **Ctrl+F3**.

3.   In the **Names in workbook** box, type **Zone**.

4.   In the **Refers to** box, type the formula
     =OFFSET(Sheet1!$A$2,0,0,COUNTA(Sheet1!$A:$A)-1).

5. Click **OK**.

6. Now define three more names: _1999, cell reference B2:B7; _2000, cell reference C2:C7; and _2001, cell reference D2:D7. In each formula, be sure to type the corresponding reference.

7. In a Series formula, manually change the reference of the names in the cells (you cannot use the F3 shortcut to paste a name into a Series formula). Select a column in a chart, and in the Formula bar, type the corresponding **Name** you defined instead of the reference.

Before changing the reference of names, carefully read the following note:

❑ Type the name into the formula after typing the name of the workbook followed by an exclamation point.

In the figure below, note the formula in the Formula bar. A new zone, Australia, has been added to the data chart. The chart was updated automatically with a new column.

Displaying Numbers in Thousands in a Chart

Charts are linked to data, and, consequently, any change to the format of numbers in the data table will lead to a corresponding change in how the numbers are displayed in the chart.

Select the data in a data table and press **Ctrl+1**. In the **Format Cells** dialog box, select the **Number** tab. In the **Category** box, select **Custom**. In the **Type** box, type **#,##0** to display a number rounded to the nearest thousand.

For more information on formatting numbers, see **Chapter 3, Formatting Numbers**.

Displaying Different Data Using a ComboBox

By adding a ComboBox and a number of formulas to a sheet, you will be able to select how to display the data for one of the zones in the chart.

For more information on techniques for working with ComboBoxes and formulas, see **Chapter 23, Using Functions and Objects to Extract Data**.

Adding a data table to which a chart will be linked

The data in the data table in row 2 in the figure below will be updated when you select the name of the zone in the ComboBox.

Define Names

MarketList - range of A5:A10.

MarketNumber – cell F1.

Data – range of A4:D10.

In the picture, note the formulas in the cells in row 2.

Go to the **Format Control** dialog box of a **ComboBox**. In the **Input range** box, type the name **MarketList**. In the **Cell link** box, type the name **MarketNumber**. Create a chart for the cell range A1:D2.

In the **ComboBox**, select the display of market data.

Format Control ? X

| Size | Protection | Properties | Web | Control |

Input range: MarketList

Cell link: MarketNumber

Drop down lines: 8

☑ 3-D shading

OK   Cancel

Adding Option Buttons to Charts

Adding **Option buttons** is similar to adding a **Combo Box**. The difference between the two is in their ease of use. When you need to select from a long list as in the previous example (list of markets), it is simpler to create a **ComboBox** and to select the name of the market from a list of markets. However, when the number of choices is small (three to four options), it is easier to use **Option buttons**.

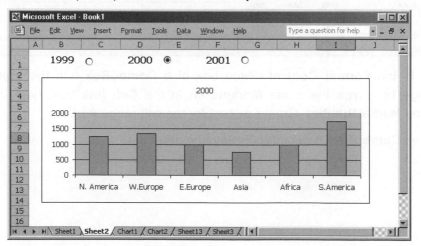

Data sheet

The **name** defined for the data table in cells A6:G9 is **Data**. In rows 3 and 4, the data is linked to a chart.

Note the formula in cell A4. The formula was typed into the cell and then copied to all of the cells through G4.

Cell H1 is linked to **Option buttons**. The **name** defined for the cell is **LinkNumber**.

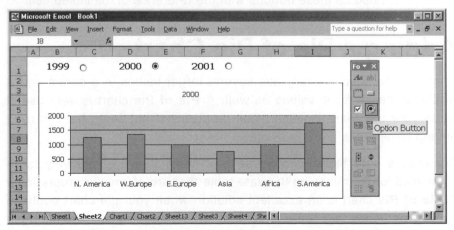

Adding option buttons to worksheets

As is the case with **ComboBoxes**, **Option buttons** are also added by using the **Forms** toolbar. Right-click a toolbar, and in the shortcut menu, select **Forms**.

1. From the **Forms** toolbar, click and drag the **Option Button** to place it in the sheet. Select and delete the text in the box. While holding down the **ALT** key, drag the **Option Button** to the appropriate cell (in the figure, to the right of the text 1999).

2. Select the **Option Button** in edit format (if it is not in edit format, right-click) and right-click. From the shortcut menu, select **Format Control**, and then select the **Control** tab.

3. In the **Cell link** box, type (**F3** does not work in this object) the reference of the linked cell, the name **LinkNumber**.

4. Add two more **Option Buttons** to the right of 2000 and 2001.

Note

Pay close attention to the order in which you copy **Option Buttons** and paste them into the sheet. The linked cell, **LinkNumber**, will return the value of the **Option Button** according to the order in which it was pasted from the **Forms** toolbar. This means that the first button will return the number 1 to the linked cell. The second button pasted will return the result 2 to the linked cell and so on.

When you add two more **Option Buttons** to the sheet, both buttons will automatically be updated with the linked reference upon being pasted into the sheet. Therefore, you do not need to update these buttons with the reference of the linked cell.

Adding a Pie of Pie Chart

A **Pie of Pie** chart typically has several larger values in a series and a whole cluster of small values as well. A **Pie of Pie** chart is very useful when your pie chart contains small proportions that seem hard to read among larger ones.

Sometimes data tables contain several items that are relatively large compared to other items in the data table that are of smaller proportions. A **Pie of Pie** chart is an excellent solution when your pie chart contains small proportions that seem to get lost among larger ones. The main pie displays the relatively large items, and the little pie presents the other items as a single, yet detailed group.

Note: In the figure below, the list of expenses contains three items which together amount to 90% of total expenses. All of the remaining items amount to 10%. A chart within a chart allows you to itemize the components that make up the 10%.

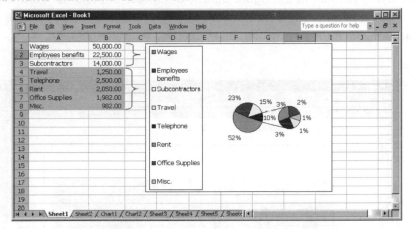

1. Select the data region.

2. Click the **Chart Wizard** icon.

3. In step 1 of 4, select the **Standard Types** tab. Under **Chart type**, select **Pie**.

4. Select (out of the six types of pie charts) **Pie of Pie**.

5. Continue creating the chart. In step 3 of 4, select the **Data Labels** tab, and then select **Show label and percent**.

6. Click **Finish**.

7. In the chart, select the **Chart Area** (select the pie wedges).

8. Right-click, and from the shortcut menu, select **Format Data Series**.

9. Select the **Options** tab.

10. In the **Second plot contains the last** box, type or select the number that matches the number of items in the small group of items. In the example, the number of expense items is 5.

11. Click **OK**.

Replacing Data Markers with Pictures

Shaking up the normal routine every once in a while cannot hurt. Jazzing up charts with interesting shapes makes a strong visual statement when displaying results. In the figure below, a number of pictures were added. You can add letters to data markers in any order you like or replace data markers with flags or anything else; just use your imagination.

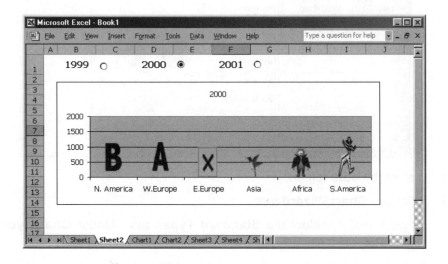

1. In the chart, select the desired data markers (if you want to replace them with the same picture).

2. From the **Insert** menu, select **Picture**.

3. From the **Insert Clip Art** pane (in Excel version 97 or 2000, choose from **File** menu), select the picture you want to use to replace the column.

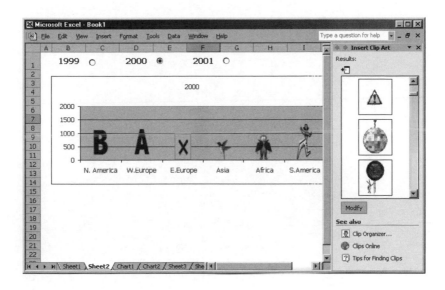

Chapter 13

Customizing Excel

As an Excel user, you know how many precious work hours you spend customizing and personalizing Excel, including changing the format of a style and saving it (see **Chapter 5, Styles**), updating headers and footers for printing, changing default font settings, changing customized lists, and so on.

In this chapter, you will become thoroughly familiar with the range of options in the **Options** dialog box, saving a workbook as a template for reuse, and more.

Changing the Window View

The default settings for the window view in Excel are determined by the Windows operating system and Excel. Minimize Excel, and right-click the desktop. Select **Properties**, and select the **Appearance** tab.

In addition to the changes described in this chapter, you can make several others through the **Item** menu. The changes described here are the most common and useful ones.

▣ **Changing the font size of the Sheet name** – the Sheet tabs in a workbook are part of the Scroll Bar. Change the font size in the Scroll Bar option to change the font size of the Sheet name in the tab.

▣ **Changing the format of cell comments and icon Tool Tips on the toolbar** – select Tool Tip, and change the background color and font.

Options Dialog box

In Excel, from the **Tools** menu, select **Options**. The **Options** dialog box has a number of tabs, each of which contains default settings that were determined by Microsoft. It is very important to become familiar with the definitions in the **Options** dialog box.

Options					? ✕
Color	International	Save	Error Checking	Spelling	Security
View	Calculation	Edit	General	Transition	Custom Lists	Chart

Show
  ☑ Startup Task Pane ☐ Formula bar ☐ Status bar ☑ Windows in Taskbar

Comments
  ○ None ◉ Comment indicator only ○ Comment & indicator

Objects
  ◉ Show all ○ Show placeholders ○ Hide all

Window options
  ☐ Page breaks ☑ Row & column headers ☑ Horizontal scroll bar
  ☐ Formulas ☑ Outline symbols ☑ Vertical scroll bar
  ☑ Gridlines ☑ Zero values ☑ Sheet tabs

Gridlines color: Automatic ▼

[OK]   [Cancel]

Displaying zero values (View tab)

Unchecking the **Zero values** box prevents the digit 0 from being displayed on the worksheet. This option is useful for printing.

Displaying gridlines (View tab)

Gridlines are controlled in two different places. To control if gridlines are displayed on the screen, use the **View** tab of the **Options** box. Uncheck the **Gridlines** box to view the spreadsheet without gridlines. This setting is great for getting a good look at your borders and lines.

By default, gridlines will not print whether they are displayed or not. To force Excel to print the gridlines, select **File**, **Page Setup**, **Sheet**. Then check the **Gridlines** box.

Recently used files list (General tab)

You can find the list of recently used files in the **File** menu. Change the default number to the maximum setting, nine files.

Set the number of sheets in a new workbook (General tab)

Set the number of sheets that open in a new workbook to avoid an excessive number of sheets. Set this number as low as possible to meet your needs. Working in a workbook with a small number of sheets is much easier.

Standard font (General tab)

The font **Arial**, size 10, is the standard font for Excel workbooks. Change the font and its size as desired.

Default file location (General tab)

A new Excel file is automatically saved for the first time (if you have not specified a location on the hard disk) in the **My Documents** folder on the **C:** drive. Change the default location as desired.

User name (General tab)

Type your name in this box. The name in the box appears in any **comment** you create in the sheet. See the section pertaining to comments in **Chapter 10, Information**.   It also appears in the file properties for any worksheet that you create.

Custom lists, in the Custom Lists tab

Add lists to the **Custom Lists**. With **Custom Lists**, you can add a list to the sheet by entering a name from this list into a cell. Copy it by dragging its handle. There is no need to type the list.

After you enter the text into the cell and copy it (by dragging the handle), Excel checks whether the text exists in one of your custom lists. If it does, Excel imports the list from **Custom Lists**.

Use **Custom Lists** to sort data according to the order of the list, instead of sorting it alphabetically. See **Chapter 17, Sorting**.

Example:

Type the text **January** in Cell A1. Drag the handle in the lower right corner of the cell to copy it to Cell A12. A list of the months of the year is entered into Cells A1:A12.

Adding a list to Custom Lists

1.   In the cells, type the list you want to save in **Custom Lists**.

2.   Select the range of cells with the list.

3.   From the **Tools** menu, select **Options** and then the **Custom Lists** tab.

4.   In the box to the left of the **Import** button, check the selected range of cells. Click **Import**.

Changing the paper size to A4/Letter (International tab)

New
In 2002

In the United States, the standard paper size is Letter, and in Europe, it is A4. Excel 2002 allows you to adjust the print area from one paper size to the other.

Saving (Save tab)

Automatic backup files are created every 10 minutes. If your computer crashes, you can restore the files from the list of restored files in the **Task Window**.

Error checking (Error Checking tab)

A nice innovation in Excel 2002 is the provision of various error-checking options. If there is an error in a formula, a **Smart Tag** is attached to the cell. Open the **Smart Tag** menu to display the type of error and evaluate the formula. For more information, see **Chapter 7, Formulas**.

Checking spelling (in the Spelling tab)

Select the dictionary language to check spelling in the sheet and access additional options.

Security (Security tab)

A new tab (see p. 218) in Excel 2002 allows you to prevent a workbook from being opened by setting a password to open it (you still have the option of setting a password from the **File** menu – select **Save As, Tools, General Options**). On this tab, you can also add a digital signature, set the level of virus protection with a macro, and even set a password to share work on a network. For an in-depth discussion of the subject of security, see **Chapter 9**, **Security and Protection**.

Options   ? X

| View | Calculation | Edit | General | Transition | Custom Lists | Chart |
| Color | International | Save | Error Checking | Spelling | Security |

New
In 2002

File encryption settings for this workbook

Password to open: ******   Advanced...

File sharing settings for this workbook

Password to modify:

☐ Read-only recommended

Digital Signatures...

Privacy options

☐ Remove personal information from this file on save

Macro security

Adjust the security level for files that might contain macro viruses
and specify names of trusted macro developers.   Macro Security...

OK   Cancel

Customizing Toolbars

Clicking an icon on a toolbar activates a macro. Adding icons to the toolbars increases the number of commands that you can activate and use. However, many useful icons are not located on the toolbars. Add important icons to toolbars based on your needs, or create a new toolbar.

Adding icons to the toolbars

Example: Add the **Page Setup** icon to the **Standard** toolbar (the first toolbar).

1. Select a toolbar.

2. Right-click, and from the shortcut menu, select **Customize**.

3. Select the **Commands** tab, and then click on the **Data** category.

4. In the **Commands** dialog box, click the **Page Setup** icon, and

![Customize dialog box showing the Commands tab with Categories list (File, Edit, View, Insert, Format, Tools, Data, Window and Help, Drawing, AutoShapes) and Commands list (Page Setup..., Set Print Area, Clear Print Area, Print Preview, Combined Preview)]

drag it to the **Standard** toolbar. Release the mouse.

Removing icons from toolbars

Select the icon you want to remove, and drag it off the toolbar while the **Customize** dialog box is open (to open this dialog box, see Steps 1-4 above, **Adding icons to the standard toolbar**).

Tip – Remove icons from the toolbar without opening the Customize dialog box

Select the icon and drag it off the toolbar while pressing **Alt**.

Tip – Remove icons that perform duplicate tasks from the toolbar

Some of the icons on the toolbar perform a double job.

For example, press **Shift** and the **Sort Ascending** icon. The sort is performed in descending order.

The duplicate icons that can be eliminated using Shift

On the **Standard** toolbar –

Print and **Print Preview**.

Sort Ascending and **Sort Descending**.

Open and **Save**.

On the **Formatting** toolbar –

Increase Indent and **Decrease Indent**.

Underline and **Double Underline**.

Center and **Merge and Center**.

Increase Decimal and **Decrease Decimal**.

Left-to-Right and **Right-to-Left** (Excel 97).

Adding icons to the menu bar

The Excel menus include a number of useful subjects, such as **Page Setup, Paste Special, Custom Views, Macro,** and more. Each one of them includes a variety of additional options, either through additional tabs or through drop-down lists. Add these necessary icons to the Excel menu bar. You will find them in the usual categories or in **Built-in Menus** in the **Customize** dialog box on the **Commands** tab.

Preventing icons from disappearing

With Excel, you can arrange the icons on the toolbars any way you like. As explained above, you can add and remove icons according to your needs. When the **Customize** dialog box is open, the entire toolbar is displayed with all its icons. After clicking **OK**, sometimes some of the icons on the right end of the toolbar disappear, because there is not enough space to display them all. To prevent these icons from disappearing, place the icons you need on the left end of the toolbar, and remove other icons that you do not need.

Adding a new customized toolbar

In addition to the regular toolbars, Excel offers the option of adding a new toolbar, giving it a name, and saving it with the existing toolbars.

1. In the **Customize** dialog box, select the **Toolbars** tab.

2. Click **New**.

3. Type a name for the toolbar.

4. Click **OK**.

5. Add icons to the toolbar.

6. Click **Close** in the **Customize** dialog box.

Saving your toolbar in the workbook

When your new toolbar is attached to a workbook, it is opened and displayed when the workbook is opened.

1. In the **Customize** dialog box, select the **Toolbars** tab.

2. Select **Attach**.

3. In the **Attach Toolbars** dialog box, select the toolbar you want from **Custom toolbars**.

4. Click **Copy**, **OK**, and **Close** in the **Customize** dialog box.

5. Save the workbook.

Removing customizations from toolbars

Select the **Toolbars** tab in the **Customize** dialog box, and click **Reset**. Selecting this option removes the additional toolbars you created.

Displaying a menu

Select the **Options** tab in the **Customize** dialog box.

Menu animations – select one of the various options for displaying a selected menu. Selecting **None** displays the entire menu as quickly as possible. The other options display the menu more slowly.

Customizing an icon

Select one of the toolbars, right-click, and from the shortcut menu, select **Customize**. Select any icon on a toolbar, and right-click.

The menu enables the following:

◙ Changing the icon name.

◙ Changing the icon image.

◙ Copying the icon image.

◙ Attaching a macro.

and a wide range of additional options.

Adding icons to an Excel menu

You can add an icon to a menu or sub-menu by using the same method you used to add icons to the toolbars or create new toolbars.

Make sure the **Customize** dialog box for toolbars is open. Drag the relevant icon to the menu or sub-menu. The sub-menu opens to allow you to place the icon there as desired.

When you add icons such as the **Custom View** icon to the Excel menu, you save toolbar space, so you can add smaller icons. See **Chapter 11, Printing**.

Saving changes to toolbars and menu

The changes made to the menu and toolbars are saved in a file called Excel.xlb in Excel 2002 and the username + the **xlb** extension in Excel 97 and 2000. When Excel is started, the file **Excel.xlb** opens the toolbars and menu as they were last saved.

To ensure that the changes to the toolbars and menu are saved (if you change computers, remove the Excel program and reinstall it, and so forth), locate files with the xlb extension by using the **Search** function, and copy them to an external backup (disk, diskette, Internet, and so forth).

Template

A workbook **template** creates a perfect copy, or image, of itself upon opening.

A **template** can be used as a substitute for office forms such as a timesheet report. Prepare a timesheet report, including formulas and formats, and save it as a **template** by using the method described below.

This section explains how to save a customized workbook as a **template** with additions and changes made according to your preferences. This includes special formats that you saved in the **Style** dialog box, **headers** and **footers** that you saved for printing and more. A **template** file is saved with the extension **xlt**, and a regular Excel file is saved with the extension **xls**. When you open a **template** file, a new file is created with the **xls** extension, and the name of the file receives a numeral.

Example:

In the course of work with Excel, you open a regular workbook by using the shortcut **Ctrl+N**. The new workbook is a perfect copy of a **template** workbook called Book.xlt (the basic Excel workbook template). The name of the new workbook is Book1.xls, and an additional workbook would be called Book2.xls.

Saving a customized workbook as a template

Open a new workbook and make changes to its default settings.

- ▣ **Format** – create or insert formats into the workbook by creating styles. See **Chapter 5, Styles**.

- ▣ **Printing** – add headers and footers. Change the default setting for the **First Page Number**. See **Chapter 11, Printing**.

- ▣ **Changing default settings** – from the **Tools** menu, select **Options**. Make the desired changes. See the beginning of this chapter for the various options.

- ▣ Add formulas and values to the **Name** box. See **Chapter 6, Name**.

Save the workbook with the changes as a **template**.

1. From the Excel menu bar, select **File**, **Save as**.

2. Select **Save as Type – Template**.

3. In **File name**, enter the name MyWorkbook (this name is only a recommendation and not mandatory).

4. Click **Save**.

5. From the Excel menu bar, select **File**, **Close** (you must close a **template** file after saving it).

The file is saved in the Templates folder.

Opening a template

A workbook **template** that you create is saved in the **Templates** folder. From the **File** menu, select **New**, and open the MyWorkbook file (the template you created and saved in the previous example). In Excel 97 and 2000, a new window is opened.

In Excel 2002, the **Task Window** is opened.

New

In 2002

Double-click the MyWorkbook file to open a new workbook called MyWorkbook1.xls. A workbook **template** called MyWorkbook is saved as a template with the name MyWorkbook.xlt. The workbook is opened as a regular workbook with the xls extension, and the name of the workbook is MyWorkbook1.xls. Start working in the workbook, and save it with any name you like, just as you would save any other workbook.

Opening a template file automatically upon starting Excel

There are two options for opening a workbook **template** automatically upon starting Excel.

First option

Save the workbook called Book.xlt, which you customized, in the sub-folder called XlStart. When Excel is started, a customized workbook Book1.xls is opened from within the template you saved, instead of the standard Book1.xls.

The XlStart sub-folder is located in the same folder as the Office program on the hard drive.

To open a new workbook, press **Ctrl+N** or in the **Standard** toolbar, click the **New** icon.

Second option

Save the **template** file you created as MyWorkbook.xlt in any folder, and enter the name of the workbook template in the **Options** dialog box.

1. From the **Tools** menu, select **Options**.

2. Select the **General** tab.

3. In the **Alternate startup file location** box, enter the full path where you saved the MyWorkbook file.

4. Click **OK**.

Note

Do not use the two selected options simultaneously, unless you have created more than one workbook. Use only one of the two options (Excel tries to open the file with the same name twice).

Inserting a sheet into the workbook from the template

After you have customized a new worksheet and saved it as a **template**, you can add a new sheet to the regular workbook from the saved workbook **template**.

Option 1 - Inserting a regular sheet to the workbook.

1. Select the sheet name of the sheet tab in the workbook.

2. Right-click, and from the shortcut menu, select **Insert**.

3. In the **Insert** dialog box, double-click **Worksheet**.

The sheet tab you inserted is a regular Excel sheet.

Option 2 – Define a new customized worksheet to be used as the default inserted worksheet.

1. To insert a sheet from a template, right-click on the sheet tab. From the shortcut menu, choose **Insert**, and then double-click Sheet.xlt.

2. Delete all of the sheets except for one.

3. Save the workbook as a template, as explained above, with the name Sheet.xlt, and close it.

Insert this customized sheet into the workbook:

1. From the menu, select **Insert** and **Worksheet**.

The sheet that you have inserted is your customized worksheet template.

Option 3 – Define more than one customized worksheet and select from them.

1. Open the customized workbook that you saved as a template.

2. Delete all the sheets except for one.

3. Save the workbook as a template, as explained above, with the name **MySheet** (or any name you choose), and close it.

Insert the saved **MySheet** into the workbook.

1. Select the sheet name in the workbook.

2. Right-click, and from the shortcut menu, select **Insert**.

3. Double-click **MySheet**.

Explanation

If you select the workbook MyWorkbook from the **Insert** menu, all the template sheets are inserted into the existing workbook. If you save the workbook with one sheet as a **template**, you can insert only a single sheet into the existing workbook.

Updating a workbook template

1. Open a workbook called MyWorkbook.

2. Make any necessary changes.

3. Save the workbook as a **template**, and select the template MyWorkbook.

4. The following message appears: "The file MyWorkbook.xlt already exists. Do you want to replace the existing file?" Click **Yes**.

5. Close the workbook.

Chapter 14

Opening, Closing and Saving Workbooks

Handling a workbook includes opening, saving and/or closing. These are actions that you routinely perform in the course of your work with Excel.

The regular performance of these routine actions justifies learning shortcuts, as it will shorten the amount of time you spend on them. This is the goal of this chapter.

Opening a New Workbook

For your convenience, Excel opens a new workbook every time you start the program. The name of the file it opens is Book1.xls. This new workbook is an exact copy of the **Template** file named Book.xlt.

Additionally, during your ongoing work in Excel, you can open a new workbook or an additional workbook by using the keyboard shortcut, **Ctrl+N** or by clicking the **New** icon in the **Standard** toolbar.

You can also open a new workbook by opening the **File** menu and selecting **New**.

Opening a Previously Saved Workbook

You can open an existing (previously saved) workbook in a number of ways. The following is the standard method for opening a workbook.

1. Press **Ctrl+O** (the letter O, not the number zero), or from the **File** menu, select **Open**.

2. Locate the file in the folder on your hard drive and open it.

This procedure is slow and inefficient. You are better off using quicker methods.

Opening a workbook from the recently used file list

Excel allows you to save a list of up to nine of the files you have used most recently. From the **File** menu, view the list of most recently used files.

To open a workbook, press **Alt+F** and the workbook number as it appears on the list.

Be sure that the recently used file list is set to the maximum of nine files. From the **Tools** menu, select **Options**, and then select the **General** tab. In the **Recently used file list** box, change the number to 9.

Saving a Workbook

By default, Excel automatically saves all new files in C:\My Documents. From the **Tools** menu, select **Options**, and then select the **General** tab. Change the default by typing a new complete path to the desired folder in the **Default file location** box. New files will now automatically be saved to that location.

Saving a workbook using Save As

Press **F12** or from the **File** menu, select **Save As**. To save the file in an existing folder, navigate in the **Save in** box to the folder where you want to store the file on your hard drive. Now save the file with a new name.

If you want to save the file in a new folder, navigate in the **Save in** box to the location on the hard drive where you want to open the new folder. Now, click the **Create New Folder** icon. In the **Name** box, type the name of the folder, and then click **OK**. In the **File name** box, type a name for the file, and click **Save**.

Inserting the path where the workbook is saved to the title bar or the status bar

When you open a workbook from some directory on the network, you do not always remember the path or name of the folder where the file is saved. Insert the full path to the title bar (the blue strip above the Excel menu bar), or to the status bar.

See the figure on next page –

A workbook called Monthly Reports is saved in the **Reports** folder on the **G:** drive.

1. In Press **Alt+F11** to open VBE.

2. **VBAProject**, double-click the module called **ThisWorkbook** to open it.

3. Above the module sheet are two drop-down lists. Open the left-hand list (**General**) and select **Workbook**.

4. A macro called **Workbook_Open** appears. In the macro, type the code as it appears in the figure below.

    Name of the title bar – **Caption**. Name of the status bar – **Status Bar**.

5. From the right-hand drop-down list, select the event (macro) **Workbook_BeforeClose**. In the macro, type the code as it appears in the figure below.

6. Save the file, close it, and then reopen it to check whether the file name and path appear in the blue title bar.

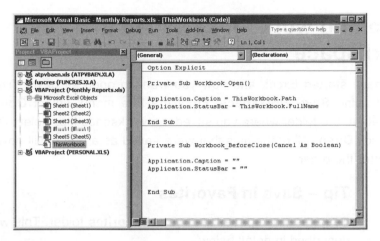

Explanation

1. When the workbook is opened, a **Workbook_Open** macro is activated. This macro performs the directions written in it.

2. When the workbook is closed, the **Workbook_BeforeClose** macro is activated. This macro deletes the path, and the title bar and status bar return to their former condition. It is very important to delete the path, because otherwise, the next workbook displays the old path.

3. Insert the macro into every workbook that you need to view the path.

Saving Workbooks in a Customized Workspace

Save Workspace allows you to create a shortcut that lets you open a group of workbooks in one step and eliminate the need to open them each individually.

From the **Window** menu, check the list of open files, and be sure that the list includes only the files want to group together as a package. Close all other files that may be open.

From the **File** menu, select **Save Workspace**, and navigate in the **Save in** box to the folder where you want to store the new file. The file name will end with the extension .xlw. The workspace file does not contain the workbooks themselves, but rather points to the files saved as a group.

Opening workbooks saved in a workspace

You have started Excel, and now you want to open all of the files you saved using **Save Workspace**. From the **File** menu, select **Open** and navigate to the folder where you saved the workspace file. Select the file, and click **Open**. All of the files that were saved as a group will now open one after the other.

Tip – Save in Favorites

Save the workspace file in your **Favorites** folder. This will be described in detail below.

Saving shortcuts to files/folders in Favorites

The Windows operating system lets you save important shortcuts to files, folders or URLs (Internet addresses) in a folder called **Favorites**. There are many of advantages to using this folder. First, create a shortcut. Then, from the **File** menu, select **Open**, and click the **Favorites** icon in the **Open** dialog box. Now, from the list of shortcuts, select the file or folder you want to open, and click **Open**.

Adding a shortcut to the Favorites folder

From the **File** menu, select **Save As**. In the **Save As** dialog box, select the workbook or folder for which you want to create a shortcut. Select **Tools** and then **Add to Favorites**.

Opening workbooks from a list of hyperlinks

Prepare a list of files in a worksheet along with a list of hyperlinks. Clicking on any of the shortcuts that were created through the hyperlinks (see column B in the figure below) will open the workbook. The figure below displays a list of files containing Excel tips.

Inserting a hyperlink

Select a cell in which you want to insert a hyperlink. Excel offers several shortcuts for opening the **Insert Hyperlink** dialog box.

1. Press **Ctrl+K**; or select the **Insert Hyperlink** icon from the **Standard** toolbar; **or** from the **Insert** menu, select **Hyperlink**.

2. In the **Insert Hyperlink** dialog box, select the workbook you want to link to, and click **OK**.

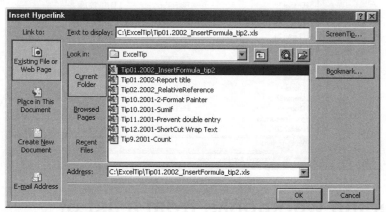

Closing a workbook / workbooks and Excel

To close a workbook, press **Ctrl+F4**.

To close all workbooks without exiting Excel, press **Shift**, and from the **File** menu, select **Close All**.

To exit Excel, press **Alt+F4**.

Chapter 15

Data

Preparing reports and performing data analysis are two of the main reasons people use Excel.

Excel offers strong and efficient data analysis tools. Select the **Data** menu to view the wide range of options Excel offers. You can sort, filter, insert subtotals, insert multilevel subtotals, consolidate data, and create incredible PivotTables from data contained in an Excel sheet.

In order to take advantage of the various features and techniques, you need to understand how Excel works. You need to learn to follow some clear and simple guidelines. Simplicity is the name of the game here, and Excel guarantees you results.

This chapter is one of the most important chapters of this book. Organizing data in the sheets of a workbook, according to Excel's data management rules, allows you to use formulas to find data, call up data needed to prepare complex reports, and use the data analysis tools that are listed in the **Data** menu.

Guidelines for Organizing Data in Excel

▣ **List structure** (also called a database): Each list of data must start with column labels in the first row, and there can only be one row of column labels. All of the cells in the column labels row must contain unique labels. Every data column should have a non-blank entry in the heading row.

A data list does not include empty rows, subtotals, or totals at the bottom of each column. The columns in a data list are adjacent to each other.

The list has distinct borders: one blank row and one blank column between the list and any other data on the sheet. To check the borders of the data list, do the following: select a cell in the list, press **Ctrl+*** and check the region selected. The entire list should be in the selected region.

◙ **Data fields**: In a list, a vertical range of data (column) is referred to as a field. The text in the column label is the **Field Name**, and the **Field Items** are the data in the cells in the column beneath the column label. Each field (column) contains one specific type of information (dates in a date field, totals in a total field, or customer names in the customer field).

◙ **Records**: In a list, a horizontal range of data (row) is referred to as a **Record**. The cells in a record (row) do not have to contain data (for example, an invoice number is missing in an invoice number field).

Tip

Create only one data list in a sheet and place it in the corner of the sheet (in the first cell in the list, A1). The remaining cells in the sheet outside the data area are empty.

The figure on the next page provides an example of a data list in a sheet.

◙ The title above the database is separated from the database by an empty row.

◙ Row 3 (the column labels row with the names of the fields) is formatted with text wrapping in the cells (for text wrapping – select row 3, press **Ctrl+1**, and select the **Alignment** tab. Now, select **Wrap text**, and click **OK**).

◙ The field names are unique (the column labels, row 3).

- There are no spaces between rows and/or between columns.

Preparing the List to Sort, Filter and Insert Subtotals

You can add more tools to the data list you created in Excel (either manually or by importing data from external systems) to help you sort, filter, and analyze data.

Using formatting to set apart the column labels row (field names)

Remember that when you create a list in Excel, you cannot leave any empty space between the rows. Make the column labels row (field names) stand out visibly by formatting them with a bold font and/or by filling the cells in a different color.

Freezing column labels

It is easier to review the data if you keep the column labels visible at the top of your worksheet as you scroll down a list.

1. Select cell A4 (the first cell beneath the first column (field) label in the database).

2. From the **Window** menu, select **Freeze Panes**.

Entering Data into the List

Excel offers a number of different ways of entering data into a list.

☐ Importing the data from external systems. See **Chapter 16, Importing Text Files**.

☐ Entering data manually. See **Chapter 2, Text**.

☐ Using **Forms** to enter data.

Using forms to enter data

Using forms to enter data allows you to add new records, delete existing records, automatically copy formulas when new records are added, search by criteria and more. Select a cell in the data list and from the **Data** menu, select **Form**.

Take a look at the **Form** dialog box:

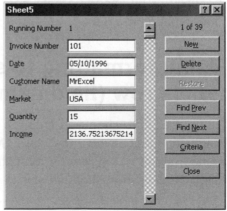

☐ The data form that appears has the same name as the sheet.

☐ You cannot enter data into fields (cells) that contain formulas.

☐ You can find data records based on criteria you specify.

Disadvantages

If you use a **Form**, you cannot use helpful tools such as **AutoComplete**, **Select from List**, and **Validation**.

Applying Color to Data Based on Criteria

Data lists contain a large variety of data representing different things. When the font color is black, the cells are white and the borders gray, and adding a color will make the data in the cells or rows stand out and will help you view data that meets certain criteria.

Example:

In an aging report, you may want to have data on customers with outstanding debts of over 60 days stand out. You might also want to use a different color to call attention to outstanding debts of over 90 days.

Later in this chapter we will discuss how to use **Conditional Formatting** to apply color to data based on criteria. See **Chapter 18, Filtering** and **Chapter 19, Subtotals** for additional techniques that can be used for coloring data based on criteria.

Using conditional formatting to color data

See the figure of a data list at the beginning of the chapter to **Format data** by using a formula:

1. Select cell A3, and press **Ctrl+*** to select the active region.

2. From the **Format** menu, select **Conditional Formatting**.

3. In the **Condition 1** drop-down list, select **Formula Is**, and type =$E3="ASIA". Click **Format**, select the **Font** tab, select the color, and click **OK**.

4. In the **Condition 2** drop-down list, select **Formula Is**, and type =$E3="AFRICA". Click **Format**, select the **Font** tab, select a different color than you selected for Condition 1, and click **OK**.

5. In the **Condition 3** drop-down list, select **Formula Is**, and type =$E3="USA". Click **Format**, select the **Font** tab, select a different color than you selected for Condition 1, and click **OK**.

6. Click **OK**.

Explanation

The cell reference in the formula is made up of the absolute reference to the column and the relative reference of the row. Excel checks each cell in the list to see if the data in the same row in column E meets the criteria you selected in **Conditional Formatting**.

A formula in conditional formatting is similar to the initial argument in an IF formula, Logical_test. If the formula evaluates to a logical value of True, the cell will be formatted as set in the **Font** tab.

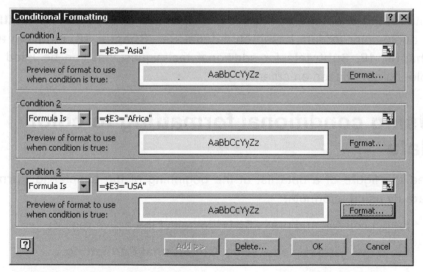

Applying color to maximum or minimum values

1. Select cell A3, and press **Ctrl+*** to select the active region.

2. From the **Format** menu, select **Conditional Formatting**. Select **Formula Is** for **Conditions 1** and **2** according to the figure with the formulas Min and Max. Select the formatting you desire.

 Note

Select the first cell in the data list before selecting the entire list. Be sure to distinguish between absolute reference and relative reference when entering the formula.

Conditional Formatting	? X
Condition 1	
Formula Is ▼ =$F3=MAX($F:$F)	🔣
Preview of format to use when condition is true: AaBbCcYyZz	Format...
Condition 2	
Formula Is ▼ =$F3=MIN($F:$F)	🔣
Preview of format to use when condition is true: AaBbCcYyZz	Format...
ⓘ Add >> Delete... OK Cancel	

Applying color to maximum or minimum values

1. Select cell A2 and press Ctrl+~ to select the active region.

2. From the Format menu, select Conditional Formatting. Select Formula is for Conditions 1 and 2 according to the figure with the formulas Min and Max. Select the formatting you desire.

Note

Select the first cell in the data list before selecting the entire list. Be sure to distinguish between absolute reference and relative reference when entering the formula.

Chapter 16

Importing Text Files

You will sometimes need to import data from external applications that originate in non-Windows operating systems (for example, the DOS operating system). This data is necessary for data analysis and preparing reports in Excel worksheets. Understanding the possible problems and solutions involved in importing text files will help you create organized data tables in Excel. This chapter explains the technique for transferring text files and also offers some common troubleshooting techniques.

Creating a Text File

Most applications that run under the DOS operating system, or under other non-Window operating systems, enable you to save a report with data in a text file by printing the report to a file instead of to a printer.

When you select the **Print to file** option (in a bookkeeping application, for example), a dialog box opens in which you type a name for the file. Enter the file name in the format of up to eight characters. The operating system automatically adds three characters which represent the file extension – for example, **.doc**.

Importing ASCII Text Files

1. From the **File** menu, select **Open**.

2. In the **Open** dialog box, select **File Type**, **All Files**.

3. In the **Search** field, select the desired text file, for example, Test.doc.

4. Click **OK**.

Tip - Copy the file you created into a different folder.

Copying the file into a different folder on your hard drive is recommended. Copy the file to the same folder in which you save the Excel workbook and from which you produce your reports.

Text Import Wizard – Step 1 of 3

1. Select the **Delimited** option.

2. In the **File origin** drop-down box, select either DOS or OS/2 for Excel 97 and MS-DOS (PC-8) for Excel versions 2000 and 2002.

3. Click **Next**.

![Text Import Wizard - Step 1 of 3 dialog box. The Text Wizard has determined that your data is Delimited. If this is correct, choose Next, or choose the data type that best describes your data. Original data type: Choose the file type that best describes your data: Delimited - Characters such as commas or tabs separate each field. Fixed width - Fields are aligned in columns with spaces between each field. Start import at row: 1. File origin: 437 : OEM United States. Preview of file C:\test1.doc. 2 11/22/2002,403,Office XP,1,10/20/2002,10,1000.00 3 11/22/2002,501,Office XP,2,9/30/2002,9,6000.00 4 11/22/2002,501,MSDN,2,11/15/2002,9,6000.00 5 11/22/2002,306,VBA CD,2,12/30/2002,6,2000.00. Cancel, < Back, Next >, Finish.]

Text Import Wizard – Step 2 of 3

Step 2 of 3 enables you to organize your data into columns.

1. Separate the data into columns by selecting one of the options. Now check the results.

2. Click **Next**.

Text Import Wizard – Step 3 of 3

Step 3 of 3 enables you to format the columns.

1. Select a column (the column will be colored black), and then click on the heading of the column.

2. Under **Column data format**, either select one of the three formats (**General**, **Text** or **Date**) or select **Do not import column (skip)** to prevent importing unnecessary columns into Excel.

3. Click **Finish**.

Tip – Format your dates in the import process

If you import a **Date** column, you must first format this column by selecting the **Date** option under **Column date format**. If you do not format the **Date** column, it will be difficult for you to use the date formatting in the entire worksheet in the workbook.

Troubleshooting problems while importing text

A minus appears to the right of the number

Problem

A negative number that is imported into Excel is often formatted as text with the minus sign (-) on the right side instead of the left. Excel does not sum up negative numbers that are formatted as text, and the results will not reconcile.

Solution

Enter the formula in the figure below to solve both problems. It will move the minus sign (-) to the left side of the number, and it will format the data in the cell as a number instead of as text.

Microsoft Excel - Trailing Minus Sign								
File	Edit	View	Insert	Format	Tools	Data	Window	Help
B1	▼	fx	=VALUE(IF(RIGHT(A1,1)="-","-"&LEFT(A1,LEN(A1)-1),A1))					
	A	B	C	D	E	F	G	H
1	5645665-	-5645665						
2								
3								

Sheet1

Ready   NUM

Breakdown of the functions used in the nested formula:

Function	Explanation
Value	Returns a change in formatting from text to number.
If	Checks True or False of the logical value.
Right	Returns the number of characters from right to left in the text.
Left	Returns the number of characters from left to right in the text.
Len	Returns the number of characters in the text.

Data that is not formatted as a number or date

Problem

Often, columns with numerical data or columns that contain date data are formatted as text columns.

Changing the formatting of the column from text to number format is often not efficient.

Solution

Multiply by 1

Enter the number 1 into the cell and copy it. Select the column that is formatted as text, right-click, and select **Paste Special**. Select **Multiply** from the dialog box, and click **OK**.

Text to Columns

Select the column that is formatted as text. From the **Data** menu, select **Text to Columns**, and then select the **Fixed width** option. Skip Step 2. In Step 3, select the **General** option from the **Column data format**, and click **Finish**. To change the column formatting to date formatting, select the **Date** option (under **Column data format**), and then click **End**.

Erase Unnecessary Characters

Trim is an important function that is used to clean up unnecessary empty characters of text that appear in a cell. From the **Insert** menu, select **Function**; from the **Paste Function** dialog box that appears, select **Text** from the list of Function categories column; and then select **Trim** from the Function name column.

```
Function Arguments                                              ? X
  ┌TRIM───────────────────────────────────────────────────────────
  │        Text │A1                              │ 🔣 │ = "Data"
  │
  │                                                   = "Data"
  │   Removes all spaces from a text string except for single spaces between words.
  │
  │
  │        Text is the text from which you want spaces removed.
  │
  │   Formula result =          Data
  │   Help on this function                    [   OK   ]  [  Cancel  ]
```

Create and Add a Function for Reversed Text Characters

Before adding a function, read about techniques for adding functions in **Chapter 7, Formulas**.

1. Click **Alt+F11** to open Visual Basic Editor (VBE).

2. From the **Insert** menu, select **Module** (to add a module).

3. Enter the following lines of code into the module:

```
Function ReverseText(Text) As String
    Dim i As Integer
    For i = Len(Text) To 1 Step -1
        ReverseText = ReverseText & Mid(Text, i, 1)
    Next i
End Function
```

Testing the function:

1. To test the function, open **Paste Function (Shift+F3)**.

2. From the **User Defined** category, select the **ReverseText** function.

3. In the function box, select any cell that contains text.

4. Click **OK**.

Chapter 17

Sorting

One of the most common operations in working with data in an Excel workbook is **Sorting** data. Read **Chapter 15, Data** and the guidelines for sorting data carefully. Understanding them is important, both to prevent problems and to get the most out of the options available.

Guidelines to consider before sorting data

▣ **Selecting cells**

Do not select a column or data range in a data list on a sheet. Select only a single cell. Click the **Sort** icon to automatically sort the entire list. The data will be sorted according to the field of the cell selected.

▣ **Formulas**

Be careful when sorting data if there are formulas in the cells. Sorting data when cells are linked to other rows or cells in other sheets could distort the calculations.

Be meticulous when sorting a list with formulas that have **Names** (which are defined with absolute references by default) or with formulas that have absolute references.

▣ **Insert a sequence column to restore original order**

Insert an additional column into the data list with ascending numbers, 1,2,3,…(do not use a formula) before sorting the data.

If a list includes a column with consecutive dates, use this column as the first sorting column.

Performing a Simple Sort

1. Select Cell E5 (see figure below).

2. Click the **Sort Ascending** icon ![icon] on the Standard toolbar.

The result – a table sorted in ascending order (alphabetically), according to the **Market** field.

> **Tip – Save space on the toolbar by removing one icon**
>
> By pressing **Shift+Sort Ascending** icon, the direction of the sort (AZ) is changed to descending (ZA).

Guidelines for Sorting Data

Excel sorts data according to a defined order.

- ◙ **Values** – Numerical values, including date and time, are sorted from the lowest (negative) to the highest (positive). Excel does not consider the format of the cell, only its contents. Date and time receive numeric values when data is sorted. (See **Chapter 4, Date and Time**).

- **Text** – Text is sorted first by symbols such as *, (,), $; then by ASCII characters; and finally, by letters of the alphabet. From the **Data** menu, select **Sort**, **Options**, and select the **Case Sensitive** box. Text with upper-case letters is sorted before text with lower-case letters.

- **Logical values** – False is sorted before True.

- **Errors** – Errors in cells that were created during calculation of formulas do not undergo internal sorting. They will appear next to last.

- **Empty cells** – Empty cells are always sorted last.

  Sort Descending changes the sort order from the last to the first, except for empty cells, which are always last.

Tip – Deleting empty rows

When importing text files into Excel, use **Sort** to delete empty rows, delimiting characters and errors, which are all automatically placed at the end of a sorted list.

Sorting a Large Number of Fields

Select a cell in the data list, and from the **Data** menu, select **Sort**. The **Sort** dialog box includes sorting options of up to three fields. To sort more than three fields in a sheet, begin the sort with the last three fields in order of importance, and continue in ascending order until you arrive at the most important field.

Sorting by Column

The default setting for sorting in ascending or descending order is by row. Occasionally you will want to sort by column.

	A	B	C	D	E	F	G	H
1	Name	Eric	John	Dennis	Josh	Freda	Will	
2	Gross Salary	1230.77	1400.00	923.08	1923.08	2500.00	1692.31	
3	Fed Tax	344.62	392.00	258.46	538.46	700.00	473.85	
4	FICA	88.62	100.80	66.46	138.46	180.00	121.85	
5	401K	73.85	84.00	55.38	115.38	150.00	101.54	
6	Net Pay	723.69	823.20	542.77	1130.77	1470.00	995.08	

Sorting by column

1. From the **Data** menu, select **Sort**, **Options**.

2. Select the **Sort left to right** option.

3. Click **OK**.

In the **Sort by** option of the **Sort** dialog box, select the number of the row by which the columns will be sorted. In the figure above (with data), the second row is selected.

Example:

The list includes salary data and will be sorted according to the employees' salaries, from the highest to the lowest. The structure of the list is such that the first row has the employee name and the second row has the gross salary. In the **Sort by** option, select the second row.

Result:

The columns in the table are sorted from the highest salary to the lowest.

Sorting by Custom Lists

As mentioned above, sorting by row is the default setting, and sorting by column is performed alphabetically, in either ascending or descending order. Occasionally, you will want to sort data according to different criteria, for example, by a list of months – January, February, March, etc., or according to a list of employees in some order other than alphabetical. A list of this kind is saved in **Custom Lists**.

The **Market** field (see page 256) contains four items – Western Europe, USA, Asia, Africa. The data will be sorted as follows – Asia, Africa, Western Europe, USA (not alphabetically).

Step 1 – saving a custom list

1. In a new sheet, in Cells A1:A4, enter the following items in this order – Asia, Africa, Western Europe, USA.

2. Select Cells A1:A4.

3. From the **Tools** menu, select **Options**, and then select the **Custom Lists** tab. Check the **Import** box to make sure that Cells A1:A4 match your selection.

4. Click **Import**.

5. Click **OK**.

Options dialog box — Custom Lists tab

Custom lists:
- NEW LIST
- Sun, Mon, Tue, Wed, Thu
- Sunday, Monday, Tuesday
- Jan, Feb, Mar, Apr, May,
- January, February, March

List entries:

Add
Delete

Press Enter to separate list entries.

Import list from cells: Import

OK   Cancel

Step 2 – sorting by a custom list

1. Select one of the cells in the list.

2. From the **Data** menu, select **Sort**, and then **Options**.

3. In the **First key sort order** drop-down list, select the list you saved in Step 1.

4. Click **OK**.

5. In the **Sort** dialog box, select **Sort by**, and then select **Market**.

6. Click **OK**.

Inserting a Line between Groups of Data after Sorting

Insert a colored line to separate between one sorting group and another. To create separating lines between customer names, use **Conditional Formatting**.

Transferring the line between customer groups

1. Select the data list without the column headings row.

2. A shortcut for quick selection is to select Cell A2 and press **Ctrl+Shift+Down Arrow**. While holding down **Ctrl+Shift**, press **Right Arrow**.

    From the **Format** menu, select **Conditional Formatting**.

3. In the **Condition 1** drop-down list, select **Formula Is**.

4. In the formula box, enter the formula =$D2<>$D3. Be sure to enter the formula with absolute reference for the column and relative reference for the row.

5. In the **Conditional Formatting** dialog box, click the **Format** button, and then select the **Border** tab. Select **underline** and the color **red**.

6. Click **OK** twice.

Explanation

When the formula is calculated, the text cells in Column D are compared. If the name of the customer changes, a red separating line is created for all the cells of the row.

Chapter 18

Filtering

Automatic filtering is a method that allows you to hide records that contain items that do not meet the specified filter criteria.

Excel offers two filtering options

▣ **AutoFiltering** of a list according to one or more criteria.

▣ **Advanced filtering** according to complex criteria.

Adding Icons to the Toolbar

Add icons from the **Data** category of the **Customize** dialog box to the toolbar to allow quick filtering and display of all data that was hidden.

AutoFilter icon

Show All icon   Show All

Once you have added the icon to the toolbar, filtering lists is easy. In the sheet, select the item in the field according to which data will be filtered, and click the **AutoFilter** icon.

To undo the automatic filter and display hidden rows, click the **Show All** icon.

To add an icon to the toolbar, select one of the toolbars and right-click. From **Customize**, select the **Commands** tab. From the **Data** category, drag the **AutoFilter** and **Show All** icons to the toolbar. Click **Close**.

AutoFilter

Select a cell list of data. From the **Data** menu, select **Filter**, **AutoFilter**.

Running Number	Invoice Number	Date	Customer Name	Market	Quantity	Income
1	101	05/10/1996	MrExcel	USA	15	2,136.75
2	102	06/10/1996	Intel	USA	17	2,270.94
3	103	07/10/1996	Motorola	Asia	20	10,152.14
4	104	08/10/1996	Pacific Bell	Western Europe	50	11,111.11
5	105	09/10/1996	Motorola	Asia	100	8,717.95
6	107	11/10/1996	Amazon	Asia	15	29,280.00
7	108	12/10/1996	Microsoft	Asia	30	6,020.00
8	109	01/10/1997	AIG	Asia	40	8,040.00
9	110	02/10/1997	Cisco	Asia	50	37,065.81
10	111	03/10/1997	MrExcel	USA	67	15,452.00
11	112	04/10/1997	Pacific Bell	Asia	77	13,032.00
12	113	05/10/1997	Amazon	Africa	89	13,095.00
13	114	06/10/1997	Intel	USA	101	23,084.00
14	115	07/10/1997	Motorola	Asia	113	23,118.00
15	116	08/10/1997	Intel	USA	125	18,495.00
16	117	09/10/1997	Microsoft	Asia	138	23,506.50
17	118	10/10/1997	AIG	Africa	150	25,129.90
18	119	11/10/1997	Pacific Bell	Africa	162	26,753.30
19	120	12/10/1997	Microsoft	Asia	174	28,376.70

A drop-down filtering list is added to the name of every **field** in the table. To open the list, click the arrow on the right side of the cell. Clicking the arrow displays a unique list of items in the field. By selecting one of these items, you are actually setting the filter criterion.

After the item is selected and the list has been filtered, the color of the filter arrow in the active-filter field changes from black to blue.

Note

Filter **on multiple fields** – you can select more than one criterion for filtering. After finishing the first filter, filter again by selecting an item from another column.

The number of items available for filtering is limited. Excel cannot filter columns in which the number of items exceeds 999 (not the number of rows). To filter when there are more than 999 items, use **Advanced Filter** (see below).

Be careful with formulas that have a relative reference. The result of the filter will distort the results of the calculation. Only perform a filter if the formulas have **Names** or absolute references.

Printing data after AutoFilter

1. Select the data list, before or after performing **AutoFilter**, by using the shortcut **Ctrl+***.

2. From the **File** menu, select **Page Setup**.

3. Set the **Print Area**.

    The Print Area is the entire data list. After filtering, only the displayed data is printed.

Saving AutoFilter criteria by using Custom Views

To save **AutoFilter** definitions as repeated criteria, add the **Custom Views** icon to the toolbar. It is located in the **View** category of the **Customize** dialog box for toolbars.

Saving a custom view

1. Filter the database with the criteria you set.

2. In the icon itself, enter the name of the view you want to save.

3. Press **Enter**.

 Note

Select and define the print area before saving the **Custom View**. See the explanation in the **Custom Views** section of **Chapter 11, Printing**. By using **Custom Views** to save filtering definitions, you can save complex definitions together with print definitions.

Deleting a custom view

From the **View** menu, select **Custom Views**. Select the view you want to delete, and click **Delete**.

Custom AutoFilter

Custom AutoFilter allows you to set complex criteria for **AutoFilter**.

Example: Selecting two customers with Custom AutoFilter.

1. Open the filter list in the **Customer Name** field.

2. Select **Custom** (third from the top of the item menu for the field).

3. In **Show rows where: Customer Name**, select **equals**, and on the right side, select the customer Cisco.

4. Select the **Or** option (as opposed to the **And** option).

5. In the second field for **Show rows where: Customer Name**, select **equals**, and on the right side, select the customer Amazon.

6. Click **OK**.

Filtering by wildcard text characters

For example, filter a customer list in which the first character is A. In the **Custom AutoFilter** dialog box, open the options from the list. Select **begins with**, and on the right side, type **A***. Click **OK**.

Filtering by the date field

Excel does not sort data according to cell format, but according to cell value. When sorting by date, Excel sorts the date according to its number. For example, the serial number of the date September 9, 2001 is 37164. If the cell format is changed to mmmm, the result of the format is **September**. When sorting the data list, Excel ignores **September** and only relates to the number 37164.

With **AutoFilter**, as opposed to **Sorting**, Excel relates to the date format and allows you to filter data according to format.

Filtering according to date by changing the format

1. Turn off the **AutoFilter**. From the **Data** menu, select **Filter, AutoFilter**.

2. Copy the **Date** column.

3. Select two columns to the right of **Date**, right-click, and from the shortcut menu, select **Insert Copied Cells** (pasting by inserting copied cells allows you to insert two columns and paste the copied column into them).

4. In Cell D1, type the heading **Month**, and in Cell E1, type the heading **Year**.

5. Select the **Month** field. To select it quickly, select Cell D2, and press **Ctrl+Shift+Down Arrow**.

6. Press **Ctrl+1** (**Format Cells**).

7. In the **Number** tab, select **Custom**.

8. In the **Type** box, enter the format, mmmm (full month format).

9. Click **OK**.

10. Select the **Year** field. To select it quickly, select Cell E2, and press **Ctrl+Shift+Down Arrow**.

11. Press **Ctrl+1**.

12. In the **Number** tab, select **Custom**.

13. In the **Type** box, enter the format, yyyy (year format).

14. Click **OK**.

15. Select one of the cells in the **Year** field, and click the **AutoFilter** icon.

The figure below illustrates the results.

Color rows according to criteria

You can use coloring to isolate data in lists and to differentiate between various types of data.

Color lists according to the criteria 1996 and 1997 (years)

1. Make sure the list is set to **AutoFilter**.

2. Filter the year **1996** according to the following criterion – from the drop-down list for the **Year** field, select **1996**.

3. Select a cell in the list of data – press **Ctrl+*** (select the current region).

4. From the **Formatting** toolbar, select **Fill Color**, and then select any color.

5. Filter the year **1997** according to the following criterion – from the drop-down list for the **Year** field, select **1997**.

6. Select a cell in the data list, and press **Ctrl+*** (select the current region).

7. From the **Formatting** toolbar, select **Fill Color**, and then select a different color from the one you selected before.

8. Turn off **AutoFilter**.

Caution

The color of the heading row in the list also changes. After coloring the data, select the heading row for the list and apply a different color.

Summing filtered data

Every change you make when selecting criteria for filtering causes the number of rows displayed in the sheet to change (assuming that the number of records in each filter is different). The SUM function sums all rows, including hidden rows. Use the SUBTOTAL function to sum only the data in displayed rows.

1.   Click the **Show All** icon.

2.   Select a cell in the **Customer Name** or **Market** field, and click the **AutoFilter** icon.

3.   Press **Ctrl+*** (select the current region).

4.   Click the **AutoSum** icon (sigma).

The SUBTOTAL function is automatically entered below the data column. The formula is =SUBTOTAL(9,F2:F42).

The digit 9 means the data displayed in the column is summed with the SUM function. To change the function of the calculation, change this digit.

You can use the formula list and the formulas' corresponding numbers in the SUBTOTAL function, as displayed in the figure below. The list was copied from the **Help** dialog box of the SUBTOTAL function (in the SUBTOTAL argument dialog box, click **Help**).

Example: in the formula =SUBTOTAL(1,F2:F42), the digit 1 represents the AVERAGE function and calculates the average of the totals in the range of cells displayed in the formula.

Num Function	Function
1	AVERAGE
2	COUNT
3	COUNTA
4	MAX
5	MIN
6	PRODUCT
7	STDEV
8	STDEVP
9	SUM
10	VAR
11	VARP

Advanced Filter

The Advanced Filter options include:

◉ Filtering according to multiple criteria.

◉ Filtering without the limit of 999 items in a field.

◉ Filtering unique lists.

Using advanced filter

1. Insert a few empty rows above the database.

2. Copy the heading row of the list, and paste it into Row 1 (see figure below).

3. In Row 2, under the name of the field, enter the filter criteria. See the figure below for an example. The filter criteria for the **Customer Name** field is **AIG Ltd.**, and the filter criteria for the **Quantity** field is >100.

4. Define a **Name** in the data table. Select one of the cells in the table, press **Ctrl+***, and then press **Ctrl+F3**. Enter the **Name** in the **Names in workbook** box, and click **OK**. For example, define the **Name** Data.

5. Define a **Name** for the criteria range. Select the range A1:I12 (heading row + criteria row). Define a **Name** as explained in the paragraph above. For example, define the **Name** CriteriaRange.

6. From the **Data** menu, select **Filter, Advanced Filter...**

7. Select the **List Range** box, press **F3**, and paste the name Data.

8. Select the **Criteria Range** box, press **F3**, and paste the name CriteriaRange.

9. Click **OK**.

Canceling advanced filter

Click the **Show All** icon, or from the **Data** menu, select **Filter, Show All**.

Note

- Do not use text that is the same as the criteria field.

- Be careful with formulas that have relative references.

- You can use names to create the filter criteria in another sheet in the workbook. In this case, it is best if you copy the results of the filter to another location. See below.

Copying the advanced filter results to another location

Excel lets you copy filter results to another location. This is excellent when you want to quickly copy the results of Advanced Filtering according to criteria.

In the **Advanced Filter** dialog box, select **Copy to another location**. In the **Copy to** box, select the reference in the worksheet into which the data will be copied.

Using the Database Functions to Sum Data According to Criteria

The **Advanced Filter** technique hides rows that do not meet the specified criteria.

You can use the SUBTOTAL function together with the **Advanced Filter** technique to sum data after it has been filtered. Change the summing function by changing the function digit in the SUBTOTAL function.

The formulas in the **Database** category in the **Paste Function** dialog box (click the icon, or press **Shift+F3**) sum data according to criteria. The syntax of the formulas in this category is as follows:

=DSUM (Data, FieldName, Criteria)

The first argument contains the data range, the second argument contains the name of the criteria field, and the third argument contains the criterion.

All the **Database** functions begin with the letter D (Data): DAVERAGE, DCOUNT, DCOUNTA, DGET, DMAX, DPRODUCT, and DSUM. The DGET function is different from the others because it returns isolated data (like the VLOOKUP function).

Disadvantage of using the Database functions

The **Database** functions require a large amount of memory. Using the **Database** functions frequently significantly reduces calculation speed.

Example: the DSUM function

```
Microsoft Excel - Book2                                          _ □ ×
File  Edit  View  Insert  Format  Tools  Data  Window  Help      _ 8 ×
    G4          ▼        =  =DSUM(Data,G1,CriteriaRange)
        A        B       C           D              E        F       G        H        I
    Running  Invoice
1   Number   Number  Date      Customer Name  Market       Quantity Income   VAT      Total
2                              AIG                          >100
3
4                                                                  169,930.80
5
    Running  Invoice
6   Number   Number  Date      Customer Name  Market       Quantity Income   VAT      Total
7        1      109  10/9/2003  AIG           Asia              40  18,881.20  3209.8   22,09
8        2      118  10/18/2003 AIG           Africa           150  70,804.50 12036.77  82,84
9        3      123  10/23/2003 AIG           Western Europe   210  99,126.30 16851.47 115,97
10       4      133  11/2/2003  AIG           USA               33  15,576.99  2648.09  18,22
11       5      138  11/7/2003  Amazon        USA              331 156,241.93 26561.13 182,8C
12       6      107  10/7/2003  Amazon        Asia             392 185,035.76 31456.08 216,49
13       7      113  10/13/2003 Amazon        Africa            15   7,080.45  1203.68   8,28
14       8      122  10/22/2003 Amazon        Africa            89  42,010.67  7141.81  49,15
I◄ ◄ ► ►I \Sheet1 /                                          ◄
```

Unique Records

A unique record is different from an ordinary record. Each item in a unique record appears only once.

Example: a unique record of the company's customers

In order to prepare an aging report, you have transferred the list of invoices and receipts from the company's accounting system to a sheet in a workbook. The names of customers are repeated several times in invoices and receipts. The customer list in an earlier report that you had prepared is not up-to-date. New customers have been added in the period between the two reports. You want to prepare an aging report with an updated customer list, in which the name of each customer appears only once.

The figure below illustrates a list of customer names that was copied from a tax receipts report.

Filtering a record into one unique record

1. Select Cell A1 (in the figure, Customer Name).

2. From the **Data** menu, select **Filter, Advanced Filter**.

3. Select **Copy to another location**.

4. In the **Copy to** box, select Cell C1.

5. Select the **Unique records only** box.

6. Click **OK**.

Result

A unique record of customers in column C.

Using the COUNTIF function to filter a record into a unique record

1. In Cell B1, enter the text **Unique Record**.

2. Select Cell B2, and enter the formula =IF(COUNTIF($A$2:A2,A2)>1,1,0).

3. Copy the formula from Cell B2 to Cell B40 (the customer list in Column A extends through Cell A40).

4. From the **Data** menu, select **Filter**.

5. Open the filtering drop-down list in Cell B1 by clicking the arrow, and select **0**.

6. Notice the unique record in Column A.

Explanation

The COUNTIF function counts the number of cells within a range that meet the given criteria.

For example, the COUNTIF function returns the number of times a customer appears in a list. The IF function uses the results of the

COUNTIF calculation. If the result of the calculation is greater than 1, the result of calculating the formula is 1. If it is not, the result is 0.

Because the range runs from an absolute cell ($A$2) to a relative cell (A2), the cell range checked by the COUNTIF functions changes when the formula is copied. With **AutoFilter**, you can filter the rows according to the criterion 0.

Coloring a unique record

1. Select Cell A2.

2. Select the customer list before filtering. Press **Ctrl+Shift+Down Arrow**.

3. From the **Format** menu, select **Conditional Formatting**.

4. In the **Condition 1** box, select **Formula**.

5. Enter the formula =COUNTIF($A$2:A2,A2)=1 (be careful about absolute and relative references).

6. Click **Format**, and select the **Pattern** tab.

7. Select any color.

8. Click **OK** twice.

Explanation

The COUNTIF function returns 1 the first time a customer name appears. In conditional formatting, the formula is the first argument in the IF function, Logical_text. If the condition exists, you can format the cell as desired.

Chapter 19

Subtotals

Adding the Subtotal Icon to a Toolbar

Add the subtotal icon to the Excel menu bar if you use subtotals regularly. Right-click a toolbar, and from the shortcut menu, select **Customize**. Select the **Commands** tab, and from the **Data** category, drag the **Subtotals** icon to the Excel menu bar (see figure on next page). Click **Close**.

Adding Subtotals

Example:

Add a subtotal for each customer in a list of invoices. See the figure below.

Note

Before you begin to use the **Subtotal** technique, you must sort the data table according to the subtotal field. This field calculates a subtotal each time an item in a field is altered. Sorting the data prevents the calculation of unnecessary, meaningless subtotals.

1. Select a cell in the **Customer Name** field (column).

2. Click the **Sort Ascending** icon.

3. Click the **Subtotals** icon, or from the **Data** menu, select **Subtotals**.

4. In the **At each change in** drop-down list, select **Customer Name**.

5. In the **Use function** drop-down list, select **Sum**. (Of course, you are not limited to this function.)

6. In the **Add subtotal to** drop-down list, select one or more checkboxes to specify the columns that contain financial data and/or quantities. In the example below, you would select Quantity, Income, VAT and Total.

7. Click **OK**.

Result

1 2 3		A	B	C	D	E	F	G	H
	1	Running Number	Invoice Number	Date	Customer Name	Market	Quantity	Income	
	2	1	109	01/10/1997	AIG	Asia	40	8,040.00	
	3	2	118	10/10/1997	AIG	Africa	150	25,129.90	
	4	3	123	03/10/1998	AIG	Western Europe	210	32,850.02	
	5	4	133	01/10/1999	AIG	USA	331	48,441.63	
	6	5	138	06/10/1999	AIG	USA	392	56,237.43	
	7				AIG Total		1,122	170,698.97	
	8	7	107	11/10/1996	Amazon	Asia	15	29,280.00	
	9	8	113	05/10/1997	Amazon	Africa	89	13,095.00	
	10	9	122	02/10/1998	Amazon	Africa	198	31,290.86	
	11	10	131	11/10/1998	Amazon	Africa	307	45,323.30	
	12				Amazon Total		609	118,989.16	
	13	12	110	02/10/1997	Cisco	Asia	50	37,065.81	
	14	13	121	01/10/1998	Cisco	Asia	186	30,000.10	
	15	14	127	07/10/1998	Cisco	Africa	259	39,086.66	
	16	15	136	04/10/1999	Cisco	Africa	367	53,119.11	
	17	16	139	07/10/1999	Cisco	Africa	404	57,796.59	
	18				Cisco Total		1,266	217,068.27	
	19	18	102	06/10/1996	Intel	USA	17	2,270.94	

G7 =SUBTOTAL(9,G2:G6)

The **Subtotals** technique automatically adds a SUM function to each customer. The **Subtotals** technique also adds Level Buttons to the left of the column labels row.

Level Button 1 Provides a total of the entire list. Hides all of the rows and only displays the grand totals.

Level Button 2 Only provides totals of visible subtotal rows. The rows of data are hidden.

Level Button 3 All rows are visible, including subtotal rows. See the figure above.

The Subtotals formula in cell F7 is =SUBTOTAL(9,F4:F6).

You can find a more detailed explanation of the SUBTOTAL function in **Summing filtered data** section of **Chapter 18, Filtering**.

Tip – **Would you like to hide the subtotal level buttons?**

Press **Ctrl+8**. To display the subtotal Level Buttons, press **Ctrl+8** again.

Removing subtotals from a list

Select a cell in the list (after you have added subtotals). Click the **Subtotal** icon (or from the **Data** menu, select **Subtotals**), and click **Remove All**.

Tip – Quickly remove subtotals

Select any cell in the data area and press the **Sort Ascending** button. Excel will automatically remove the subtotals.

Adding subtotals according to two fields

You can add subtotals according to two fields, the primary and secondary sort order.

Example:

Add subtotals: The first level of subtotals is **Market**, and the second level is **Customer Name**.

1. In the **Subtotals** dialog box, click **Remove All** to remove the subtotals.

2. Sort the data in each field. The order for sorting is the opposite of the order of subtotals according to the primary and secondary fields. The primary field is **Customer Name**, and the secondary is **Market**.

3. Click the **Subtotal** icon. In the **At each change in** drop-down list, select **Market**.

4. Click **OK**.

5. Click the **Subtotal** icon. In the **At each change in** drop-down list, select **Customer Name**.

6. Clear the checkbox beside **Replace current subtotals** (keep subtotals for the **Market** field).

7. Click **OK**.

8. Click **Level Button 2**.

You can see the result in the figure below. There are four Level Buttons here compared to three Level Buttons when you subtotal according to a single field. Level Buttons 2 and 3 enable you to subtotal according to primary and secondary fields.

Adding additional subtotals and using additional functions

You can continue to insert additional subtotals by ensuring that the checkbox beside **Replace current subtotals** is not selected. In the **Subtotals** dialog box, select additional functions such as AVERAGE, COUNT, and others.

Adding subtotals to a date field

When discussing **AutoFilter** (see **Chapter 18, Filtering**), we explained how to use **AutoFilter** to handle dates. **AutoFilter** recognizes date formats and allows you to filter by format.

Problem: When working with **Subtotals**, you cannot use the technique of changing the date format.

Solution: Subtotals according to month and year.

Add two additional columns to the list. In the first column, enter the MONTH function. It will return the month of a date represented by a serial number. In the second column, enter the YEAR function. It will return the year corresponding to a date. Copy the formulas to all the cells in the columns.

Caution

Sort the list according to primary and secondary sort order, as explained earlier, before adding subtotals.

Printing

In the **Subtotals** dialog box, select the checkbox beside **Page break between groups**. Each group of subtotaled data will be printed on a separate page.

Copying consolidation of subtotals

Problem: You cannot use the standard copy-and-paste techniques to copy a consolidation of subtotals. If you copy and paste a list of consolidated subtotals, all of the data, including the hidden rows of data, are copied.

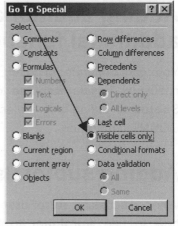

Solution: Select   the   visible   cells before copying.

1. Be sure that the rows of data are hidden and that only the summary of the subtotals is visible on the sheet.

2. Select a cell in the data region, and press **Ctrl+***.

3. To select visible cells, press **Alt+;** or press **F5**.

4. In the **Go To** dialog box, click **Special**.

5. In the **Go To Special** dialog box, select **Visible cells only**.

6. Click **OK**.

Now copy and paste the consolidation of the subtotals into a different sheet. Only the values of the data are pasted.

Applying colors to subtotal rows

We have already discussed the importance of applying colors to specific records. Applying colors to subtotal rows will allow you to easily distinguish them from the other rows of data in the sheet.

Applying colors to subtotal rows

Select the visible cells (see **Copying a consolidation of subtotals**). Click the **Fill Color** icon on the **Formatting** toolbar, and select a color. Display the hidden rows in the sheet, and check the results.

Applying colors to subtotal rows according to the subtotal level

Changing Styles

1. Insert subtotals.

2. From the **Data** menu, select **Group and Outline**, **Settings**.

3. Click **Apply Styles**.

4. Select a cell at subtotal level 2. From the **Format** menu, select **Style**.

5. For the style called RowLevel2, click Modify, change the style as desired, and click OK.

6. Use this technique to change the styles of all the subtotal levels.

Conditional Formatting

When you insert subtotals, some cells remain empty in the rows containing the subtotals. See the figure in **Adding subtotals according to two fields**.

1.   Select Cell A1, press **Ctrl+***, and select the data table.

2.   From the **Format** menu, select **Conditional Formatting.**

3.   In the first argument, select **Formula Is**.

4.   In the formula box, enter the formula =ISBLANK($D1).

5.   Click **Format**, and select the desired formatting.

6.   Click OK.

7.   Repeat these steps for the second argument.

8.   Click OK.

Replacing/deleting the word *Total*

When you insert subtotals to a list, the word *Total* is added automatically to each subtotal.

To delete the word *Total*, select the column in which the text appears and press **Ctrl+H** (or from the **Edit** menu, select **Replace**). In the **Find**

what box, type the word *Total*. Leave the **Replace with** box empty. Now click **Replace All**.

Caution

The SUBTOTAL function includes the characters that form the word *Total*. Therefore, it is important that you only select the column containing the word *Total* before you perform the search and replace operation. If you do not select a defined region, the characters in the word *Total* will be deleted from all of the subtotal functions. If you do this, you will end up with a SUB function instead of a SUBTOTAL function (if there even is such a thing).

Chapter 20

Grouping and Outlining

In a report made up of numerous levels of subtotals, it is difficult to view a vertical or horizontal summary of the results. The **Grouping and Outlining** technique is designed to allow you to hide rows and/or columns, making it easier for you to view a report of summarized data.

The **Subtotals** feature automatically enters a SUBTOTAL function into the cells and enables **Subtotals** for columns alone. In **Grouping and Outlining**, you determine the subtotal levels according to the reports you created. As can be seen in the figures below, the grouping and outlining levels are different.

Grouping and Outlining Guidelines

Enter data and functions into the sheet using the guidelines below. After you have finished entering the data and the functions and adding the SUBTOTAL functions (manually, not automatically from the **Data** menu), from the **Data** menu, select **Group and Outline**, **Auto Outline**.

Auto Outlining is done according to the following guidelines:

▣ **SUBTOTAL and GRAND TOTAL functions**

Outlining is possible because of the insertion of SUBTOTAL and GRAND TOTAL functions. When you create an outline, Excel identifies the subtotals and uses them to determine the outline levels.

▣ **No empty rows or columns**

Data lists do not contain empty columns or rows.

Adding Icons to Toolbars

If you use **Grouping and Outlining** regularly, you will want to add several icons to the toolbar.

Add the **Auto Outline**, **Clear Outline**, and **Show Outline Symbols** to the toolbar.

Right-click a toolbar, and from the shortcut menu, select **Customize**. Select the **Commands** tab, and from the **Data** category, drag the icons to the **Standard** toolbar.

Tip – Hide outline symbols

The **Show Outline Symbols** icon also lets you hide the outline symbols. The outline symbols reduce the size of the data region in the window.

Alternatively, use the **Ctrl+8** shortcut. To restore the outline symbols, press **Ctrl+8** again.

Adding Manual Outlining

Manual outlining allows you to determine the outline levels for each group without requiring total data organization based on the guidelines presented at the beginning of this chapter.

Select cells A2:A4 (income items, see figure below). From the **Data** menu, select **Group and Outline** and then select **Group**. Select **Rows** and click **OK**. Rows 2-4 are grouped, and you can now view the total of that group in Row 5, Total Income. By clicking the + symbol, you can expand the group to show the details.

An additional technique for grouping and outlining is to select a number of rows or columns and press **Alt+Shift+Right Arrow**. To clear the outlining, select the same rows or columns, and press **Alt+Shift+Left Arrow**.

In the figure below, the income items (Row 5), the expense items for Depart1 (Row 11), and the Quarter 1 items (Column E) are grouped.

	A	B	C	D	E	F	G	H	I
1	Income	January	February	March	*Quarter1*	April	May	June	*Quarter2*
2	Sales	350,000	370,000	390,000	*1,110,000*	410,000	430,000	450,000	*1,290,000*
3	Interest	5,000	6,000	7,000	*18,000*	8,000	9,000	10,000	*27,000*
4	Other Income	7,500	8,500	9,500	*25,500*	10,500	11,500	12,500	*34,500*
5	Total Income	362,500	384,500	406,500	*1,153,500*	428,500	450,500	472,500	*1,351,500*
6	Wages Depart.1	70,000	75,000	80,000	*225,000*	85,000	90,000	95,000	*270,000*
7	Office Exp Depat.1	25,000	30,000	35,000	*90,000*	40,000	45,000	50,000	*135,000*
8	Car Exp. Depart.1	12,000	14,000	16,000	*42,000*	18,000	20,000	22,000	*60,000*
9	Telephone Depart1	16,000	18,000	20,000	*54,000*	22,000	24,000	26,000	*72,000*
10	Other Exp. Depart1	39,000	40,000	41,000	*120,000*	42,000	43,000	44,000	*129,000*
11	Total Exp. Depart1	162,000	177,000	192,000	*531,000*	207,000	222,000	237,000	*666,000*
12	**Wages Depart.2**	41,000	42,000	43,000	*126,000*	44,000	45,000	46,000	*135,000*
13	**Office Exp Depat.2**	5,000	7,500	10,000	*22,500*	12,500	15,000	17,500	*45,000*
14	**Car Exp. Depart.2**	10,000	12,000	14,000	*36,000*	16,000	18,000	20,000	*54,000*
15	**Telephone Depart2**	13,000	15,000	17,000	*45,000*	19,000	21,000	23,000	*63,000*
16	**Other Exp. Depart2**	69,000	76,500	84,000	*229,500*	91,500	99,000	106,500	*297,000*
17	**Total Exp. Depart2**	231,000	253,500	276,000	*760,500*	298,500	321,000	343,500	*963,000*
18	*Net income*	*131,500*	*135,000*	*130,500*	*397,000*	*130,000*	*135,000*	*129,000*	*394,000*
19	**Interest Exp.**	15,000	16,000	17,000	*48,000*	18,000	19,000	20,000	*57,000*
20	**Net income After interest Exp.**	**116,500**	**119,000**	**113,500**	**349,000**	**112,000**	**116,000**	**109,000**	**337,000**
21	**Income Tax**	41,940	42,840	40,860	*125,640*	40,320	41,760	39,240	*121,320*
22	**Net After Income Tax**	74,560	76,160	72,640	*223,360*	71,680	74,240	69,760	*215,680*
23									

Clearing the outline

From the **Data** menu, select **Group and Outline**, **Clear Outline**.

Combining Automatic and Manual Outlining

You can combine automatic and manual **Group and Outline**. Add **Auto Outline**, and then add manual outline levels. The result will be totals and details for subgroups.

Copying or applying color to reports created by grouping and outlining

Select **Visible cells only** before copying reports created by **Group and Outline**.

1. Consolidate outline levels as desired.

2. Press **Alt+;** to select visible cells.

3. Copy and paste the data into a different sheet, or apply color to the visible cells by clicking the **Fill Color** icon on the **Formatting** toolbar and selecting a color.

Chapter 21

Consolidating Data

Consolidating data from a number of different tables is a task that is not easy for Excel users to perform. Excel offers data consolidation techniques that use formulas, and consolidation techniques that do not use formulas (Consolidate).

Below are several examples of the types of data organized in lists and tables that you consolidate in your work in Excel workbook sheets.

▣ Consolidation of monthly tables containing sales receipt data.

▣ Consolidation of tables containing salary data for various departments in the organization.

▣ Consolidation of trial balance tables to create tables that will become the basis for preparing financial statements and profit and loss statements.

▣ Consolidation of tables with budget data broken down by department/profit center.

Consolidating Data Tables

There are several methods for consolidating data tables.

Consolidate with formulas if the row & column headers of all worksheets are identical

If you have several worksheets and every worksheet has an identical structure - that is, the headings in row 1 and column A are identical from sheet to sheet, you can create a total worksheet using simple formulas.

Example: In the workbook, the sheets January, February and March contain tables with salary data. On every sheet, the items in cells A2:A8 are identical. On every sheet, the employees listed in B1:H1 are identical and never change.

Add a new worksheet called Total. Use a formula like the one shown in cell B2 to add the other sheets.

	A	B	C	D	E	F	G	H	I
1		Eric	Nancy	John	Lee	Ana	Stephen	Total	
2	Gross	9,839	9,366	9,453	7,870	18,056	18,004	72,588	
3	Income Tax	1,597	1,452	1,393	1,210	2,881	2,701	11,233	
4	Social Security	496	467	473	379	891	900	3,606	
5	401K	301	241	203	187	541	334	1,805	
6	Other Deductions	1,655	1,579	1,444	1,272	4,024	1,197	11,170	
7	Total Deductions	13,888	13,105	12,966	10,917	26,393	23,135	100,403	
8	Net	-4,049	-3,739	-3,513	-3,047	-8,337	-5,131	-27,815	
9									

The cell reference box shows **B2** and the formula bar shows `=SUM(January:March!B2)`. Sheet tabs: January / February / March / **Total** / Consolidate / PivotTable / Cons.

The formula in Cell B2 is =SUM (January:March!B2).

The technique for entering a formula to sum a single cell on a number of sheets

1. Select Cell B2 in the sheet called **Total**.

2. In the cell, type =SUM, and press **Ctrl+A** (the shortcut for displaying the formula argument box).

3. In the first argument box, select the name of the first sheet in the range **January**.

4. Press **Shift**, and select the last sheet in the range **March**.

5. Click **OK**.

Consolidate with Copy & Paste if the columns of all worksheets are identical but the rows contain different records

By using the technique described below, you can easily consolidate tables to a single data table, as well as sort, filter and create subtotals.

You may have several worksheets with identical columns, for example, months. These worksheets all have similar text in column A, but the text labels in each row differ from worksheet to worksheet.

Example: a budget workbook with expenses for each department. Every worksheet has identical columns, but each department has a different list of expense items in column A.

	A	B	C	D	E	F	G
1	Budget Department 1	January 2002	February 2002	March 2002	April 2002	May 2002	June 2002
2	Wages	100	110	120	130	140	150
3	Car Exp.	15	16	13	13	13	13
4	Advertising	10	12	6	6	6	6
5	Printing	4	4	4	4	4	4
6	Office Exp	6	6	6	6	6	6
7	Rent	10	10	5	3	1	1
8	Office Supplies	4	4	4	4	4	4
9	Taxes	5	5	5	5	5	5
10	Other	1	1	1	1	1	1
11							
12	Total	155	168	164	172	180	190
13							

Microsoft Excel - Book2

File Edit View Insert Format Tools Data Subtotals... Window Help

Type a question for help

Department1 / Department2 / Department3 / Consolidate /

Adding a department name column to each table

Add a column to each table that contains the name of the department in all the cells.

1. Add a column (see the figure on next page), and type the department name in the first cell.

2. Copy the department name to all the cells in the range, to the end of the list of items.

Consolidating the tables

Select the sheet **Department 1**; select and copy the data table (without the totals); and paste (press **Enter**) the table for **Department 1** into Cell A1 in the **Consolidate** sheet in the workbook. From the **Department 2** table, copy the table without the headers or the totals, select the **Consolidate** sheet, select the first empty cell at the end of the table in Column A, and paste the **Department 2** table (press **Enter**). Repeat this procedure, and copy the **Department 3** table without the headers into the **Consolidate** sheet, below the new table.

The result – A single data table (see the figure below).

At this stage, you can sort, filter and create a PivotTable, as necessary.

Consolidation

From the Data menu, select **Consolidate**.

Rules for consolidating data with the Consolidate technique

▣ The structure of the tables must be identical. The headings of all rows and the left-most columns in the tables must contain the same topic. The number of columns and the number of rows do not have to be identical; neither does the internal order of the text.

▣ Tables must have a single label row and a single column for labels.

▣ The cells in the table's data range must contain only numeric data.

Excel consolidates data by identifying corresponding text crossed between the header row and the leftmost column.

Example:

In the figure below, the top header row holds the employee name, and the leftmost column contains Gross Salary & Deductions. The number of employees and the order of their names in the header row, and the number and order of Gross Salary & Deductions in the leftmost column, do not correspond across all tables.

The data range contains all the cells from Cell B2 (see figure below).

	A	B	C	D	E	F	G	H	I
1		Eric	Nancy	John	Lee	Ana	Stephen	Total	
2	Gross Salary	2,540	3,256	2,928	1,987	3,854	3,285	17,850	
3	Income Tax	381		3	8	578	493	2,678	
4	Social Security	127	1	46		193	164	893	
5	401K	76		88	60	116	99	536	
6	Total Deductions	584	749	673	457	886	756	4,106	
7	Net	1,956	2,507	2,255	1,530	2,968	2,529	13,745	
8									
9									

January / February / March / Total / Sheet1 /

Crossing the employee name **Eric** with **Gross Salary** in the table **January** (see figure) returns the result in Cell B2. The amount in the cell is 2,540. In the table **February**, the crossed cell of the text **Eric** with **Gross Salary** is E2, and the amount in the cell is 2,758. The **Consolidate** technique identifies the crossed text in the tables and returns a total.

Consolidation options

▣ Consolidating data **without** links to the source data.

▣ Consolidating data **with** links to the source data.

Consolidating without links

Stage 1 – definition of names in the data tables

In the tables, select only the data range, including headers (without selecting subtotals or totals).

1. Select the sheet **January**, select Cell G5, press **Ctrl+Shift+Home** (to quickly select a range from any cell in the sheet, up to A1).

2. Press **Ctrl+F3** (the **Define Name** dialog box).

3. In the **Name** box in the workbook, enter the name **AJanuary**. Click **OK**.

4. Select the sheet **February**, select Cell F6, and perform steps 1-3. In step 3, enter the name **BFebruary**.

5. Select the sheet **March**, select Cell E5, and perform steps 1-3. In step 3, enter the name **CMarch**.

Explanation

▣ Defining **Names** in the tables makes it easier to perform the consolidation.

▣ Referring to **Names** in the data table should not include the total rows or columns.

▣ In defining **Names**, assign the names alphabetically.   This is particularly important when using multiple consolidation ranges in a pivot table as discussed at the end of this chapter.

Press **F3** to open the **Paste Name** dialog box. The names are sorted alphabetically.

Stage 2 – the Consolidate dialog box

1.   Open a new sheet in the workbook.

2.   Select Cell A1. From the **Data** menu, select **Consolidate**.

The Function Box

Select the function for consolidating the data. The default function is **SUM**.

The Reference Box

In this box, enter the reference (**Name**) temporarily, until the reference is transferred to the **All References** dialog box.

You can consolidate data tables from three sources: data tables in the active workbook, data tables in an open workbook, and data tables in a closed workbook.

▣ **Data table in the active workbook**

Select the **Reference** box, and press **F3**. Select the **Name** of the reference, and click **OK**.

▣ **Data table in an open workbook**

Select the **Reference** box. From the Excel menu, select **Window**, and select the open workbook. Choose the sheet containing the data table, select it, and substitute the table reference in **Name**, after the file name and the exclamation point.

▣ **Data table in a closed workbook**

Select the **Reference** box, and click **Browse**. Select the name of the file containing the table to be consolidated, enter the **Name** you defined for the data table, and then click **Add**. The **Name** of the reference is transferred from the **Reference** box to the **All References** dialog box.

Add other data tables. Select the **Reference** box, press **F3** (if the data table is in the active workbook), select the **Name** of the reference, and click **Add**.

The All References Dialog box

The **All References** dialog box contains the names of the tables that will be consolidated.

Use Labels In

Select both the checkboxes in the **Use Labels In** option. The names of employees and Gross Salary & Deductions are the labels in the example presented. Selecting these boxes causes the text to be transferred to the consolidation table in the sheet.

The Delete Button

Use this button to delete a table from the **All References** dialog box. Select the **Name** of the table in the **All References** dialog box, and click **Delete**.

Stage 3 – Consolidate the data

1. In the **Consolidate** dialog box, select the **Reference** box, press **F3**, and select the name **AJanuary**.

2. Click **OK**, and click **Add**.

3. Repeat steps 1-2, and add the tables **BFebruary** and **CMarch** to the **All References** dialog box.

4. Select both checkboxes in the **Use Labels In** option.

5. Click **OK**.

The result: the consolidation of data tables into values without formulas.

	A	B	C	D	E	F	G	H	I	J
1		Eric	Nancy	John	Lee	Ana	Stephen			
2	Gross Salary	8,297	9,506	9,995	3,539	7,612	6,270			
3	Income Tax	1,220	1,455	1,620	531	1,142	988			
4	Social Security	415	461	504	177	381	312			
5	Other Deductions	35	50	25	25	100				
6	401K	249	283	319	106	228	192			
7										
8										
9										
10										

Microsoft Excel - Book1

File Edit View Insert Format Tools Data Subtotals... Window Help

Type a question for help

January / February / March / Total \ Consolidate /

Refreshing data

The result of consolidating data tables is only in the values. Changing the data in the source tables does **not** update the data in the consolidated tables.

Solution

Delete the data in the **Consolidate** sheet. Select Cell A1, and from the **Data** menu, select **Consolidate**. In the **All References** dialog box, you will see the names of the data tables. The names are saved in the **Consolidate** dialog box, in **All References**. Click **OK**.

Adding or changing a consolidation formula

1. Delete the data in the **Consolidate** sheet, and select Cell A1.

2. From the **Data** menu, select **Consolidate**.

3. Open the **Function** option, and select the **Count** function.

4. Click **OK**.

The result of consolidating with the **Count** function returns the number of appearances of every Employee Name and/or Gross Salary & Deductions in the table.

In the figure below, the consolidation was performed three times in the same sheet. In each consolidation, a different function was chosen. Each time the technique is performed, select a different cell in the sheet and perform the **Consolidation**.

Consolidating with links

1. Delete the data in the consolidated table, and select Cell A1.

2. From the **Data** menu, select **Consolidate**.

3. Select the **Create links to source data** option.

4. Click **OK**.

Note the results of the consolidation. The formula cells contain links to the source data in the tables. On the left side of the sheet, in the continuation of the sheet's header row, notice the subtotal buttons. Pressing **Button 1** will show only the subtotals. Pressing **Button 2** will open and expand the data.

Click the + sign to the left of one of the items. Notice the **Gross Salary** details of the employee **Eric**, as well as the total (SUM formula) of his gross salary.

As opposed to consolidating without links, refreshing data is automatic provided you do not add other data tables or add rows or columns to the tables.

Adding data tables

Delete the consolidated data from the sheet by selecting the sheet. Select the button in the corner of the sheet's header row and column, right-click, and select **Delete** (do not press the **Delete** key, since only the data is deleted without the subtotal buttons). Select Cell A1, and from the **Data** menu, select **Consolidate**.

Select the **Reference** box, and press **F3**. Select the name of the new table you defined, and click **OK**. Click **Add** (to transfer the reference to **All References**), and click **OK**.

Copying and coloring rows in the subtotals

Try to copy the results of the consolidation. Select a single cell in the current region, press **Ctrl+***, and press **Ctrl+C**. Select a new sheet, and press **Enter**.

Note the results – all the data is copied, including data in the hidden rows.

Solution

Select the visible cells and isolate them from the hidden cells.

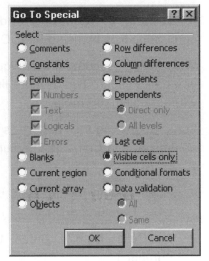

1. Press **Group & Outline Button 1** (to the left of the header row) to show sub-totals.

2. Select one of the cells in the current region, and press **Ctrl+***.

3. Press **F5**, or from the **Edit** menu, select **Go To Special**.

4. In the **Go To** dialog box, click **Special**. Select **Visible cells only**.

5. Click **OK**.

The result – only visible cells are selected.

6. Copy the visible cells. Press **Ctrl+C**.

7. Move to another sheet in the workbook, select Cell A1, and press **Enter.**

Note the results – only the subtotals are copied, and the results are only values.

Color the subtotal rows

1. Return to the sheet with the subtotals. Use the technique described above to make sure only the visible cells are selected, and repeat steps 1-7.

2. Click the **Fill Color** icon on the **Formatting** toolbar, and select any color.

3. Click **Button 2**. Only rows with subtotals are colored.

Comparing Lists

The data consolidation technique allows you to compare lists quickly and easily.

In **Chapter 8, Summing and Counting**, refer to the technique for comparing lists by using the COUNTIF formula.

With the consolidation technique, you can compare two or more lists without using a formula.

Look at the figure: **List 1** is in column A, and **List 2** is in column B.

1. Add Column B. In Cell B1, type "List number".

2. In Cells B2:B7, enter the number 1.

3. In Cells D2:D7, enter the number 2.

4. Cut Cells C2:D7 and paste them into Cell A8.

The result is shown in figure to the right.

1. Select cell A1. Press **Ctrl+***, press **Ctrl+F3**, and define a name for the list.

2. From the **Data** menu, select **Consolidate**.

3. In the **Reference** box, press **F3** and paste the Name you defined for the list.

4. Click **Add,** select both **Use labels in** checkboxes, and click **OK**.

The result is shown in the figure.

The number that appears in Column B is the total number of lists in Column B before **Consolidation**.

If the result = 1, the name appears in List 1 and does not appear in List 2.

If the result = 2, the name appears in List 2 and does not appear in List 1.

If the result = 3, the name appears in both lists (1+2=3).

Comparing Three or More Lists

Using the technique described above, paste these lists one list below the other.

Note – the list number should be factors of 2 (or any other mathematical combination that you choose).

For List 1, use 2^0 or the number 1. For List 2, use 2^1 or the number 2. For List 3, use 2^2 or the number 4.

The consolidation results in a series of numbers from 1 to 7, in which:

1,2,4 = the name appears in only one list.

3,5,6 = the name appears in two lists, 3=2+1, 5=4+1,6=2+4.

7 = the name appears in all three lists.

Consolidating Data Tables by Using a PivotTable, Multiple Consolidation Ranges

Another technique for consolidating data is using **PivotTable**, **Multiple Consolidation Ranges**. For further information and an explanation of the use of **PivotTables** for data analysis, see **Chapter 22, PivotTable**.

1. Use the examples that are presented here – salary tables using the **Consolidate** technique.

2. Select an empty sheet in the workbook. Select Cell A1.

3. From the **Data** menu, select **PivotTable Report**.

4. In the **PivotTable Wizard**, in Step 1, select the **Multiple Consolidation Ranges** option and click **Next >**.

5. In **Wizard Step 2A**, leave the default setting, **Create a single page field for me**, and click **Next >**.

6. In **Wizard Step 2B** (the consolidation tables are located in the active workbook), select the **Range** option.

7. Press **F3**, select the first name AJanuary, and click **OK**.

8. Click **Add**. The name of the table is transferred to the **All Ranges** box.

9. Repeat this step for the names BFebruary and CMarch (both tables), and transfer them to the **All Ranges** box.

In order to consolidate data from an open or closed workbook, follow the same steps under the Reference box section of this chapter.

10. Click **Next >**.

11. In Excel 97 for Step 3 of 4, click **Next >**.

12. In the final step, click **Finish**. Notice the PivotTable in the sheet.

If the **PivotTable** toolbar is not displayed? Select one of the toolbars, right-click, and select **PivotTable**.

13. Format the data in the PivotTable – select one of the cells in the active region, and from the **PivotTable** toolbar, click **PivotTable Field**.

14. In the **PivotTable Field** dialog box, make sure the function for summing data is the **SUM** function. Click **Number**, and select the number formatting you prefer.

15. Click **OK**, and click **OK** again.

Change the names of the fields in the PivotTable by double-clicking the gray buttons with the text – row, column and page 1 (Cells A4, B3, A1).

16. Instead of Row, type Gross Salary & Deductions.

17. Instead of Column, type Employee Name.

18. Instead of Page 1, type Month.

Organize the rows and columns in the PivotTable

The default order the rows is alphabetical. To reorder into a logical format:

Example 1:

Select Cell A6, Gross Salary. Move the mouse to the upper border of Cell A6. When the mouse cursor changes, click the mouse, drag the row, and place it as the first row, before Row 5.

Example 2:

The item Gross Salary is located in the center of Gross Salary & Deductions. To move Gross Salary to the beginning of the list, type *Gross Salary in Cell A6 (the asterisk goes before the text), select Cell

A5, and click the **Sort Ascending** icon. This will force Gross Salary to the top of the list.

Example 3:

Put the cellpointer in A5 and type Gross Salary. Hit **Enter**, and the 401k entry in A5 will move to Row 6.

Move the location of the fields from column and row to page

Click and drag the Gross Salary & Deductions field from Row to Page. Drag to the upper left area of the PivotTable, below Month.

Click and drag the Employee Name field from Row to Page. Drag to the upper left area of the PivotTable, below Month.

	A	B
1	Month	(All)
2	Employee Name	(All)
3	Gross Salary & Deductions	(All)
4		
5	Sum of Value	Total
6	Total	58035.79

PivotTable

January / February / March \ PivotTable / Total / Consolidate

List the names of the months (tables) in the Month field

1. Click and drag the Month field to a row in the PivotTable (see figure on page 314).

2. Change the text Item 1 by typing directly into the cell January.

3. In the same fashion, change the text Item 2 to February, and Item 3 to March.

Item 1 represents Table number 1. In the example, the name of the table is AJanuary. Make sure the PivotTable does not relate to the names of the tables, but that it relates to the entire reference range as an item.

Be careful to define names in alphabetical order, to prevent errors in identification when changing the name of an item.

Refreshing, adding or deleting a data table

Select one of the cells in the table, and click the **PivotTable Wizard** button in the **PivotTable** toolbar. In step 3 in the dialog box that opens, select **<Back**.

To delete a data table, select the name of the table, and click **Delete**.

To add a data table, select the **Range** box, press **F3**, click **Add**, and click **Finish**.

To refresh data, click **Refresh Data** (red exclamation point on the **PivotTable** toolbar).

In the figure below, the example report contains a list of gross salaries according to employee name.

Chapter 22

PivotTable

Of all the techniques that Excel offers for data analysis, PivotTables are the most exciting; the variety of options for data analysis is huge, and the results are immediate.

A PivotTable can sort, filter, create dynamic subtotals by dragging the mouse, add calculated formulas, create a chart that is automatically linked to various dynamic data, and more.

The data for creating a PivotTable can come from a variety of sources, including data organized in an open or closed workbook sheet, a number of tables in sheets in different workbooks, and data drawn from external systems.

With a PivotTable, you can create multiple queries and subtotals that are grouped according to daily totals or totals by days of the week, months, quarters or years; add calculated formulas; and more.

Basic Concepts: Terminology Used in PivotTables

- **Field** – the header at the top of a column in a data table.
- **Item** – numeric data or text in the **Field** column.
- **Data** – area detailing the data in the lower part of the PivotTable, including columns with numeric data.
- **Row Field** – a **Field** that is positioned as a row in the lower left of the PivotTable.
- **Column Field** – a **Field** that is positioned as a column in the row above the data in the PivotTable.

▣   **Page Field** – a **Field** that is positioned in the upper left of the Pivot Table.

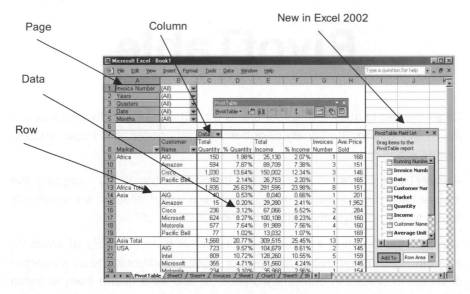

Creating a PivotTable

Rules for organizing data to create a PivotTable

▣   The data table can have only one header row.

▣   All the cells in the header row must contain text; each header must be unique.

▣   The table cannot have subtotal rows, empty rows or columns, or totals.

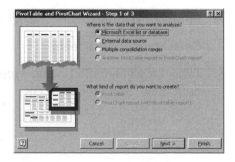

Running Number	Invoice Number	Date	Customer Name	Market	Quantity	Income
1	101	05/10/1996	MrExcel	USA	15	2,136.75
2	102	06/10/1996	Intel	USA	17	2,270.94
3	103	07/10/1996	Motorola	Asia	20	10,152.14
4	104	08/10/1996	Pacific Bell	Western Europe	50	11,111.11
5	105	09/10/1996	Motorola	Asia	100	8,717.95
6	107	11/10/1996	Amazon	Asia	15	29,280.00
7	108	12/10/1996	Microsoft	Asia	30	6,020.00
8	109	01/10/1997	AIG	Asia	40	8,040.00
9	110	02/10/1997	Cisco	Asia	50	37,065.81
10	111	03/10/1997	MrExcel	USA	67	15,452.00
11	112	04/10/1997	Pacific Bell	Asia	77	13,032.00
12	113	05/10/1997	Amazon	Africa	89	13,095.00
13	114	06/10/1997	Intel	USA	101	23,084.00
14	115	07/10/1997	Motorola	Asia	113	23,118.00
15	116	08/10/1997	Intel	USA	125	18,495.00

Defining a name for the data table

1. Select the data table from the sheet.

2. Select a cell in the data area, and press **Ctrl+***.

3. Press **Ctrl+F3** (the **Define Name** dialog box).

4. Type the text in the **Names in Workbook** box. For example, the name **Data** is defined.

5. Click **OK**.

Steps 1 and 2

1. Select Cell A1 from another sheet in the workbook.

2. From the **Data** menu, select **PivotTable and PivotChart Report**.

3. In **Step 1 of 3**, select **Microsoft Excel list or database**.

4. Click **Next**.

5. In **Step 2 of 3**, select the **Range** box.

6. Press **F3** (**Paste Name** dialog box).

7. Paste the name **Data**.

8. Click **OK**.

9. Click **Next**.

PivotTable and PivotChart Wizard - Step 2 of 3	? ×
Where is the data that you want to use?	
Range: Data	Browse...
Cancel < Back Next > Finish	

Caution

Did you have a problem continuing to Step 3? Cancel the PivotTable, return to the data sheet, and check that the text in each cell in the header row is different than the text in the other cells. Do not leave an empty cell without a header.

Data table in another workbook, open or closed

In the example, you created the PivotTable in the workbook in which the data table is located. If you want to create a PivotTable from a data table located in another workbook, open or closed, define a **Name** for the data table in the source workbook before beginning to construct the PivotTable.

In the explanation above, the work steps from Step 5 change (**Paste the Name** of the data table).

Data table in an open workbook

1. Select the **Range** box.

2. From the **Window** menu, select the open workbook.

3. Select one of the sheets.

4. Type an exclamation point, type the **Name** that you defined for the data table, and then click **OK**.

Data table in a closed workbook

1. Select the **Range** box.

2. Click **Browse**, and select the workbook after locating it in the directory on the hard drive.

3. Type an exclamation point, type the name that you defined for the data table, and then click **OK**.

Step 3

Click **Layout** (Excel 97 does not include this button).

Construct the PivotTable by dragging fields to **Data** and **Page**.

There are three types of PivotTable fields:

1. Data fields.

2. Query/Data filter fields.

3. Fields not relevant to the PivotTable.

For example:

1. Data fields – **Quantity, Income**.

2. Query/Data filter fields – **Date, Invoice Number, Market, Customer**.

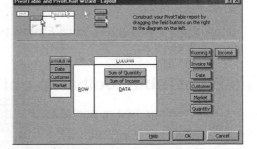

Transfer the data fields to **Data**. Click and drag the **Quantity** field to the white **Data** area. Click and drag the **Income** field to the white **Data** area. Transfer query/data filter fields to **Page**. Click and drag the **Invoice Number** field to the white **Page** rectangle. Repeat this action to drag the fields **Date**, **Market** and **Customer**.

Formatting data fields in a PivotTable

Format each data field separately. You can format or change the formatting later on by clicking the **Field Settings (PivotTable Field in Excel 97)** icon on the **PivotTable** toolbar.

Format the Total Data column with the SUM function

1. Double-click the field **Sum of Quantity**. Excel uses the header text at the top of the column as the **Source Field** Name. In the **Name** box, the text **Sum of Quantity** points to the **SUM** function, according to which the field items are summed. Change the text in the box to something else. For example – **Quantities**. You cannot use the Source Field name **Quantity**.

2. Click **Number**.

3. Click **OK** twice.

4. Repeat steps 1-3 to format the **Income** field.

5. Click **OK**.

6. In the **Step 3** dialog box, click **Finish** (in Excel 97, go to Step 4 and click **Finish**).

The PivotTable toolbar is not displayed

Select any toolbar in the toolbar area, right-click, and from the toolbar shortcut menu, select **PivotTable**.

Notice the figure of the PivotTable. The query fields are in the upper left, and the itemized data fields are in the lower section of the PivotTable.

The **Quantities** and **Income** data fields are displayed as rows. Change the direction of the data displayed in the PivotTable from rows to columns. Simply click and drag the gray data field button (in the figure, the field is called Data) slightly up and to the right, and release the mouse.

The result:

Regular Work with the PivotTable

Filtering and inserting a query into the PivotTable

Place the cursor in the upper left of the sheet and select an item in one of the **Page** fields (open the list of items by clicking the arrow in the box of one of the fields). This action filters the data in the PivotTable. The results of the filter are displayed in the lower section of the PivotTable.

Inserting a complex query

Example:

Click and drag the **Market** field from **Page** to **Row**. Notice the figure – the **Market** field is located to the left of the **Customer Name** field, and there is a subtotal below all the items in the **Market** field. Insert an additional query by selecting an item in the **Page** field (in the upper left of the PivotTable).

Caution

Dragging a field's button outside of the PivotTable area in the sheet deletes it. If you drag the button outside the PivotTable area, an X sign appears. If you release the mouse at this point, the field is deleted. To cancel this action and return the deleted field to the PivotTable, press **Ctrl+Z**, or click the **Undo** icon on the toolbar.

Inserting subtotals

With a PivotTable, you can insert automatic subtotals, delete subtotals, or insert subtotals and additional functions.

Drag at least two fields to the row area and position them next to one another in a row. In the figure, the two fields that are placed in the row are the **Market** field and the **Customer Name** field.

The subtotals you insert are calculated for the items in the first field – **Market**. Double-click the **Market** field name (gray button). In the **PivotTable Field** dialog box, there are three options for subtotals.

☑ Automatic

☑ Custom

☑ None

Automatic subtotals

Excel uses the SUM formula as the default for inserting subtotals for an item in the **Market** field.

Custom subtotals

Select the **Custom subtotals** option, and select additional functions (see figure). Click **OK**.

None

Data is displayed without subtotals.

Hiding items

You can hide items to calculate sums for only the displayed items.

In Excel 97, double-click the name of the **Market** field, and in **Hide Items**, select the item called **Africa**. Click **OK**.

In Excel 2000 and 2002, click the arrow to the right of the **Market** field, and in the drop-down list, cancel the selection of the items you wish to hide.

In the figure, notice the item Africa is not included in the list of items and the data for the displayed items is totaled.

Problem

There is a significant difference between the Hide techniques in Excel 97 and Excel 2000 and 2002.

In Excel 97, if you wish to display just a few items from a long list of customers, you must uncheck every hidden customer name separately. You can use **Shift** to select a contiguous series, but this is not a simple solution.

In Excel 2000 and 2002, this problem does not exist. You simply cancel the selection of **Show All** and select the items you want to display. The rest are already hidden.

Solution

In Excel 97, use **Grouping** (see the explanation below) to group all the customer names you want to hide. Leave the rest of the names ungrouped, hide the grouped customers, and leave the ungrouped list of customers displayed.

Canceling "hide items"

Caution

Cancel **Hide Items** immediately after finishing the data analysis. In the PivotTable, there is no icon or any other way to automatically cancel **Hide Items**, and later in your work with the PivotTable, you will not remember which items are hidden.

Canceling "Hide Items"

In Excel 97, double-click the name of the field, for example, the **Market** field. Select the item **Export**. The selection changes color from blue to white. Click **OK**.

In Excel 2000 and 2002, select the boxes you had previously hidden.

Sorting items

You can sort PivotTable items according to a selected field, according to Excel's sorting rules. Select an item in the **Row** field. Click the **Sort Ascending** or **Sort Descending** icon, or from the **Data** menu, select **Sort**.

Displaying Top 10 Records with AutoShow

You can set the PivotTable to display only the top or bottom ten invoices using the **AutoShow** feature.

You can set the PivotTable to display the top 10% of records.

New In 2002

In the example shown, the PivotTable is showing data for a number of invoices. A common requirement would be to provide a list of the top ten invoices.

	A	B	C	D	E
1	Customer Name	(All)			
2	Date	(All)			
3	Market	(All)			
4					
5		Data			
6	Invoice Number	Total Quantity	Total Income		
7	101	15	2,137		
8	102	17	2,271		
9	103	20	10,152		
10	104	50	11,111		
11	105	100	8,718		
12	107	15	29,280		
13	108	30	6,020		
14	109	40	8,040		
15	110	50	37,066		
16	111	67	15,452		
17	112	77	13,032		
18	113	89	13,095		
19	114	101	23,084		
20	115	113	23,118		
21	116	125	18,495		
22	117	138	23,507		
23	118	150	25,130		

▣ Double click the gray invoice field in cell A6 in order to display the PivotTable Field dialog.

PivotTable Field

Name: Invoice Number

Subtotals
● Automatic
○ Custom
○ None

Sum
Count
Average
Max
Min
Product

☐ Show items with no data

[OK] [Cancel] [Hide] [Advanced...] [Layout...] [Number...]

▣ Click the **Advanced...** button on the right side of this dialog.

◙ In the **PivotTable Field Advanced Options** dialog, click the **On** button under **Top 10 AutoShow**. Change the **Show** fields to either Top 10 or Bottom 5 as appropriate.

PivotTable Field Advanced Options

Page field options

⊙ Retrieve external data for all page field items (faster performance)

○ Query external data source as you select each page field item (requires less memory)

☐ Disable pivoting of this field (recommended)

AutoSort options

⊙ Manual (you can drag items to rearrange them)

○ Ascending

○ Descending

○ Data source order

Using field:

Invoice Number

Top 10 AutoShow

○ Off

⊙ On

Show: Top   10

Using field:

Total Quantity

OK   Cancel

◙ Indicate how Excel should rank the items. In this case, it would make sense to see the top ten based on either quantity or revenue.

◙ Click OK to close the **Advanced Options** dialog. Then click **OK** to close the **Pivot Table Field** dialog.

Result: only the top ten invoices in terms of quantity are displayed.

Microsoft Excel - Book1

File   Edit   View   Insert   Format   Tools   Data   Window   Help

PivotTable ▾

	A	B	C	D	E
1	Customer Name	(All)			
2	Date	(All)			
3	Market	(All)			
4					
5		Data			
6	Invoice Number ▾	Total Quantity	Total Income		
7	131	307	45,323		
8	132	319	46,882		
9	133	331	48,442		
10	134	343	50,001		
11	135	355	51,560		
12	136	367	53,119		
13	137	380	54,678		
14	138	392	56,237		
15	139	404	57,797		
16	140	416	59,356		
17	Grand Total		3,614	523,395	
18					

I◀ ◀ ▶ ▶I \ **PivotTable1** / Sheet3 / Sheet4 / Invoi ◀

Refreshing data

The PivotTable is not automatically linked to the data table. During the construction of the PivotTable, data is drawn from the data table to the computer's memory. Update the data in the memory by refreshing it – click the **Refresh Data** icon (red exclamation point) on the **PivotTable** toolbar.

If the data table changed its size, or rows or columns were added to it, you must refresh the **Name** reference that you defined. The **Name** of the data table must include all the data in the table.

Inserting a sub-detail as an item

With a PivotTable, you can insert a sub-detail as an item without changing the structure of the PivotTable fields.

Example: in the customer called **Cisco**, insert a detail according to the **Market** field.

1. Select an item in the **Customer Name** field.

2. Double-click.

3. In the **Display Detail** dialog box, select the name of the sub-detail's field.

4. Click **OK**.

Sending drill-down detail to a new sheet

1. Select a cell in the data area in the customer row for which you want details. For example, select Cell C9 for a customer called **Cisco**.

2. Double-click.

3. A new sheet is automatically inserted with an itemized data table showing all rows included in the selected cell.

Result: see the figure below.

PivotTable Fields

You can insert fields into a PivotTable; this includes inserting the same **Field** of data several times into the data area. You can format each **Field** differently by using different functions; inserting a calculated **Field** (a **Field** with a formula); and using a variety of additional options that will be explained later in the chapter.

Additional options are as follows:

▣ Insert a field.

▣ Delete a field.

▣ Group items and insert a new field.

▣ Group fields with numeric items or dates.

▣ Group dates.

◼   Insert a calculated field.

◼   Insert a data field and change the method of calculation.

Inserting a field

Did you forget to insert a field while constructing the PivotTable, or did you mistakenly delete a field (see **Deleting a Field** below)? Select a cell in the area of the PivotTable, click the **PivotTable Wizard** icon on the **PivotTable** toolbar, and select **Layout** (in Excel 97, there is no **Layout** button). Drag the field to **Page** or **Data**, click **OK**, and click **Finish.**

Deleting a field

Click the **PivotTable Wizard** icon on the **PivotTable** toolbar, and select **Layout**. Drag the field outside the data area of the PivotTable, click **OK**, and click **Finish**.

Grouping items and inserting a new field

Group text items. In the figure, notice the field **Customer Name.**

If you group two items into one, you can create subtotals for groups of items with the same properties. For example, group customers according to their properties.

1. Select the items (Cells A7-A10) in **Customer Name**. Press **Alt+Shift+Right Arrow** or right-click the cell; from the shortcut menu, select **Group and Outline**, and then select **Group**.

2. Select Cell A7 (with the text Group 1), and type **Customer Group 1**.

3. Drag the **Customer Name** field to **Page** (upper left section).

Result

You inserted a new **Customer Name** field.

Change the name of the **Customer Name 2** field by double-clicking the gray **Customer Name 2** button. Type the new name of the field, and click **OK**.

Alternatively, type directly onto the gray button.

Grouping a field with items that are numbers or dates

Grouping data in a field, or in the language of the PivotTable – items, requires that all the items in the field have the same properties. In other words, a date column will have dates in all the cells. A cell without a date is a text cell, and the PivotTable cannot group incomplete dates or numeric data.

If, while grouping dates, you receive the message **Cannot group that selection**, you must return to the data sheet and check that the date column contains only dates.

After checking, repairing and completing the data, return to the PivotTable. Refresh the PivotTable by clicking the **Refresh Data** icon on the **PivotTable** toolbar, and try again to group the field as described below.

Example:

Group the **Invoice Number** field.

1. Return the PivotTable fields to **Page**. The data area contains one Total row.

2. Click and drag the **Invoice Number** field to a row.

3. Select one of the cells with an invoice number. For example, select Cell A9.

4. Right-click, select **Group and Outline** from the shortcut menu, and then select **Group**.

5. In the **Group** dialog box, enter the grouping method in the third box. The example has groups of ten invoices.

6. Click **OK**.

Grouping a date field

Grouping dates and inserting total fields by day, month, quarter, year and/or grouping and summing by day

By grouping the **Date** field, you can create filtering queries and sum data according to day, month, quarter, year, and even by the number of days.

Adding three new fields: month, quarter, year

1. Restore the PivotTable to its original structure, in which the fields are located in the upper left of the PivotTable (Page) and are not filtered. Notice the appearance of the word **All** in the **Field Name** box. The data area includes one total row for the data.

2. Click and drag the **Date** field from **Page** to **Row**.

3. Select one of the dates under the **Date** field name.

4. Right-click, select **Group and Outline** from the shortcut menu, and then select **Group**.

5. In the **Grouping** dialog box, select **Days, Months, Quarters, Years**.

6. Click **OK**.

Three fields have been added to the PivotTable – **Years, Quarters, Months**. (The least aggregate grouping selected – in this case, days – is shown in the **Date** field.

7. Click and drag each of the three new fields from **Row** to **Page**.

Grouping dates by days

1. Drag the **Date** field from **Page** to **Row**. Select one of the dates under the **Date** field name.

2. Right-click, select **Group and Outline** from the shortcut menu, select **Group**, and select **Days**.

3. In **Number of Days,** enter a number, or select the number of days. For example, select 7.

4. Click **OK**.

The result of grouping dates in groups of seven days:

Note

You cannot group according to **Number of Days**, and also according to months, quarters or years in the same PivotTable.

If you group by **Number of Days**, the date groups that you created earlier become ungrouped (the three new groups that you created are removed). You cannot simultaneously group according to **Number of Days** and insert the three new columns of months, quarters and years.

If you want to save the PivotTable with grouping by days and grouping by months, quarters and/or years, you must construct an additional PivotTable (see explanation below of inserting additional PivotTables into the workbook.

Grouping dates by weeks

You will certainly want to create groups of seven days that begin with the first day of the week. To do so, you must locate the first Sunday or Monday of the data table and define it as a date to begin grouping the dates.

Often, the location of the first Sunday will be before the first date of the data table. For example, the first date of the data table is 5/10/1996. To determine if this is a Sunday:

1. In any cell outside the PivotTable, enter the date 5/10/96.

2. Select the cell and press **Ctrl+1** (Format Cells).

3. Select the **Number** tab.

4. Select **Custom**.

5. In the **Type** box, type dddd.

6. Click **OK**.

7. The result – Friday. The conclusion – the first Sunday before 5/10/96 is 5/5/96.

8. Drag the date field and position it in **Row**.

9. Select one of the dates in the **Date** field.

10. Right-click, select **Group and Outline** from the shortcut menu, and select **Grouping**.

11. In the **Starting at** box, type 5/5/96, and leave the check box empty.

12. Select **Days**.

13. For the number of days, type 7.

14. Click **OK**.

Inserting a calculated field

Calculated fields are fields with formulas. The dynamic formulas you insert into the PivotTable will allow you to perform calculations between fields or in a single field.

Example: calculate the average price of an item sold to a customer or conversion according to the dollar exchange rate of the Income field. In the example, insert a field that calculates the average price per unit.

1. Select one of the cells in the data area of the PivotTable.

2. On the **PivotTable** toolbar, select **PivotTable, Formulas, Calculated Field**.

3. In the **Name** box, type the name of the formula. This name will be the name of the calculated field, and the formula will be saved along with the field name.

4. In the **Fields** box, select the **Income** field and click **Insert**. In the **Formula** box, insert the division sign (/).

5. In the **Fields** box, select the **Quantity** field, and click **Insert**.

6. Click **OK**.

Formatting a calculated field

1. Select one of the cells in the column of the **Total of Average Unit Price Sold** calculated field.

2. On the **PivotTable** toolbar, click **Field Settings**.

3. In the **Name** box, change the field name to **Average Unit Price Sold**.

4. In **Summarize by**, check the function for summing the data.

5. Click **Number**, and format as desired.

6. Click **OK**.

							H
	A	B	C	D	E	F	G
1	Invoice Number	(All)					
2	Years	(All)					
3	Quarters	(All)					
4	Date	(All)					
5	Market	(All)					
6	Customer Name2	(All)					
7	Months	(All)					
8							
9		Data					
10	Customer Name	Total Quantity	% Quantity	Total Income	% Income	Invoices Number	Ave.Price Sold
11	AIG	1,122	14.87%	170,699	14.04%	5	152
12	Amazon	609	8.07%	118,989	9.79%	4	195
13	Cisco	1,266	16.76%	217,068	17.85%	5	172
14	Intel	809	10.72%	128,260	10.55%	5	159
15	Microsoft	979	12.97%	151,668	12.47%	5	155
16	Motorola	811	10.74%	127,957	10.52%	5	158
17	Pacific Bell	939	12.44%	146,221	12.02%	5	156
18	MrExcel	1,015	13.44%	155,118	12.76%	5	153
19	Grand Total	7,550	100.00%	1,215,980	100.00%	39	161
20							
21							

Updating a calculated field / deleting a formula

1. Select one of the cells in the PivotTable.

2. On the **PivotTable** toolbar, select **PivotTable, Formulas, Calculated Field**.

3. Open the **Name** box, and select the name of the formula. Update the formula in the **Formula** box, or click **Delete** to remove the calculated field.

Adding a data field and changing the calculation method

With a PivotTable, you can insert additional data fields that you have already used and change the calculation function by which you create new calculated columns.

Insert an additional data field, the **Quantity** field.

1. Click and drag the **Customer Name** field to **Row**.

2. Select an item in the **Customer Name** field (one of the customer names).

3. Right-click, and from the shortcut menu, select **Wizard, Layout** (in Excel 97, there is no need to select **Layout**).

4. Drag the **Quantity** field to the data area.

5. Click **OK** and **Finish** (in Excel 97, click only **Finish**).

Changing the calculation function and formatting the field

1. Select a cell in the data area of the new field you inserted, **Sum of Quantity**.

2. From the **PivotTable** toolbar, select **Field Settings** (in Excel 97, select **PivotTable Field**).

3. In the **Name** box, type Invoices Number.

4. In **Summarize By**, select Count. Click **Number**, and select the number format.

5. Click **OK**.

Use the same method to insert the **Quantity** and **Income** fields. Change the calculation functions for each field to a different function, including Average, Maximum, Minimum or statistical functions.

In the figure, notice that the **Quantity** field is used to create additional data columns, each with a different calculation function.

Inserting fields to calculate % and more

Insert various additional calculated fields by using the **Options** button in the **PivotTable Fields** dialog box.

Select a cell in the data area of the new column field you created, **Invoice Numbers**. On the **PivotTable** toolbar, click the **Field Settings** button, and press the **Options** button to view the **Show data as** options:

▣ Regular

▣ Difference From

▣ % Of

▣ % Difference From

▣ Running Total In

▣ % of Row

▣ % of Column

▣ % of Total

▣ Index

The figure below illustrates examples and uses of the options found in
Show data as:

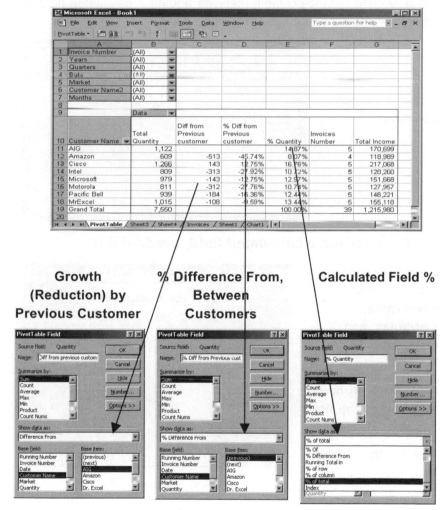

Adding a running balance column

Adding a running balance column involves adding a calculated field and changing the calculation function of the new field.

In the figure, notice Column D

Stage 1 – inserting a calculated field, credit-debit

1. On the **PivotTable** toolbar, select **PivotTable, Formulas,** and **Calculated Field**.

2. In the **Name** box, type **Calc Running Balance** as the field Name.

3. Select the **Credit** field from the list of fields, and click **Insert**.

4. Select the minus sign (–) in the **Formula** box.

5. In **Fields**, select the **Debit** field, and click **Insert**.

6. Click **OK**.

Stage 2 – display data as a running balance

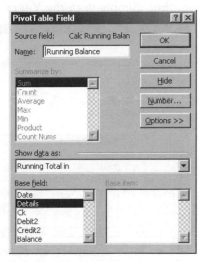

1. Select a cell in the data area in the **Calc Running Balance** column field.

2. On the **PivotTable** toolbar, click **Field Settings**.

3. In the **Name** box, type **Running Balance**.

4. Click **Options**.

5. Open **Show data as**, and select **Running Total In**.

6. In the **Base Field** box, select the **Details** field, and click **OK**.

Changing the presentation of multiple data fields in a PivotTable

This PivotTable is unique in that there are two fields in the Data section – Quantity and Income. Excel struggles with how to best present the PivotTable with two data columns. By default, this awkward presentation is used.

Invoice Number	(All)									
Customer Name	(All)									
Quarters	(All)									
Date	(All)									
Months	(All)									
	Years	Data								
	1996		1997		1998		1999		Total Total	Tota
	Total	Total	Total	Total	Total	Total	Total	Total		
Market	Quantity	Income	Quantity	Income	Quantity	Income	Quantity	Income		
Africa			400	64,978	763	115,701	771	110,916	1,935	29
Asia	165	54,170	592	133,139	469	72,205	343	50,001	1,568	30
USA	32	4,408	294	57,031	1,587	239,197	1,873	270,273	3,786	57
Western Europe	50	11,111			210	32,850			260	4
Grand Total	247	69,689	1,286	255,148	3,029	459,953	2,988	431,190	7,550	1,21

You may prefer this presentation where all of the Quantity fields are kept together. Simply drag the Years field to the right side of the Data field.

The other option (not shown) is to drag the Data field to the left of the Market field.

Formatting a PivotTable

1. Select a cell in the PivotTable.

2. In Excel 97, click the **Format Tables** icon in the **PivotTable** toolbar. From the **Format** menu, select **AutoFormat**.

3. Select one of the format options.

4. Click **OK**.

Printing a PivotTable

1. Select one of the cells in the PivotTable.

2. Press **Ctrl+*** (select the current region).

3. Select **File**, **Set Print Area**.

For further information, see **Chapter 11, Printing**.

Note

For users of Excel 97 and 2000, pressing **Ctrl+*** selects the entire PivotTable, including the fields in **Page Field**. Select the itemization rows in the detailed lower section of the PivotTable, without using the shortcut mentioned above, and set the print area.

The options dialog box

Select a cell in the PivotTable. On the **PivotTable** toolbar, select **PivotTable**, **Table Options**, or right-click and select **Table Options** from the shortcut menu.

PivotTable Options	? X
Name: PivotTable1	

Format options

☑ Grand totals for columns
☑ Grand totals for rows
☑ AutoFormat table
☐ Subtotal hidden page items
☐ Merge labels
☑ Preserve formatting
☑ Repeat item labels on each printed page
☐ Mark Totals with *

Page layout: Down, Then Over
Fields per column: 0
☐ For error values, show:
☑ For empty cells, show:
☐ Set print titles

Data options

Data source options:
☑ Save data with table layout
☑ Enable drill to details
☐ Refresh on open
☐ Refresh every 0 minutes

External data options:
☐ Save password
☐ Background query
☐ Optimize memory

OK   Cancel

Important topics in the options dialog box

▣ **Grand totals for columns and/or rows**

Select or clear the selection of the relevant checkbox in **Format Options**.

▣ **Save data with table layout**

Selecting this option saves PivotTable data when the workbook is saved and closed. This option is unnecessary if you selected the **Refresh on open** option.

▣ **Page Layout**

Changing the page layout to **Down**, **Then Over** changes the positioning of the fields in the upper left of the PivotTable (see figure).

Define a number different than the default, and the fields are displayed as groups. This action is crucial for working with PivotTables that have a large number of fields.

Inserting Additional PivotTables from a Single Data Table

The PivotTable enables dynamic analysis of data. The data in the table varies with filtering and with changing the structure of the table by moving fields from Page to Row or Column.

To produce regular reports, the fields in the PivotTable must be set. That is, PivotTables must have a defined structure for row and column fields. For example, construct a single PivotTable to analyze sales per customer, a sales report by customer in a different sheet that is linked to this PivotTable, an additional PivotTable to analyze sales by market, and a sales report by market in a different sheet that is linked to this PivotTable.

The solution – construct several PivotTables from a single data table.

Note

The PivotTable is created from data that is drawn from the computer's cache. Inserting duplicate or triplicate data is unnecessary and slows the computer down. To avoid inserting duplicate data into the memory, use the data that is already in the memory to insert a PivotTable from a single data source.

Select a new sheet in the workbook in which you constructed the PivotTable.

1. Select Cell A1.

2. Select **Data**, **PivotTable and PivotChart Report**.

3. In Step 1 of 3, select **Another PivotTable or PivotChart** (checkbox no. 4).

4. Click **Next**.

5. Select the name of the PivotTable you created in the workbook.

6. Click **Next**.

7. Continue constructing the PivotTable.

> **PivotTable and PivotChart Wizard - Step 2 of 3**   [?] [X]
>
> Which PivotTable report contains the data you want to use?
>
> [Book1.xls]Sheet4!PivotTable2
> [Book1.xls]Sheet1!PivotTable1
> [Book1.xls]PivotTable!PivotTable2
>
> [?]   Cancel   < Back   Next >   Finish

Quickly creating several PivotTables from a single data table

An easier way to create additional PivotTables from a single PivotTable is to copy and paste the existing PivotTable.

1. In the first PivotTable you created, select one of the cells.

2. Right-click, choose **Select** from the shortcut menu, and select **Entire Table**.

3. Press **Ctrl+C** (copy).

4. Select a new sheet or workbook.

5. Select Cell A1, and press **Enter**.

Another method is to copy the entire sheet.

1. Select the tab of the sheet with the PivotTable.

2. Press **Ctrl**. Click and drag the sheet to a new location. Release the mouse and the **Ctrl** button.

Continue inserting additional sheets with the PivotTable, and change the structure of the PivotTables as necessary.

 Note

◙ Refreshing one PivotTable refreshes all the additional PivotTables.

◙ You cannot use this method if you have selected the **Number of Days** grouping. In this case, you cannot create a second pivot table from the data in memory. You would have to create a new pivot table with the usual method.

Retrieving Data from a PivotTable

The use of a PivotTable saves you enormous use of formulas. After creating a PivotTable, you can create complex reports in other workbook sheets by using the GETPIVOTDATA function to extract cells from the PivotTable.

The easiest way to extract data from the PivotTable and insert it into the cells of other sheets to prepare reports is to insert simple formulas linking the cells in the regular sheet to the cells in the PivotTable. The PivotTable is, by nature, a dynamic data table. Changing the data in the data table and refreshing the PivotTable also refreshes the PivotTable's resulting data and the reports it creates.

There is a problem with changing the structure of a PivotTable and refreshing the data – the data table includes the invoice data for the company. The total income (see the PivotTable in the figure) is $1,215,980. The result is located in Cell D16.

Upon refreshing the PivotTable after recording additional invoices, it seems as if a new customer has been added. The total in the PivotTable is in Cell D19.

Inserting a row of data into a PivotTable is natural and expresses the dynamic character of the PivotTable; however, this damages the reports that you have prepared by inserting data from the PivotTable.

The solution is to use formulas to locate and extract PivotTable data

1. Use the INDEX formula in combination with the MATCH formula.

2. Use the SUMIF formula in combination with the OFFSET formula.

3. Use the GETPIVOTDATA formula.

For an explanation, see **Chapter 23, Using Functions and Objects to Extract Data.**

The INDEX and MATCH formulas

The INDEX and MATCH formulas belong to the LOOKUP family (the formulas are part of the Lookup & Reference category).

The second formula has two names that have been defined in the PivotTable sheet: the name of the sheet is PivotTable, and the name of Column A is ColA. In order for the calculation to succeed, make sure that the text *Grand Total* is identical in both sheets, in the PivotTable sheet and in the sheet with the formula.

The SUMIF and OFFSET formulas

The solution is similar to the earlier one, as the SUMIF and OFFSET formulas are combined.

The GETPIVOTDATA formula

This is a special formula for extracting data from a PivotTable.

Example:

The formula extracts the total income from sales for 1998.

The arguments for the formula are as follows:

Argument 1 – the name of the data **field**.

Argument 2 – PivotTable reference.

Arguments 3+4 – **Field+Item**. The rest of the arguments are the **Field+Item** pair.

In the figure, note the formula arguments.

Data_Field – the name of the data field is surrounded by quotation marks – "Income".

PivotTable – the PivotTable reference – the reference is a single cell – A9.

Field1 – the field for the row – "Customer Name".

Item1 – an item in the Customer Name field – "Intel".

Inserting a Chart from PivotTable Data

Insert a **chart** while constructing the PivotTable. The chart is automatically linked to the data in the PivotTable, and every change in the PivotTable data results in a change in the chart.

Excel 97 does not include this option. The PivotTable is treated like a regular table. Changing the structure of the data in a PivotTable results in an undesired change in the chart. The solution is to insert a PivotTable with a set structure for the row and column fields, in addition to the PivotTable you use for filtering and creating queries.

In Step 1 of 3, for **What kind of report do you want to create**, select the second option, **PivotChart Report (with PivotTable report)**. Construct the PivotTable according to the explanations provided in this chapter.

In addition to the PivotTable you constructed in the sheet, a sheet called **Chart1** is added. In this sheet, notice the chart with buttons for the PivotTable fields.

You can change the field structure of the PivotTable or filter data. The chart changes automatically. A change in the structure of the PivotTable in the PivotTable sheet results in a change in the chart in the Chart1 sheet.

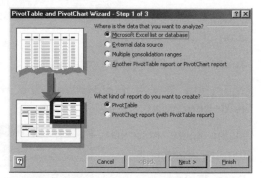

Creating a PivotTable by Consolidating Several Data Ranges

See **Chapter 21, Consolidating Data**.

Chapter 23

Using Functions and Objects to Extract Data

Chapter 15, **Data**, explains the principles and rules for organizing data in tables in your Excel worksheet. It is important to organize your data in your data tables according to these clear, well-defined principles. This will allow you to take advantage of the features Excel offers, such as sorting, automatic filtering and using pivot tables.

In order to prepare reports that are based on data taken from the data tables in your worksheet, remember to use formulas to locate and return data from data tables. Summarize your data according to criteria from within the data tables.

This chapter explains how to use formulas for these tasks, including formulas for locating and returning data. These include **Lookup & Reference** in the Paste Wizard function, **Sumif** and **Offset** functions, and combining functions with combo boxes and validation techniques.

Prepare the data table for use with formulas, assign names and insert an ascending numbered column.

Assign names to the data table and add a column with consecutive numbers

Assign names

Assign names to the following data in the data table: the data table itself and the fields of data (columns). See **Chapter 6, Names** for an explanation of the importance of defining names.

Define a name for the worksheet in the data table

Create only one data table in the sheet. The first cell in the data table should always be A1. This placement of the data table, which always contains the first active cell (A1), aligns the numbering of rows and columns in the sheet; aligns the row and column numbers in the data table; and prevents the problem of updating the name of the data tables when rows or columns are added to the data table.

 Note

Do not assign the **Name** of the sheet when you are working with a pivot table. To work with a pivot table, only define a **Name** of the data table.

Define a name for the sheet

Select the sheet by either pressing **Ctrl+A** or clicking on the button to the left of the worksheet's heading (to the left of column A, above row 1). Then press **Ctrl+F3**, enter name into the **Names in workbook** box, and then click **OK**.

Define a name only for the data table

Select a cell in the data table, and press **Ctrl+***. Then press **Ctrl+F3**, insert the name of the data table in the **Names in workbook** box, and click **OK**.

Define names for fields in the data table

Fields in the data tables refer to columns in the data tables. The field name is the text of the heading cell of the column.

Select a cell in the data table, and press **Ctrl+***. Press **Ctrl+Shift+F3**, or from the Insert menu, select **Name, Create**. Then select the **Create names in top row** option, and click **OK**.

Define a name for a single cell

Select the first cell (heading cell) in one of the fields, and then select the data range in the field (press **Ctrl+Shift+Down Arrow**). Enter name in the **Names in workbook** box, and click **OK**.

Add a first field with ascending consecutive order

The **VLookup** formula finds a number or text value in the first left column of the table and returns a value from a cell which is in the intersection between the row, which is in column 1, and the column number you set in the data table. Nesting the **Match** formula in the **VLookup** formula requires that there be an initial left column in the data table with consecutive, ascending numbering that is automatically updated whenever there is a change in the records, in other words, during **Sort**.

Insert a first left column in the database. Enter the name of the field of the first cell in the head of the column, which is cell A1 (assuming that you added a column in the top corner of the sheet). In cell A2, enter the formula =ROWS ($A$2:A2). Copy the formula down until the last cell of the data table.

explanation

The Rows formula returns the calculation of the number of the row in a formula cell range from the first cell until the current address. The first cell address is absolute, while the address of the last cell in the range is relative (relative distance).

result

Excel automatically calculates and updates the number of the row. You may sort the table according to any field that you desire, and you may delete or add rows. The result is Excel calculates a new row number and updates it in ascending order.

The Lookup formula group

The **Lookup** formula group (explained below) returns one value from a cell in the data range or the data table. Note that the **Match** formula is different and returns the consecutive (ordinal) *number* of the cell in the cell range and not the *value* of the cell.

List of **Lookup** formulas discussed in this chapter:

Lookup   Returns one value from a cell in the range of the corresponding data table.

Hlookup   Returns one value from a cell in the data table, horizontal design.

Vlookup   Returns one value from a cell in the data table, vertical design.

Match   Returns an ordinal number of a cell in the cell range, either horizontal or vertical.

Index   Returns one value from a cell in the data table.

Lookup formula

Select a cell in the sheet, and press **Shift+F3**. From the **Lookup and Reference** category, select the **Lookup** function. Or enter =Lookup in the cell, and then press **Ctrl+A** (shortcut for displaying the **Select Arguments** dialog box of the formula).

In the **Lookup** formula, there are two possible calculations for returning a value from a cell:

☐ Searching a data range and returning a value from a cell in the same range, or

☐ Searching a data range and returning a value from a cell in a parallel range.

Returning a value from one data range

Select the second argument in the **Select Arguments** dialog box (the shorter argument), and click **OK**.

Example: In order to calculate the Consumer Price Index (CPI) to the date of March 15, 2001, you must first locate the CPI published closest to the date of the computation.

Result: See the list of the dates in the figure. The date closest to the desired date of March 15, 2001 is March 1, 2001.

Calculation method of the Lookup formula

In the **Lookup formula**, Excel searches for the value March 15, 2001 in the range of cells. The search method is from the end to the beginning (when the date range is sorted from the lowest to the highest, in ascending order). The formula returns a result that is equal to or lower than the value that was checked; in the example here, the value is March 1, 2001.

Note

Be consistent in the type of value you check and the range of cells in which you check for the value (date/dates, number/numbers, etc.).

The Lookup formula in the Function Arguments

Function Arguments		? X

LOOKUP

Lookup_value H3   = 36965

Array Dates   = {"Dates";36892;369;

= 36951

Looks up a value either from a one-row or one-column range or from an array. Provided for backward compatibility.

Array is a range of cells that contain text, number, or logical values that you want to compare with Lookup_value.

Formula result =   36951

Help on this function   [OK] [Cancel]

The Lookup formula has two arguments. In the first argument box, select a cell that contains the value for which the calculation takes place.

In the second argument box, paste the name for the cell range, or select the cell range (vertical range only) in the worksheet in which you carry out the search.

example

To retrieve text from the list sorted in ascending order, type the text **Int** in cell C2. Enter the **Lookup** formula in cell D2.

result

Excel retrieves the text Cisco (see cell A4), which is the first value that is lower (alphabetically) than Int.

```
Microsoft Excel - Book1                                                    _ □ X
  File  Edit  View  Insert  Format  Tools  Data  Window  Help    Type a question for help  ▼ _ ∂ ×
     D2        ▼        fx  =LOOKUP(C2,A:A)
         A            B       C       D       E      F      G      H      I
 1  Customer Name
 2  AIG                      Int    Cisco
 3  Amazon
 4  Cisco
 5  Intel
 6  Microsoft
 7  Motorola
 8  MrExcel
 9  Pacific Bell
10
|◄ ◄ ► ►|\ Sheet1 \Sheet2 / Sheet3 / Sheet4 / Sheet5 / Sheet6 /   |◄|
```

The Lookup formula: returning a value from a parallel range

```
Microsoft Excel - Book1                                                    _ □ X
  File  Edit  View  Insert  Format  Tools  Data  Window  Help    Type a question for help  ▼ _ ∂ ×
     E4        ▼        fx  =LOOKUP(E3,Dates,CPI)
      A      B           C       D         E        F      G      H      I      J
 1
 2        Dates        CPI                 2
 3       01/01/2001   100.00         03/15/2001
 4       02/01/2001   110.00            120
 5       03/01/2001   120.00             12
 6       04/01/2001   130.00              3
 7       05/01/2001   140.00             12
 8       06/01/2001   150.00
 9       07/01/2001   160.00
10       08/01/2001   170.00
11       09/01/2001   180.00
12       10/01/2001   190.00
13       11/01/2001   200.00
14       12/01/2001   210.00
15       01/01/2002   220.00
16
|◄ ◄ ► ►|\ Sheet1 / Sheet2 / Sheet3 / Sheet4 / Sheet5 \Sheet6 /   |◄|
```

The Lookup formula (see figure) returns the Income for the date March 15, 2001.

Two names are defined in the example:

▣ **Dates** – cell range B3:B15

▣ **CPI** – cell range C3:C15

Note

The two cell ranges (**CPI** and **Dates**) are of equal length (13 cells). The ranges MUST be of equal length in order to obtain correct results.

Enter three arguments in the Lookup formula

1. Select cell E4, type =Lookup and press **Ctrl+A**. The **Function Arguments** dialog box appears.

2. In the **Function Arguments** dialog box, select the first option, and click **OK**. The **Function Arguments** dialog box appears.

Function Arguments		? X
LOOKUP		
Lookup_value E3	= 36965	
Lookup_vector Dates	= {36892;36923;3695	
Result_vector CPI	= {100;110;120;130;1	

= 120

Looks up a value either from a one-row or one-column range or from an array. Provided for backward compatibility.

Lookup_value is a value that LOOKUP searches for in Lookup_vector and can be a number, text, a logical value, or a name or reference to a value.

Formula result =   120

Help on this function   OK   Cancel

3. In the first argument, **Lookup_Value**, select cell E3.

4. In the second argument, **Lookup_Vector**, click F3, and paste the name **Dates**.

5. In the third argument, **Result_Vector**, click F3, and type the name **CPI**.

6. Finish entering the formula, and click **OK**.

result

The formula searches (in the **Dates** range) for a date that is equal or less than March 15, 2001. The date that fulfills this condition is March 1, 2001 (cell B5). The results are returned from the corresponding cell in the Income fields; the value that the formula returns is 120 (cell C5).

The VLookup formula

The **VLookup** formula returns a value from a cell in one of the table columns. The **VLookup** formula is an extension of the **Lookup** formula.

The letter V at the beginning of the formula is an abbreviation for vertical. **VLookup** searches for a value in the leftmost column of a table and then returns a value in the same row from a column you specify in the table.

Row: The formula that returns the number of the row in the table is **Lookup**.

Column: Consecutive number of the column in the table.

Question

What was the Consumer Price Index (CPI) on March 15, 2001?

Answer

The CPI that was known is 120 (see figure).

Explanation

The value of 120 is located in the cell which intersects the row in the data table with a date equal or less than March 15, 2001 (the date that fulfills this criteria is March 1, 2001) and the second column on the data table, which is the CPI column.

Enter the VLookup formula

Step 1: Define a name for the table

1. Select a cell in the data table, select an active area, and press **Ctrl+***.

2. Press **Ctrl+F3**, and enter the name Data in the **Names in workbook** field.

3. Click **OK**.

Step 2: Type the formula

1. In cell F2, type the number 2 (the number of the CPI column in the data table).

2. Select cell F5. In the formula bar, type =Vlookup, and press **Ctrl+A**. The **Function Arguments** dialog box appears.

3. In the **Lookup_value** (first) argument box, select cell F3 (the value for which the calculation is made).

4. Select the **Table_array** (second) argument box, click F3, and paste the name Data.

5. In the **Col_Index_num** (third) argument box, select F2 (the number of the column in the data table).

6.   Click **OK**.

Results of calculating the formula: The CPI on 3/15/2001 is 120.

explanation

When a **Name** (or a cell range) of a data table is entered as the second argument of the **VLookup** formula, Excel calculates the number of the columns in the data table. Remember not to enter a column number that is greater than the number of columns in the data table; this will cause Excel to return an erroneous result.

The fourth argument: Range_Lookup

In the first argument in the **VLookup** formula, the value that is entered is the value of the row number in the first column in the table.

The default in the fourth argument (**Range_lookup**) is empty. This means that Excel will look for a value in the first column that is equal or less than the original value.

To find an exact match, enter False in the fourth argument. If you do so, you do not need to sort the data according to column A. The **VLookup** function looks to find the exact match in the left unsorted column.

The Match formula

The **Match** formula returns the ordinal number or *position* (and not the *value*) of a cell within the range of the cells that are searched.

example

Cell B12 is the tenth cell position within the range of the cells that have been assigned the name called Dates (B3:B15).

Enter the Match formula

The date 3/15/2001 shown in cell E3.

1. Select cell E6.

2. In the formula bar, type =Match and then press **Ctrl+A**. The **Function Argument's** dialog box appears.

3. In the **Lookup_Value** argument box (first), select cell E3.

4. In the **Lookup_Array** argument box (second), click F3, and paste the name **Dates**.

5. Click **OK**.

The third argument box: Match_type

The third argument box validates the first argument's value within the range that is searched. For example, the value in the first argument's box is the date March 15, 2001; this date does not appear in the range that was assigned the name of Dates.

Enter 0 to search for an exact match in the **Match_type** argument. In this example, the result will be the error type #N/A.

The Index formula

The Index formula returns a value corresponding to the intersection of the row number on the data table and the column number in the data table.

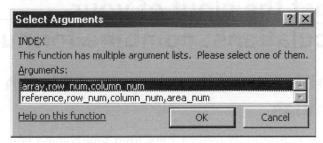

Index formula returns one of two possibilities:

☐ Short formula arguments which return a value from a cell.

☐ Long formula arguments which return a reference.

Example, see the figure above:

Cell E2 contains the number of the row in the data table.

Cell E6 contains the number of the column in the data table.

The **Name** of the data table is Data. The result of the calculations is 110 in cell E7.

Boost the clout of your calculations: combine formulas

Combine the VLookup and Match formulas

The **VLookup** formula returns data from any column you choose in the data table; simply change the number of the column in the third argument.

Although it sounds simple, there is a catch. How can you determine the number of a column in a data table that contains numerous columns? How can you easily change the number of the column in the third argument of the **VLookup** formula? How can you easily change the column number in multiple formulas in a worksheet from which complex reports are prepared or in a sheet that contains multiple **VLookup** formulas?

solution

Combine the **Match** formula with the third argument of the **VLookup** formula.

Combining the VLookup and Match formulas:

1. Calculate the column number by using the **Match** formula.

2. Combine the two formulas into one.

	A	B	C	D	E	F	G	H	
1	Account Number	Account Name	P&L	January 2001	February 2001	March 2001	April 2001	May 2001	Jur
2	101	Sales	Income	25,235	27,586	30,251	26,585	28,965	
3	201	Salary & Wages	General Exp.	7,625	7,076	7,425	7,901	8,722	
4	202	Employee Benefits	General Exp.	1,524	1,762	1,554	1,822	1,726	
5	203	Utilities	General Exp.	928	1,098	887	1,625	1,423	
6	204	Rent	General Exp.	3,500	3,500	3,500	3,500	3,500	
7	205	Advertising	General Exp.	1,425	2,765	1,233	1,928	1,324	
8	206	Sales Exp.	General Exp.	2,415	1,928	2,665	2,981	1,728	
9	207	office supplies	General Exp.	526	332	162	345	625	
10	208	Office Exp.	General Exp.	442	654	425	336	554	
11	209	Telephone	General Exp.	887	987	769	886	654	
12	210	Depreciation	General Exp.	250	250	250	250	250	
13									
14									
15									

In the figure above, the column number of April 2001 is 7.

Calculation - The first three columns In the table are Account Number, Account Name, P&L (profit and loss), plus four columns for the months January-April.

Task - To calculate the column number according to the text heading of the column.

Tip – add new headings to the data table

In cell D1, enter the date 1/1/2001; in cell E1, enter the date 1/2/2001. Select the two cells and drag the fill handle to the right to copy them to the rest of the cells in Row 1. Select all the cells, and press **Ctrl+1**; the **Format Cells** dialog box appears. Select the **Number** tab, and then under **Category**, select **Custom**. In the **Type** box, type **mmmm yyyy** and click **OK**.

Step 1: Define 2 names

1. Select Row 1, press **Ctrl+F3**, type the name **Row1** in the **Names in workbook** field, and click **OK**.

2. Select the entire sheet by pressing **Ctrl+A**. Then press **Ctrl+F3**, enter Data in the **Names in workbook** field, and click **OK**.

Step 2: Enter the Match formula

1. Open an adjacent worksheet, and select cell A1.

2. In cell A1 type 4/1/2001.

3. In cell B1, enter the formula =MATCH (A1, Row1, 0). (Be careful to enter the value 0 in the third argument to specify the search for an exact value.)

4. Results of calculation: 7.

Step 3: Enter the Vlookup formula

1. Enter the account number 201 into cell A2.

2. Enter the formula =VLOOKUP(A2,Data,B1) in cell B2. In the third argument of the **VLookup** formula, select a cell which contains the **Match** formula.

3. Calculation results: 7,981.

Step 4: Combine the formulas

In the formula bar (**Match** formula) of cell B1, select the formula without the = sign, press **Ctrl+C**, and click the Cancel sign (from the left of the formula in the formula bar). Select cell B2, and in the formula bar, select the address B1. Press **Ctrl+V** and press **Enter**.

The final result is a nested formula is

=VLOOKUP (A2, Data, MATCH(A1, Row 1, 0))

Combine the Index and Match formulas

Step 1: Define a name

Define a **Name** to column B. In the example, the **Name** is ColB.

Step 2: Enter the Match formula

1. Select a new sheet. In cell A1, enter one text from the expenses list.

2. Calculate the row number. In cell B1, enter the formula =MATCH (A1, ColB, 0). The result of the calculation is 9.

3. In cell A2, enter the date 4/1/2001.

4. Calculate the column number. In cell B2, enter the formula =MATCH (A2, Row1, 0). The result of the calculation is 7.

Step 3: Enter the Index formula

In cell C1, enter the formula =INDEX(Data, B1, B2). The result is 345.

Step 4: Combine (nesting) the formulas

Now you will use the technique of copying and pasting a formula from the formula bar (without the = sign) into a different formula.

From the formula bar of cell B1, copy the **Match** formula without the = (equal) sign. Then click the X to the left of the formula (to cancel); select the C1 cell; in the formula bar, select the B1 address; and press **Ctrl+V**.

Use the same technique to copy the **Match** formula from the B2 cell to the formula bar in cell C1 (instead of the B2 address).

The combined formula is (see figure on page 372):

=INDEX(DATA, MATCH(A1, ColB, 0), MATCH(A2, Row 1,0)

```
┌─────────────────────────────────────────────────────────────────────────────┐
│ Microsoft Excel - Book1                                           _ □ X        │
│ File  Edit  View  Insert  Format  Tools  Data  Window  Help    Type a question for help  ▾ _ ⊟ X │
│   C1        ▾         fx  =INDEX(Data,MATCH(A1,ColB,0),MATCH(A2,Row1,0))       │
│      A           B         C         D      E      F      G      H      I    J  │
│ 1 office supplies  9         345                                              │
│ 2    April 2001    7                                                          │
│ 3                                                                             │
│ 4 Function in cell B1   =MATCH(A1,ColB,0)                                      │
│ 5 Function in cell B2   =MATCH(A2,Row1,0)                                      │
│ 6 Function in cell C1   =INDEX(Data,MATCH(A1,ColB,0),MATCH(A2,Row1,0))        │
│ 7                                                                             │
│ 8                                                                             │
│ 9                                                                             │
│ I◄ ◄ ► ►I\Sheet1 /Sheet2 /Sheet3 /Sheet4 /Sheet5 /Sheet6 /    │◄│            │
└─────────────────────────────────────────────────────────────────────────────┘
```

Combo Box

You added the **Match** formula to the **VLookup** formula in order to calculate the column number.

You added two **Match** formulas to the **Index** formula in order to calculate the row and column numbers.

Choosing an item from a list in the **Combo box** returns a number. The number then replaces the use of the **Match** formula to calculate the column number in the **VLookup** formula and replaces the use of the **Match** formula to calculate the column number in the **Index** formula.

Where do I find the Combo Box?

Select one of the toolbars and right-click the mouse. From the shortcut menu that appears, select **Forms**.

Working with the combo box

A list of the cell ranges in the sheet is attached to the **Combo Box**. After an item is selected from the list, the **Combo Box** enters into the linked cell the *ordinal number* of the item that is selected on the list.

Example:

The figure below displays a profit and loss statement as compared to the previous year. Changing the month in the **Combo Box** will automatically change the display of data according to the selected month.

Add a combo box

Step 1: Define names

1. Enter the months January-December into the cells A1 to A12 in the new worksheet.

2. Select the list of months, press **Ctrl+F3**, enter the text **MonthsList** into the **Names In workbook** box, and click **OK**.

3. Select Cell B1, press **Ctrl+F3**, enter the text **MonthNumber** into the **Names in Workbook** box, and click **OK**.

Step 2: Add a combo box to a worksheet

1. Select one of the toolbars, right-click, and select the **Forms** toolbar.

2. Copy the **Combo Box** by clicking the **Combo Box** icon, and then release the mouse. Create a rectangle with the mouse in the worksheet, and then release the mouse.

Step 3: Format the combo box

1. Select the **Combo Box**; right-click; and from the shortcut menu that appears, select **Format Control**. Then select the **Control** tab.

2. In the **Input range** box, type the name **MonthsList**. (You cannot press **F3** to paste a name with an object.)

3. In the **Cell link** box, type the name **MonthNumber**.

4. Click to select the **3-D shading** box (more aesthetic).

5. Click **OK**.

Exit the formatting mode of **Combo Box**, and select a cell in the sheet. Open the list of items in the **Combo Box**, and select a month. Note that the new month number is shown in cell B1.

Advantages of working with names in a combo box

Attaching a list with **Define Names** causes your list references to be updated automatically in the **Combo Box**. Sorting the list in the sheet will automatically sort the list in **Combo Box** as well.

Deleting a combo box

Select the object; right-click; and from the shortcut menu that appears, select **Cut**.

Deleting all the objects in a worksheet

Press **F5**, click the **Special** button, select the **Objects** check box, click **OK**, and then click **Delete**.

Adjusting the size of the combo box to the cells

Select the **Combo Box** and right-click; the **Combo Box** is now in editing mode. Adjust the width or height of the **Combo Box** by dragging one of the corner boxes; adjust the placement of the **Combo Box** on the worksheet by clicking anywhere inside the box and dragging it.

Automatic adjustment of the combo box

Hold down the **Alt** key while you click the mouse to adjust the size of the **Combo Box**.

Combine the VLookup formula and the Combo Box

Attach a list of 36 months (starting from January 2001) to the **Combo Box**.

	A	B	C	D	E	F	G
			Consolidate Account				
1	**Account Name**	**P&L**	**Name & P&L**	**January 2001**	**February 2001**	**March 2001**	**April 2**
2	Sales	Revenue	Revenue - Sales	(1,000,001)	(1,001,002)	(1,002,003)	(1,003
3	Interest	Revenue	Revenue - Interest	(10,101)	(10,202)	(10,303)	(10
4	Other Income	Revenue	Revenue - Other Income	(1,001)	(1,002)	(1,003)	(1,
5	Car Exp.	G&A	G&A - Car Exp.	5,001	5,002	5,003	5
6	Office Supplies	G&A	G&A - Office Supplies	301	302	303	
7	Computers Exp.	G&A	G&A - Computers Exp.	201	202	203	
8	Insurance	G&A	G&A - Insurance	1,001	1,002	1,003	1
9	Audit	G&A	G&A - Audit	1,101	1,102	1,103	1
10	Rent	G&A	G&A - Rent	5,001	5,002	5,003	5
11	Head Hunting	G&A	G&A - Head Hunting	7,501	7,502	7,503	7
12	Courses	G&A	G&A - Courses	901	902	903	
13	Other	G&A	G&A - Other	101	102	103	
14	Utilities	G&A	G&A - Utilities	1,251	1,252	1,253	1
15	Maintenance	G&A	G&A - Maintenance	1,501	1,502	1,503	1
16	Taxes	G&A	G&A - Taxes	951	952	953	
17	Salaries	G&A	G&A - Salaries	250,001	250,002	250,003	250
18	Legal	G&A	G&A - Legal	2,501	2,502	2,503	2
19	Office Exp.	G&A	G&A - Office Exp.	1,201	1,202	1,203	1
20	Cleaning	G&A	G&A - Cleaning	251	252	253	
21	Telephone	G&A	G&A - Telephone	3,001	3,002	3,003	3

1. In Row 1, select and copy the list of months. Select cell D1, click the left arrow plus **Ctrl+Shift**, and press **Ctrl+C**.

2. Select a new sheet in your workbook. Select cell A1, right-click, and select **Paste Special** from the shortcut menu. In the **Paste Special** dialog box, select **Transpose**. The reason: the input range in the **Combo Box** must be vertical.

3. To define a **Name** for the list of months, click **Ctrl+F3**, enter the name **MonthsList** in the **Names in workbook** box, and then click **OK**.

4. Select cell B1, press **Ctrl+F3**, enter the name **MonthNumber** in the **Names in workbook** box, and then click **OK**.

5. Select one of the toolbars, right-click, and select **Forms**.

6. Add a **Combo Box** to the sheet from the **Forms** toolbar (see previous instructions).

7. In the **Input range** box, enter **MonthsList**. In the **Link to cell** box, enter **MonthNumber**. Then click **OK**. (Note that you cannot paste a name to cells through the **F3** shortcut here).

8. Open the **Combo Box**, and select March 2001.

The result: the number 3 is entered into cell B1, which is named **MonthNumber**.

Adjust the number of the column in the data table to the number that is linked to the combo box

The number 3 that appears in the **MonthNumber** cell is the number of the month that you select in the **Combo Box**. The number corresponding to the **March 2001** column (in the data table) is 6: three columns for the Account Number, Account Name, and P&L (Profit and Loss); and three columns for the months January 2001 to March 2001. This number, the column number of **March 2001,** must be inserted as the third argument of the **VLookup** formula.

The **VLookup** formula is =VLOOKUP (B3,DATA,MonthNumber+3).

Combine the Index formula, Validation and Combo Box

The **Combo Box** is an excellent, easy-to-use technique that serves us well when we need to calculate the column number. The number in the cell is linked to the **Combo Box,** and it replaces the use of the **Match** formula in calculating the column number in the **VLookup** and **Index** formulas.

However, the **Combo Box** does not help us in calculating the number of the *row* in the **Index** formula.

Example: Prepare a report of the Expenses list for the month of March 2001.

To calculate the column number, add a **Combo Box** with a list of months, as explained above. The number in the cell is linked to the **Combo Box** and matches the columns of the sheet. Excel returns the results of the calculation of the column in the data table, and this, in turn, is the column number in the third argument in the **Index** formula.

Calculating the row number – How can you calculate the row number, which is the second argument of the **Index** formula? Suppose you try to define a list for **Account Name** (column B, cell range from B2 until the end of the list), and then attach the list to a **Combo Box**. You see the problem: you would have to create numerous combo boxes in all of the cells, and in each **Combo Box** you would select only one account name. This is not a practical solution.

Solution

Attach a **Validation** list to the cells.

For a detailed explanation of the Validation technique see **Chapter 2**, **Text**.

	Microsoft Excel - P&I						
	File Edit View Insert Format Tools Data Window Help				Type a question for help		
	C2	fx	=B2&" - "&A2				
	A	B	C	D	E	F	G
1	Account Name	P&L	Consolidate Account Name & P&L	January 2001	February 2001	March 2001	April
2	Sales	Revenue	Revenue - Sales	(1,000,001)	(1,001,002)	(1,002,003)	(1,00
3	Interest	Revenue	Revenue - Interest	(10,101)	(10,202)	(10,303)	(1(
4	Other Income	Revenue	Revenue - Other Income	(1,001)	(1,002)	(1,003)	(
5	Car Exp.	G&A	G&A - Car Exp.	5,001	5,002	5,003	
6	Office Supplies	G&A	G&A - Office Supplies	301	302	303	
7	Computers Exp.	G&A	G&A - Computers Exp.	201	202	203	
8	Insurance	G&A	G&A - Insurance	1,001	1,002	1,003	
9	Audit	G&A	G&A - Audit	1,101	1,102	1,103	
10	Rent	G&A	G&A - Rent	5,001	5,002	5,003	
11	Head Hunting	G&A	G&A - Head Hunting	7,501	7,502	7,503	
12	Courses	G&A	G&A - Courses	901	902	903	
13	Other	G&A	G&A - Other	101	102	103	
14	Utilities	G&A	G&A - Utilities	1,251	1,252	1,253	
15	Maintenance	G&A	G&A - Maintenance	1,501	1,502	1,503	
16	Taxes	G&A	G&A - Taxes	951	952	953	
17	Salaries	G&A	G&A - Salaries	250,001	250,002	250,003	25(
18	Legal	G&A	G&A - Legal	2,501	2,502	2,503	

P&L / Details for P&L / Total Expenses / Lists & Formulas \ ActualData

Add a validation list

Step 1: Define a name

Select the Account Name list in column A by selecting cell A2 and pressing **Down Arrow+Ctrl+Shift**. Press **Ctrl+F3**, enter the **IndexList** name in the **Names in workbook box**, and click **OK**.

Step 2: Attach a list to the cells

1. Open the worksheet in which you will prepare the report, and select the cells from B5 on.

2. From the **Data** menu, select **Validation**.

3. Select the **Settings** tab, and under **Allow**, select **List**.

4. Select the **Source** box, press **F3**, paste **AccountName**, and click **OK**.

5. Open each validation list in any cell from cell B5 on, and choose the account item.

Step 3: Enter the Index formula

Enter the **Index** formula in cell D5 (see figure).

Explanation: In the second argument in the **Match** formula, use the selection technique from the **Validation** list in order to easily select an item from the list. The **Match** formula returns the ordinal number of the text that was selected in the **Name** column. This is the ColB column in the data table.

Summarize data according to criteria from the data table

The combination of formulas in the **Combo Box** and **Validation** returns only one value from the data table.

The **SUMIF** formula summarizes data according to criteria (see **Chapter 8, Summing and Counting**). The **OFFSET** formula enables us to change the reference. The combination of the two formulas and the addition of a **Combo Box** allow you to easily summarize data according to criteria from the data table.

Example, see figure below

Task: Summarize the Profit and Loss by P&L items (see P&L, column B) for the month of January 2001 or any other month that you choose.

	A	B	C	D	E	F	G
1	Account Name	P&L	Consolidate Account Name & P&L	January 2001	February 2001	March 2001	April 2
2	Sales	Revenue	Revenue - Sales	(1,000,001)	(1,001,002)	(1,002,003)	(1,003,
3	Interest	Revenue	Revenue - Interest	(10,101)	(10,202)	(10,303)	(10,
4	Other Income	Revenue	Revenue - Other Income	(1,001)	(1,002)	(1,003)	(1,
5	Car Exp.	G&A	G&A - Car Exp.	5,001	5,002	5,003	5,
6	Office Supplies	G&A	G&A - Office Supplies	301	302	303	
7	Computers Exp.	G&A	G&A - Computers Exp.	201	202	203	
8	Insurance	G&A	G&A - Insurance	1,001	1,002	1,003	1,
9	Audit	G&A	G&A - Audit	1,101	1,102	1,103	1,
10	Rent	G&A	G&A - Rent	5,001	5,002	5,003	5,
11	Head Hunting	G&A	G&A - Head Hunting	7,501	7,502	7,503	7,
12	Courses	G&A	G&A - Courses	901	902	903	
13	Other	G&A	G&A - Other	101	102	103	
14	Utilities	G&A	G&A - Utilities	1,251	1,252	1,253	1,
15	Maintenance	G&A	G&A - Maintenance	1,501	1,502	1,503	1,
16	Taxes	G&A	G&A - Taxes	951	952	953	
17	Salaries	G&A	G&A - Salaries	250,001	250,002	250,003	250,
18	Legal	G&A	G&A - Legal	2,501	2,502	2,503	2,
19	Office Exp.	G&A	G&A - Office Exp.	1,201	1,202	1,203	1,
20	Cleaning	G&A	G&A - Cleaning	251	252	253	
21	Telephone	G&A	G&A - Telephone	3,001	3,002	3,003	3,

P&L / Details for P&L / Total Expenses / Lists & Formulas \ ActualData

Step 1: Specify a name for column B in the worksheet

Select column B, press **Ctrl+F3**, enter ColB in the **Names in worksheet** box, and then click **OK**.

Step 2: The SUMIF formula

The **SUMIF** formula summarizes data according to criteria.

see **Chapter 8, Summing and Counting**.

Function Arguments   ? X

SUMIF
Range │ColB│   =
Criteria │b3│   = "Revenue"
Sum_range │D:D│   = D:D

= -1011103

Adds the cells specified by a given condition or criteria.

Range is the range of cells you want evaluated.

Formula result =   (1,011,103)

Help on this function   OK   Cancel

The formula has 3 arguments

1. First argument – **Range** – ColB (column B in the data table sheet).

2. Second argument – **Criteria** – b3 (the text: **Revenue)**.

3. Third argument – **Sum_range** – **D:D** (column D, January 2001). This is the data range from which the data-by-criteria will be summarized.

Problem

The **SUMIF** formula is excellent for summarizing data according to criteria. However, there is a limitation: you cannot make any changes in the summary range when you use the **SUMIF** formula. In the example above, you summed up the data from the January 2001 column. How, then, can you easily change the range of the sum in order to sum from the column of March or April (instead of from January)?

There is a third argument in the **VLookup** formula: changing the column number also changes the number of the intersected column. The **Index** formula is much more flexible; you can change both the number of the row and the number of the column. The **SUMIF** formula needs help, and the solution is to add the **OFFSET** formula.

Step 3: The OFFSET formula

The **OFFSET** formula returns a reference to a range that is a specified number of rows and columns from a cell or range of cells. The reference that is returned can be a single cell or a range of cells. You can specify the number of rows and the number of columns to be returned.

The formula in the figure above returns a value from a cell that is a given distance from the base cell of B4. The distance is 0 rows, 2 columns. The cell address is D4.

Step 4: Combining the OFFSET and SUMIF formulas

In the combined formula below, the data from January 2001 is summarized according to a criteria.

The formula is =SUMIF(ColB,B3,OFFSET (ColB,0,2))

Changing the third argument in the **OFFSET** formula will offset (reposition) the data summary range. In order to accomplish this, add a **Combo Box** to the sheet.

Step 5: Combo box

Add a **Combo Box** as explained earlier in this chapter. The name of the cell linked to the combo box is **MonthNumber**.

In the figure below, see the third argument of the **SUMIF** formula in the formula bar. The name of the cell that is linked to the **Combo Box** appears here.

Combining **SUMIF**, **OFFSET** and a **Combo box** provides an incredibly powerful tool for querying and summing data from a report.

Chapter 24

Loans

Formulas that calculate loan payments, principal, interest and more are found in the **Financial** category in the **Paste Function** dialog box. In the figure below is a list of functions and necessary syntax for loan calculations. See the formulas in the gray cells, and the syntax in rows 12-16.

	A	B	C	D	E	F	G
1	Functions	PMT	PPMT	NPER	RATE	PV	IPMT
2							
3	Principal	100,000	100,000	100,000	100,000	113,922	75,000
4	Interest rate	10%	10%	10%	83%	12%	12%
5	Total No. of Payments	36	36	36	36	48	48
6	Monthly payment	3,227	3,227	3,227	3,227	3,000	
7							
8	First Month Payment		-2,393				
9	Principal first year		-33,057				
10	Principal last year		-33,610				
11	Interest first month						750
12	Function Syntax	=PMT(B4/12,B5,-B3)		=NPER(D4/12,D6,-D3)		=PV(F4/12,F5,F6)*-1	
13					=RATE(E5,-E6,E3)*100		=IPMT(G4/12,1,G5/12,-G3)
14	Principal first year		=PPMT(C4/12,1,C5,C3)				
15	Principal last year		=PPMT(C4/12,1,C5/12,C3)				
16	Interest first month		=PPMT(C4/12,3,C5/12,C3)				
17							
18							

Syntax for loan calculation functions

Rate   The interest rate per period.

Per   The period for which the interest rate is calculated.

Nper   The total number of payments.

Pv   The present value, the total amount that a series of future payments is worth now.

Fv   The future value or a cash balance you want to attain after the last payment is made.

Type   The timing of the payment, either at the beginning or end of the period.

            Numbers 0 or 1 represent the payment date. The number 0 represents payment at the end of the period, and the number 1 represents payment at the beginning of the period. The default (empty argument) is 0. The calculation is at the end of the period.

PMT (Rate, Nper, -Loan Amount)

Calculates the payment for a loan based on constant payments and a constant interest rate.

Returns the regular monthly payment on the loan (principal + interest) when the interest for each of the monthly payments is constant.

Example: The principal of a loan is $100,000, and the term of the loan is three years. The monthly payment during the term of the loan is calculated at $3,227; see column B in the figure below.

PPMT (Rate, Which Period, Nper, -Loan Amount)

Returns the amount on the principal for a given period for a loan based on periodic, constant payments and a constant interest rate.

Returns the sum of the principal within the monthly payment (the monthly payment is comprised of the principal + interest). See various examples of calculations in column C, rows 8:10, and the formula syntax in rows 14:16.

IPMT (Rate, Which Period, Nper, -Loan Amount)

Returns the interest payment for a given period for a loan based on periodic, constant payments and a constant interest rate.

Returns the amount of the interest within the monthly payment (the monthly payment is comprised of the principal + interest). See the calculation in cell G11 and the formula syntax in G13.

NPER (Rate, Pmt, -Loan Amount)

Returns the number of loan payments with a constant interest rate. See the formula syntax in D12.

RATE (Nper, Pmt, -Loan Amount)

Returns the interest rate per period of a loan. RATE is calculated by iteration and can have zero or more solutions.

Returns the percentage of interest on the loan, when the number of payments is constant.

PV (Rate, Nper, Pmt)

PV is the present value — the total amount that a series of future payments is worth now.

Returns the current value for a series of payments with a constant interest rate.

Create an Amortization Schedule

Simple amortization schedule

See the example of an amortization schedule in the figure below:

Formulas that do not appear in the figure:

The formula in cell C17 is =LOAN (LOAN is the name of cell C4).

The formula in cell C18 is =G17; copy the formula from cell C18 to all the cells in column C, starting from C18.

Amortization schedule with a grace period

The difference between a regular amortization schedule and one with a grace period is that in the latter, the repayment of the principal is delayed. The loan agreement stipulates the month in which the repayment of principal begins. The interest on the loan is calculated, and the first interest payment starts with the first month *after* the month that the loan was accepted.

See the example in the figure below. Note that the formulas used are not PPMT and IPMT; these formulas are not appropriate when the calculations are not linear.

	A	B	C	D	E	F	G
1							
3			Data			Results	Function syntax
4	Principal		100,000	Monthly payment		3,227	=PMT(C5/12,C6,-C4)
5	Interest rate		10%	Total interest paid		21,162	=SUM(D:D)
6	No. of payments		36	Total principal paid		100,000	=SUM(E:E)
7	Grace Period		7	Total grace period+no. of payments		42	=IF(C7=0,C6,C6+(C7-1))
9	Function in cell C16			=C4			
10	Function in cell D16			=IF(B13<=$F$7,C13*($C$5/12),0)			
11	Function in cell E16			=IF(B13<$C$7,0,IF(B13<=$F$7,$F$4-D13,0))			
12	Function in cell F16			=D16+E16			
13	Function in cell G16					=IF(B16<=$F$7,C16-E16,0)	
15	Return date	Payment number	Principal balance at the beginning of month	Interest	Principal	Monthly payment	Principal balance end of month
16	01/10/2000	1	100,000.00	833.33	0.00	833.33	100,000.00
17	01/11/2000	2	100,000.00	833.33	0.00	833.33	100,000.00
18	01/12/2000	3	100,000.00	833.33	0.00	833.33	100,000.00
19	01/01/2001	4	100,000.00	833.33	0.00	833.33	100,000.00

Amortization schedule for random payment

See the formulas in the figure below for calculating the sum of the principal and interest in every payment.

The dates of the loan repayment are random. The interest is calculated according to the number of interest days divided by 365 days in a year.

	A	B	C	D	E	F	G
1							
2			Data			Results	
3			Cell Name			Function syntax	Total
4	Principal		Loan	100,000	Total Interest paid	=SUM(E:E)	419
5	Date Loan received		Date	15/01/01	Total principal paid	=SUM(F:F)	22,081
6	Interest rate		Int	12%			
7							
8	Function in cell C16			=Loan			
9	Function in cell C17			=IF(G16=0,0,G16)			
10	Function in cell D16			=IF(B16=0,0,IF(A16<Date,"Ck return date",A16-Date))			
11	Function in cell E16			=IF(A16<Date,0,B16*D16/365*Int)			
12	Function in cell F16			=IF(E16=0,0,B16-E16)			
13	Function in cell G16			=IF(E16=0,0,C16-F16)			
15	Return date	Principal paid	Beginning principal balance	No. of days	interest	Principal return	Ending principal balance
16	15/02/2001	10,000	100,000	31	102	9,898	90,102
17	20/03/2001	7,500	90,102	64	158	7,342	82,760
18	22/04/2001	5,000	82,760	97	159	4,841	77,919
19			77,919	0	0	0	0
20			0	0	0	0	0

Table for Calculating Payments for a Loan with Two Variables

The amount of money you want to borrow depends on your ability to make regular monthly payments. The monthly repayment sum is, in turn, affected by the amount of the loan, the period of the loan, and the amount of interest.

To help you make a decision as to how much money you can safely borrow, see the table below which displays various loan repayment sum calculations when one of the three variables is constant and the others vary. The table is created by using **Table**, **Data Table**. For additional explanations about using the **Table** technique, see **Chapter 25, What If**.

The data and formula in the table:

Number of payments is constant—36 (you can change this number at will).

First variable—Amount of the loan, between $10,000 and $100,000; see row 6 in the figure.

Second variable—Interest rate, between 4% and 10%; see column B in the figure.

Formula PMT is in cell B6. This formula returns the amount of the monthly loan payment (principal plus interest). The cells that input the formula are D2:D4.

The formula in the formula bar in the table:

The formulas from a value called **TABLE** return the monthly payment sum. The two variables that input the formula are in the column and the row.

The formulas from a value called **TABLE** are automatically input into the cells by using the **Table** technique. The formula syntax is =**TABLE** (D4, D2). You cannot enter the function directly. You must follow the steps in the next section, "How to create a table with two variables."

	10,000	40,000	50,000	75,000	100,000
3,226.72	10,000	40,000	50,000	75,000	100,000
4.00%	295	1,181	1,476	2,214	2,952
4.50%	297	1,190	1,487	2,231	2,975
5.00%	300	1,199	1,499	2,248	2,997
5.50%	302	1,208	1,510	2,265	3,020
6.00%	304	1,217	1,521	2,282	3,042
6.50%	306	1,226	1,532	2,299	3,065
7.00%	309	1,235	1,544	2,316	3,088
7.50%	311	1,244	1,555	2,333	3,111
8.00%	313	1,253	1,567	2,350	3,134
8.50%	316	1,263	1,578	2,368	3,157
9.00%	318	1,272	1,590	2,385	3,180
9.50%	320	1,281	1,602	2,402	3,203
10.00%	323	1,291	1,613	2,420	3,227
10.50%	325	1,300	1,625	2,438	3,250
11.00%	327	1,310	1,637	2,455	3,274
11.50%	330	1,319	1,649	2,473	3,298

Data Table
Interest rate — 10%
No. of payments — 36
Loan Principal — 100,000
Function =PMT(D2/12,D3,D4)
C7 — {=TABLE(D4,D2)}

How to create a table with two variables

1. Enter the loan data in the sheet according to the example in the figure, in rows 1-4.

2. Enter the PMT formula =PMT(D2/12,D3,-D4) in cell B6. In the formula's arguments, select the D2:D4 cells.

3. Enter the various interest percentages in column B under the PMT formula. Enter the various loan sums in the heading row of the table, in cells C6 until G6.

4. Select the B6:G40 range (the PMT formula in the upper corner).

5. From the **Data** menu, select **Table**. The dialog box below appears.

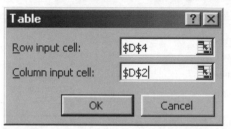

6. In the **Row input cell** box, select D4, the amount of the loan.

7. In the **Column input cell** box, select cell D2, the interest %.

8. Click **OK**.

Chapter 25

What-if

Excel also offers a number of techniques called **What-if** analyses for calculating profitability and enhancing decision-making. This chapter will also cover:

- ▣ Performing sensitivity analysis by using **Data Tables**.

- ▣ Using **Goal Seeking** to find solutions.

- ▣ Using **Solver** to find the optimal solutions under constraints.

- ▣ Creating various economic models using **Scenarios**.

Sensitivity Analysis (Data Table)

Chapter 24, Loans, explained how to use a **Table** to create two-variable **Data Tables**. **Table** generates and displays the results of the calculation for monthly loan payments when one of the three arguments in the calculation is a constant and the other two are variable.

Example: See figure below - Calculating the **Break-Even Point**.

	A	B	C	D	E	F	G	H
1								
2								
3	Sales				Sales – Units	Sales	Expenses	Net income
4	Units	3,000						
5	Sale price	5.30				=Sales	=Expenses	=F6-G6
6	Total Sales		15,900			15,900	19,000	-3,100
7					2,500	13,250	17,500	-4,250
8	Direct Cost				3,000	15,900	19,000	-3,100
9	Materials (per unit)	2.00			3,500	18,550	20,500	-1,950
10	Labor cost (per unit)	1.00			4,000	21,200	22,000	-800
11	Total direct cost	3.00	9,000		4,500	23,850	23,500	350
12	Fixed cost		10,000		5,000	26,500	25,000	1,500
13	Total direct & fixed cost		19,000		5,500	29,150	26,500	2,650
14					6,000	31,800	28,000	3,800
15	Net income		-3,100		6,500	34,450	29,500	4,950
16								
17								

Sheet1 / Sheet2 / Sheet3 / Scenario Summary / Scenario PivotTable

The **Break-Even Point** in a model is the result of the following calculation: the quantity of sales required to cover both direct and fixed costs. Any quantity that is sold above the calculated break-even point will yield net income; any quantity that is sold below the calculated break-even point will yield a loss.

Data regarding sales and costs have been input into the worksheet above in columns A:C. The results of the calculations appear in cell C15 and represent the loss from the sale of 3000 units.

Creating a Data Table

Enter the sales and cost data into the worksheet (according to the example).

1. Assign the following names: cell C6 – **Sales**, cell C13 – **Expenses**.

2. Enter the following formulas into cells F6:H6, according to the list below:

Cell	Insert this:
F6	Formula: =Sales
G6	Formula: =Expenses
H6	=F6-G6 (the difference between sales and expenses).

3. Enter different quantities of sales into range E7:E15.

4. Select the table in range E6:H15. Be careful to include the header row that contains the formulas, as well as the left column with the sales quantities.

5. From the **Data** menu, select **Table**.

6. In **Row input cell**, select cell B4.

7. Click **OK**.

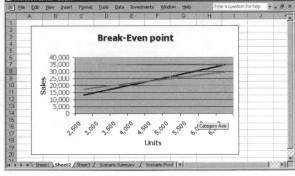

View the results (in the graphic in the previous page). In the cell range F7:H15, formulas of the **TABLE** type appear. The break-even point in the example is between 4,000 and 4,500 units (the exact result is 4,348 units).

Adding a Break-Even Point

1. Select the range E6:G15 (without the formulas in column H).

2. Click the **Chart Wizard** option in the Standard Toolbar.

3. In Step 1 of 4, select the **Standard Type** tab. Under **Chart type**, select **Line**, and click **Next**.

4. In Step 2 of 4, click **Next**.

5. In Step 3 of 4, type **Break-Even Point** in the **Chart title** box. Type Units in the **Category (X) axis** box. Type Sales in the **Value (Y) axis** box. Click **Next**.

6. In Step 4 of 4, click **Finish**.

7. Select the chart, right-click and select **Cut**.

8. Select another worksheet in the workbook, and click **Ctrl+V (Paste)**.

Modify and improve the chart as you wish.

Finding a Solution by Goal Seeking

By using the **Goal Seek** technique, you can compute an unknown value that produces the result you want. **Goal Seek** varies the value in one specific cell until a formula that is dependent on that cell returns the result you want. See the examples below which clarify this principle.

Calculating the sales required to achieve desired profits

Calculate the number of units you must sell of Item 1 in order to achieve net income of $50,000. The result is 30,713 units.

The Optimal Solution for Constraints: Solver

Using goal seeking, you obtained the answer to the question: how many units do you have to sell in order to obtain net income of $50,000.

Note that the calculation in this example was carried out without constraints. Suppose, however, that there are constraints. If you are limited in the number of units that you can produce or the sale price is fixed and cannot be changed, how would you solve the problem?

The add-in called **Solver** seeks and returns optimal calculations subject to constraints; that is, it takes into consideration limitations in unit numbers, sale price, and more. Note that **Solver** is not an integral part of Excel; rather, it is an add-in that you must install.

Installing the Solver Add-In in Excel Versions 97 and 2000

1. From the **Tools** menu, select **Add-Ins**.

2. Select the **Solver** checkbox, and click **OK**.

In Excel Version 2002

The Solver Add-in does not appear in the list of **Add-ins**.

1. From the **Tools** menu, select **Add-Ins**.

2. Click **Browse** to search for and select the **Solver** file; it is usually located in the following directory:

   c:\Program_files\MicrosoftOffice\Office\Library.

3. Select the **Solver** add-in check box, and click **OK**.

Work Techniques With the Solver

Maximize net income according to the data in the economic model that was input into the worksheet. The constraints that you determine will influence the result of the calculation.

![Microsoft Excel - Book1 spreadsheet showing Product1, Product2, Total columns with Units, Sale price, Income, Direct cost (per unit), Cost of goods, Indirect cost, Total costs, and Net income rows]

	Product1	Product2	Total
Units	27,500	30,000	57,500
Sale price	13	15	
Income	357,500	450,000	807,500
Direct cost (per unit)	5	5	
Cost of goods	137,500	150,000	287,500
Indirect cost	197,853	297,853	495,705
Total costs	335,353	447,853	783,205
Net income	22,147	2,147	24,295

Solver Parameters

Set Target Cell: $D$9

Equal To: ● Max ○ Min ○ Value of: 0

By Changing Cells:

$B$2:$C$3,$B$5:$C$5,$B$7:$C$7

Subject to the Constraints:

$B$2 <= 30000
$B$3 <= 14
$B$7 <= 200000
$C$2 <= 32500
$C$3 <= 15
$C$7 <= 297000

Solve · Close · Guess · Options · Add · Change · Reset All · Delete · Help

Setting Solver parameters:

1. Type into the worksheet the data and formulas according to the model in the figure above.

2. Select the cells that contain values without formulas. Assign them **Names** and highlight them. (This will later help you to locate these cells in the stage when you determine constraints for the **Solver**.)

Tip – Select only the cells which contain values

Highlight the area with data (without column A that contains text), click F5, select **Special**, select the **Constants** option, and click **OK**.

3. From the **Tools** menu, select **Solver**.

4. Enter the target cell in the **Set Target Cell** box, for example, D9.

5. In the **Equal To** section, select the **Max** option.

6. In the **By Changing Cells** box, select the data that **Solver** is allowed to change when it finds a solution. Note that the cells with values were already highlighted by you.

7. Click **Add**; the **Add Constraint** dialog box appears.

    Adding constraints:

    a. In the **Cell Reference** box, enter the address of the cell in which **Solver** will insert the new value. Select the relationship you want to add or change (**<=**, **=**, **>=**, **Int**, or **Bin**) between the referenced cell and the constraint.

    b. Then enter the constraint—a number, cell or range reference, or formula—in the box to the right.

    c. Click **Add** to add additional constraints or **OK** to finish.

8. Click **Solver** to find the optimal solution. The **Solver Results** dialog box appears.

9. To save the solutions as a scenario, click **Save Scenario**. See details on **Scenarios** later in this chapter.

10. Select the reports from the list in the **Reports** box that you want **Solver** to create.

Creating reports with Solver

The reports are created automatically in the new worksheets in the workbook.

Answer Report

The report displays the original numbers of the reports, in contrast to the results of the constraint values.

Limits Report

This report displays the maximum values of the variables without constraints.

Sensitivity Report

This report supplies information about the sensitivity level of the target cell regarding the constraint values.

Solver Options

In the **Solver Parameters** dialog box, click **Options**.

Selecting the various options in this dialog box changes the calculations and solutions offered by the **Solver**.

Tip

Too many constraints, or illogical constraints, may prevent **Solver** from finding a solution. If **Solver** does not find a solution, try these two troubleshooting techniques:

1. Limit the number of constraints or determine different ceilings for the calculations.

2. Run the solver on only one constraint at a time; after you receive one solution on a single constraint, then run Solver again on another constraint, etc.

Solver on the Internet

The **Solver** add-in appears in its current version from Excel version 5 and on. The add-in has not been updated. If, however, you need solutions to more complex problems, a more advanced and updated version of **Solver** is available (for a fee) from the manufacturer. The URL is www.solver.com.

Scenarios

You can save and display various scenarios for one economic model by changing the underlying premises of the scenario. **Scenarios** create summary reports and PivotTable reports for review of the various scenarios.

In the process of preparing a business plan, you assume that you will sell a certain quantity of the product that the company produces and sells. The business results of the company are derived from this assumption. Economic caution, then, requires that you present at least three forecasts (regarding the number of products you hope to sell) and the effect of these different forecasts on the business results. These forecasts, or scenarios, would be: pessimistic, average and excellent forecasts, sometimes also called best/worst scenario forecasts.

Adding Different Scenarios

A profit and loss forecast model of a company is displayed in the figure below. The company sells only one product, and the input data is based on past experience. The cells highlighted in gray in columns B and C contain values (without formulas). The rest of the (non-highlighted) cells in columns B and C contain formulas for calculating results. Column E contains the list of names that were assigned to the cells of columns B and C.

Tip

Make sure to define names for all cells that contain data BEFORE using **Scenarios**. See below for an explanation of the importance of defining names.

	A	B	C	D	E
		Week	Year		Cell name
1					
2	Average income per customer	34.78			Average_income_per_customer
3	Direct Cost	30.12			Direct_Cost
4	Gross income	4.66			Gross_income
5	Average number sales per month	33,759			Average_number_sales_per_month
6	Gross income - week	157,317			Gross_income____week
7	Gross income - year		8,180,481		Gross_income____year
8					
9	Fixed cost				
10	labor		3,494,046		labor
11	Rent		1,635,511		Rent
12	Depreciation		453,305		Depreciation
13	Advertising		291,647		Advertising
14	Office exp.		496,944		Office_exp.
15	Other exp.		1,295,828		Other_exp.
16	Total Fixed costs		7,667,281		Total_Fixed_costs
17	Net income		513,200		Net_income
18					

Microsoft Excel - Book1

File Edit View Insert Format Tools Data Investments Window Help   Type a question for help

K1

Scenario Summary Scenario PivotTable Sheet4 Sheet5

Step 1: Define Names

Trick to quickly define a name for a single cell. Select cell B3 and press **Ctrl+F3**. The **Define Name** dialog box will appear and will propose using the label from A3 - Direct_Cost - as the name for the cell. Click **OK**. Excel will replace any spaces or dashes with an underscore character (see a list of names created in column D above).

This trick will not work in rows 10:17 where the row labels are separated from the target cells by a blank column. In this case, copy A10:A17 to B10:B17. Use the following method to assign names. Then erase the temporary cells in B10:B17.

Trick to define names for many cells. After copying A10:A17 to B10:B17, select B10:C17. Press **Ctrl+Shift+F3**. In the **Create Names** dialog box, select the **Right Column** checkbox, and click **OK.**

Step 2: Create Scenarios

1.   From the **Tools** menu, select **Scenarios**.

2.   In the **Scenario Manager** dialog box, select **Add**.

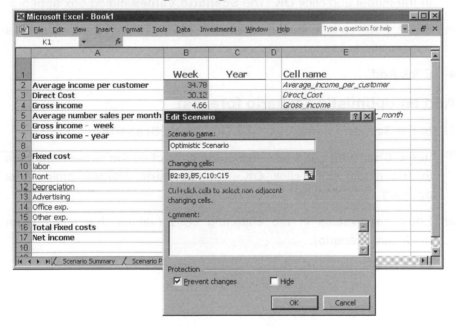

Add an original scenario forecast

1. In the **Scenario name** box, type **Original Scenario**.

2. In the **Changing cells** box, select the cells of all the values/variables in the model, and click **OK**. The **Scenario Values** dialog box appears.

3. Enter new values for the changing cells, and click **Add**.

Add a pessimistic scenario forecast

1. In the **Scenario name** box, type **Pessimistic Scenario**.

2. In the **Changing cells** box, select the cells of all the values/variables in the model and click **OK**. The **Scenario Values** dialog box appears.

3. Enter new values in the changing cells (values that indicate a pessimistic scenario).

4. Click **Add**.

Add an optimistic scenario forecast

1. In the **Scenario name** box, type **Optimistic Scenario**.

2. In the **Changing cells** box, select the cells of all the values/variables in the model, and click **OK**. The **Scenario Values** dialog box appears.

3. Enter new values in the changing cells (values that indicate an optimistic scenario).

4. Click **Add**.

Enter values using a temporary formula

Scenario Values

Enter values for each of the changing cells.

1:	Average_income	34.78
2:	Direct_Cost	30.12
3:	Average_number	33759
4:	labor	3494046
5:	Rent	1635511

OK
Cancel

In the **Scenarios Values** box, enter a function or formula, and then click **OK**. The formula is now replaced by values.

Example: In the **Average_income** box (E2), enter the formula =B2*1.25 (growth of 25%). After saving the change, the value in the **Average_income** cell will be greater by 25% than the value in cell B2.

Updating data in a scenario

In the **Scenario Manager** dialog box, select the scenario, click **Edit**, and update the scenario values.

Show the scenario in the worksheet

In the **Scenario Manager** dialog box, select the scenario, and click **Show**. Note that in your worksheet, the scenario values replace the previous values in the cells.

Scenario Manager

Scenarios:
Original Scenario
Optimistic Scenario
Pessimistic Scenario

Show
Close
Add...
Delete
Edit...
Merge...
Summary...

Changing cells:
$B$2:$B$3,Average_number_sales_p

Comment:

Adding a Scenario icon to your toolbar

From the **View** menu, select **Toolbar**, select **Customize**, and then select the **Commands** tab.

Under the **Tools** category (in the **Commands** tab), select and drag the **Scenario** icon to your toolbar.

Reports

In the **Scenario Manager** dialog box, click **Summary**. The **Scenario Summary** dialog box appears.

Two types of reports are available for the scenarios you create:

▣ Scenario summary

▣ Scenario PivotTable report

Scenario Summary Report

1. Select the **Scenario summary** option.

2. In the **Result cells** box, select all the cells with summary formulas and calculations. If there are too many, select only the important cells: gross income, fixed costs and net income.

3. Click **OK**.

Note

Note how the names have replaced the cell addresses in column B in your sheet. The importance of defining names before creating your scenarios is apparent; without names, the reports are indecipherable. Column D contains the current values of the model. Saving the original values (column E) under the name Original Scenario is recommended in order for you to refer to them for comparison purposes and to enable you to reconstruct your original data if necessary.

PivotTable Report

1. In the **Scenario Summary** dialog box, select the **Scenario PivotTable report**.

2. In the **Result cells** box, select all the cells with summary formulas and calculations. If there are too many, select only the important cells: gross income, fixed costs and net income.

3. Click **OK**.

	A	B	C	D	E
1	$B$2:$B$3,Average_number_sales	(All)			
2					
3		Result Cells			
4	$B$2:$B$3,Average_number_sales_per_month,$C$10:$C$15	Gross_income year	Total_Fixed_costs	Net_income	
5	Optimistic Scenario	14,560,000	7,667,281	6,892,719	
6	Original Scenario	8,180,481	7,667,281	513,200	
7	Pessimistic Scenario	-4,680,000	7,667,281	-12,347,281	
8					
9					
10					
11					

Microsoft Excel - Book1 | File Edit View Insert Format Tools Data Investments Window Help   Type a question for help

Scenario Summary \ Scenario PivotTable / Sheet4 / Sheet5 /

Printing Scenarios

Use Report Manager to print all the scenarios in succession. See the **Report Manager** section of **Chapter 11, Printing**.

1. Select the Scenario area in the sheet, and define correct printing options for the selected section.

2. From the **View** menu, select **Report Manager**.

3. Click **Add**. The **Edit Report** dialog box appears.

4. In the **Report Name** box, type a name for the report.

5. Under **Section to Add**, select the **Scenario** check box.

6. Select the first scenario on the list, and click **Add**; it now appears in the **Sections in this Report** box. Continue to select and add all the scenarios in the drop-down text box until they all appear in the **Sections in this Report** box.

7. Click **OK**.

Printing the scenarios:

Open **Report Manager** (under **View**). Select the scenarios, and click **Print**. Each report is printed on a separate page.

Chapter 26

Running a Macro

Even if you have never learned programming, this chapter will help you write lines of code easily before you ever need to take a course in programming.

First of all, to set things straight, "macro" is an old term used for Excel's programming language, before Excel adopted the Visual Basic for Applications language (abbreviated as VBA).

Open the first chapter of the book again. In **Chapter 1, Time is Money, Give the Mouse a Rest**, you learned to move quickly around a worksheet from cell to cell, to select cells, to move between sheets and more, without using the mouse.

In a moment, you will begin relearning all the topics that were presented in Chapter 1; only this time, you will write the lines of code that make work happen with the keys of the keyboard and without use of the mouse.

Start by selecting a cell. Selecting a cell is the most fundamental action that you carry out in Excel.

The line of code for selecting a single cell:

```
Range("A1").Select
```

Explanation: use Range to select a cell or cells, a row or a column.

To select a number of cells:

```
Range("A1:D5").Select
```

To select a number of rows:

```
Range ("1:5").Select
```

To select a column:

```
Range ("A:A").Select
```

To select a number of columns:

```
Range ("A:D").Select
```

Now that you know how to write lines of code in the VBA macro language, you are very probably asking yourself where to write the code and how to activate the macro.

Press the keyboard shortcut **Alt+F11**.

VBE (Visual Basic Editor) opens.

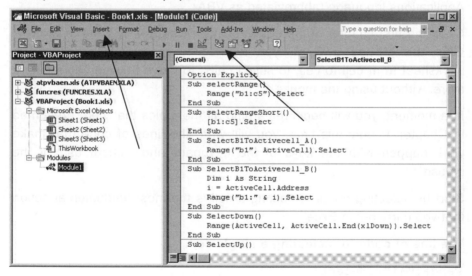

You don't see a dialog box that resembles the dialog box in the picture?

1. On the left side, you don't see the **VBA Project** dialog box (with the names of the files and sheets)? Click the ProjectExplorer icon (note the arrow which points to the 14th icon from the left).

2. The window is gray, and there is no white pane on the right side? Add a module by selecting the name of a file (for example, Book1). Select **Insert**, **Module**. The sheet of the module you inserted is added to the workbook Book1.

Adding a macro to a module

For the macro syntax, see the figure below. All of the lines of code are written in the Module sheet, in Sub.

The Sub line contains the name of the macro. The name is written as a series of characters (similar to a defined name for a cell). There are parentheses after the name. At the end of the Sub line, there are the words End Sub.

To make your work easier, write the word Sub, leave a space, and after it, the name of the macro. Press **Enter**, and both the parentheses and the extra line End Sub are inserted automatically.

In the macro, type one line of code to select a cell in a sheet.

After you type the closing parenthesis of the cell address and type a period, a list opens from which you can select the correct word to complete the action. Find the word Select, and press **Enter** or use the **Tab** key to insert the word into the line of code.

Running a macro from the VBE dialog box

Have you finished typing the line of code in the macro? Do you want to run the macro?

With the mouse, select any area within the macro and press **F5**. That's right, nothing happens. In order to view the activation of the macro, you must minimize the VBE dialog box on top of the Excel window.

The technique: go back to the Excel window, and press **Alt+F11** again. Click the Maximize button, return to the VBE dialog box, and double-click the blue title bar at the top of the dialog box to minimize it.

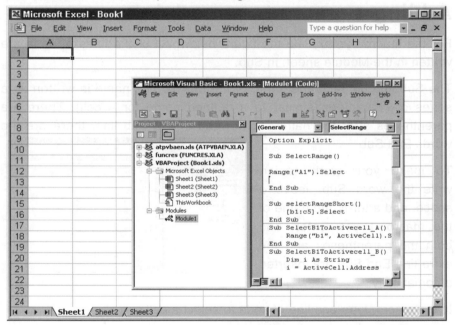

Now use **F8** to run the macro. The **F8** key allows you to run the macro one line at a time, and view the results. The **F8** key is vital for debugging. The **F5** key runs the macro from start to finish.

You have begun to run the macro. Before the macro begins, its syntax is checked for errors and more by the VBA program (Visual Basic for Applications). This is the macro program for Excel and other Office programs. Error messages are displayed so that you can correct the syntax and the errors.

If you have received a **Run-time error**, click the **Debug** button. The result – the line containing the bug is colored yellow. Check this line, correct the mistake and continue running the macro using **F8**, or click the **Reset** icon (the blue square on the toolbar) to stop running the macro.

While in Debug mode, hover your mouse pointer over any variable to see the current value of the variable.

> **Microsoft Visual Basic**
>
> Run-time error '1004':
>
> Method 'Range' of object '_Global' failed
>
> | Continue | End | Debug | Help |

Running a macro up to a stopping point

As you write more lines of code to build a more complex macro, the number of times you run it to examine it grows. You certainly will not want to check a line of code over and over again, if it has already been checked.

The technique is to run the macro quickly by using the **F5** key, up to a particular stopping point, and then to continue running the macro one line at a time by using the **F8** key.

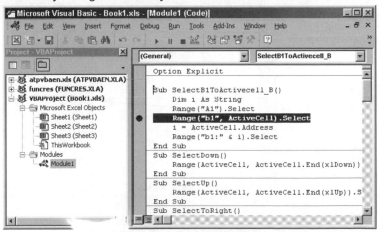

Select a line in the code and press **F9**, or click the gray line to the left of the line of code. The stopping point is indicated by a brown circle, and the line of code is colored brown. To remove this indication, press **F9** or click the brown circle.

Stopping a macro

You have run the macro, and it becomes clear that you have made terrible mistakes. You have to stop the running macro. Press **Ctrl+Break**. Do not forget to click the **Reset** icon after stopping the macro.

Using an icon to run a macro

Run a macro in an Excel sheet by attaching the macro to a button.

You can attach a macro to various types of objects – a button, an icon, a menu, a picture, a text box, and more.

To insert a button into a sheet, display the Forms toolbar. Select one of the toolbars, right-click, and select **Forms**. Click the button image, select a cell in the sheet, and left-click to draw the button. When you finish drawing and release the mouse, the **Assign Macro** dialog box opens. Select the macro and click **OK**, Click the button to run the macro.

Attaching a macro to an icon on a toolbar

Attach a macro to a button or object such as a picture or text box in order to activate a specific macro, which is activated only within the sheet containing the button.

If you want to create a macro that assists you in your work in Excel, store the macro in a personal workbook, and attach it to an icon.

1. Select one of the toolbars, right-click, and select **Customize**.

2. Select the **Commands** tab.

3. From **Categories**, select **Macros**.

4. Select **Custom Button** (with the yellow smiley-face), and drag it onto a toolbar.

5. Select the icon (do not close the **Customize** dialog box), and right-click.

6. Select **Assign macro**, select the macro, and click **OK**.

7. Close the **Customize** dialog box.

Recording a macro

Recording a macro allows you to type lines of code into the macro in a module without using the keyboard.

The technique for recording a macro is very useful when you begin using the VBA program, do not know the program, or do not have enough experience in writing lines of code in a macro. As you gain more knowledge and experience, you will begin to record lines of code less and less frequently.

To record a macro, display the **Visual Basic** toolbar, or from **Tools**, select **Macro, Record New Macro**.

To insert a macro icon into the Excel menu (recommended and easy to use):

Select one of the toolbars, right-click, and from the shortcut menu, select **Customize**. Select the **Commands** tab. From **Categories**, select **Built-In Menus**, drag the **Macro** icon to the Excel menu, and position it after **Tools** or **Data**. Click **Close**.

Begin recording. Click the **Record Macro** icon (blue circle) on the Visual Basic toolbar, or from the Macros menu, in **Macro Name**, type a name for the macro. Be sure to type continuous characters; for example, type Macro1 and not Macro 1 (with a space).

Shortcut keys

In **Shortcut key**, type an upper or lower case letter. The use of shortcut keys allows you to use shortcuts to activate the macro.

Storing a macro

When you record the macro, you also determine where to record it; that is, you determine where you want to save the macro that you record.

Storing a macro in a personal workbook

The **personal workbook (Personal.xls)** is not an open workbook. It is created immediately after you record a macro, when you choose to save the recording in the personal workbook.

The purpose of the **personal workbook** is to save a macro in a workbook that will open automatically when you open Excel, thereby enabling you to use the macro that is stored in a module in this workbook. After Excel is started, the workbook is hidden. If you want to display it, select **Unhide** from the **Window** menu.

It is not recommended you use the **personal workbook** for every macro you save. In the **personal workbook**, save only those macros that will assist you in general tasks, and not in tasks that are performed in a specific sheet or workbook.

After you select the location where you want to store the macro, click **OK**.

Now perform the same lines that you typed in the macro at the beginning of the chapter. Select cell(s), row(s), or column(s).

Stop recording

You finished recording. Click the **Stop Recording** button (blue square) on the toolbar, or select **Tools, Macro, Stop Recording**.

Checking the lines of code you recorded

Press **Alt+F11**, and double-click the name of the module in **VBAProject (Book1)** (in the example, the macro was recorded in the Book1 workbook). The result is usually not perfect, to put it mildly. You will usually record unnecessary lines of code, such as selecting a cell or cells that you did not intend to select.

The solution: delete the unnecessary lines, and insert lines of code manually. In short, fix the macro.

Another way to check or enter the macro that you want to edit is to use the **Alt+F8** shortcut in the Excel sheet, which provides a list of all the macros that are stored in every open workbook in the **Macro** dialog box. Select the macro you want to edit, and click **Edit**.

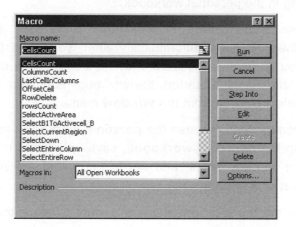

Visual Basic Editor – VBE

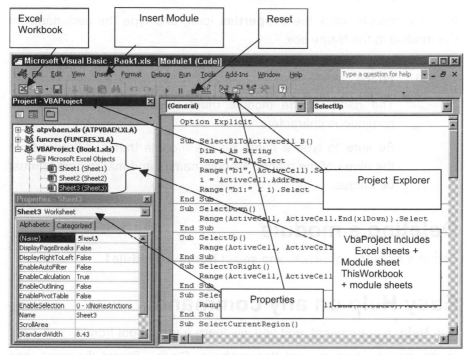

Colors in lines of code

1. **Blue** – keywords such as Sub, End Sub.

2. **Green** – information, comments, or a skipped line of code. Select the ' (apostrophe) sign before a line of code. The color changes to green, and the macro skips the line while it runs. Comments are useful for explaining your macro in English so that you can recall several months later what you were trying to do.

3. **Red** – syntax error that must be checked and corrected.

4. **Yellow** – step mode run of a macro by using the **F8** key, or a line containing a bug.

5. **Brown** – break point for the macro.

Changing the module name

Select a module, click the **Properties** icon, and type the new name of the module in the Name box.

Note

The name of the module must be a single word, that is, continuous characters.

Be sure to type a name for the module that is different from the name of the macro. Module names and macro names must be unique.

Deleting a module

Select a module, right-click, and select **Remove Module1**.

Easy Help on any command

Use **Help**. It is excellent, and you will learn a great deal from it.

In the module, type a word (for example, Close). Select the word, and press **F1**.

Have you found the solution to your question? Copy the line of code into the module from the help topic.

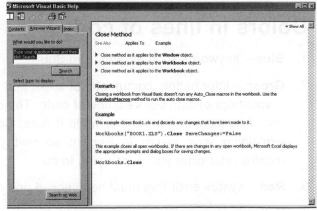

Using the recording as help

Record every action that you want to turn into a line of code. Select the relevant lines in the macro you recorded. Copy the lines by clicking **Ctrl+C**. In the macro you are creating, select the location to paste, and press **Ctrl+V**.

Chapter 27

Write Your First Program

The best way to write a program is simple: write, make mistakes, fix bugs, but most important – do not be afraid.

Writing a Program to Consolidate Data Tables

Sheets 1, 2 and 3 (January, February and March) have tables containing balance data for three months.

The required program is the consolidation of the three tables into a single data table in Sheet 4, one table below the other. In order to identify which data belongs in which table, you have to insert the name of the table in an additional column. With a consolidated table, you can sort, filter, insert subtotals, and/or create PivotTables.

Sound complicated? Follow the workflow and the lines of code one step at a time.

January Sheet   **Consolidate Tables** Sheet

Stage 1: Enter text into a cell

In Cell C1 (header), in all three sheets, enter the text **Month**.

You do not have to select the sheet. In the lines of code, refer to the address of the sheet and the cell.

```
Sheets("January").Range("C1").Value = "Month"
Sheets("February").Range("C1").Value = "Month"
Sheets("March").Range("C1").Value = "Month"
```

Stage 2: Enter the name of the table

In every sheet, in Column C, in every cell that corresponds to the items (Column A), enter the name of the table. In the example, table name = sheet name.

Follow the steps:

1. Select the sheet **January.**

    ```
    Sheets("January").Select
    ```

2. Jump from Cell A1 to the last cell in the range (Ctrl+down arrow).

    ```
    Range("A1").End(xlDown).Select
    ```

    After End, you can choose to move in four directions – xlDown, xlToRight, xlToLeft.

3. Select a corresponding cell in Column C; that Is, offset the selection two cells from the active cell.

    ```
    ActiveCell.Offset(0, 2).Select
    ```

    Use Offset to move between cells. The first number in parentheses represents the number of rows, and the second number represents the number of columns. In the example, you offset the selection two columns to the right.

4. Enter the name of the sheet in the cell range, from the active cell, cell C14 (refer to the sheet **January** in the figure), until cell C2.

    ```
    Range(ActiveCell, "C2").Value = ActiveSheet.Name
    ```

    In the selection of the cell range, the comma symbol means until. That is, from the active cell (ActiveCell) until a cell with the specific address C2.

    Alternatively, you can enter text in the cells. For a range, write the text between quotation marks.

    ```
    Selection.Value = "January"
    ```

5. To summarize, here are the lines of code for Stage 2.
    ```
    Sheets("January").Select
    Range("A1").End(xlDown).Select
    ActiveCell.Offset(0, 2).Select
    Range(ActiveCell, "C2").Value = ActiveSheet.Name
    ```

6. Copy the lines of code and paste them twice. In the first row, change the name of the sheet from **January** to **February**, and in the next, change it to **March**.

Another technique is to select a range that corresponds to the selection of the cell range in the column. Offset the selection two columns to the right and select.

```
Range(("A2"), Range("A1").End(xlDown)).Offset(0, 2).Select
Selection.Value = ActiveSheet.Name
```

Stage 3: Copy and consolidate the tables

From the sheet **January**, copy the table, and paste it into the sheet **Consolidate Tables**.

1. Select the sheet **January**.

    ```
    Sheets("January").Select
    ```

2. Select the data table. Use the Excel shortcut **Ctrl+*** for selecting the current region.

    ```
    Range("A1").CurrentRegion.Select
    ```

3. Copy the current region that you selected.

    ```
    Selection.Copy
    ```

4. You can combine steps 2 and 3 into a single line.

    ```
    Range("A1").CurrentRegion.Copy
    ```

5. Select the Consolidate Tables sheet, select a cell, and paste.

    ```
    Sheets("Consolidate Tables").Select
    Range("A1").Select
    ActiveSheet.Paste
    Application.CutCopyMode = False
    ```

6. After copying, clear the clipboard. Look at the last line; it is the same as pressing the **Esc** key.

7. Copy the tables from the sheets **February** and **March**. From these sheets, copy the data range without the header row.

8. Select the sheet **February**.

```
Sheets("February").Select
```

9. Select the data without the header row.

To copy the data range without the header row, you have to select the data range from Cell A2 until the last cell in Column C.

```
Range("A2").End(xlDown).Select
ActiveCell.Offset(0, 2).Select
Range(ActiveCell, "A2").Copy
```

10. Paste the data in the **Consolidate Tables** sheet. In order to paste, you have to select the first empty cell in Column A, under the data tables you pasted earlier.

```
Sheets("Consolidate Tables").Select
Range("A1").End(xlDown).Select
ActiveCell.Offset(1, 0).Activate
ActiveSheet.Paste
Application.CutCopyMode = False
```

11. Repeat this technique and paste the data for the table for the month of **March**.

Another technique is you can copy data from the sheets **February** and **March** by copying the rows from Cell A2 until the end of the data range.

```
Range(("A2"), Range("A2").End(xlDown)).EntireRow.Copy
```

To select the rows instead of copying them, use Select instead of Copy.

To select entire columns, use

```
.EntireColumn
```

Your final code should look like this:

```
Sub MyFirstProgram()
    Sheets("January").Select
    Range("C1").Value = "Month"
    Range("A1").End(xlDown).Select
    ActiveCell.Offset(0, 2).Select
    Range(ActiveCell, "C2").Value = ActiveSheet.Name

    Sheets("February").Select
    Range("C1").Value = "Month"
    Range("A1").End(xlDown).Select
    ActiveCell.Offset(0, 2).Select
    Range(ActiveCell, "C2").Value = ActiveSheet.Name

    Sheets("March").Select
    Range("C1").Value = "Month"
    Range("A1").End(xlDown).Select
    ActiveCell.Offset(0, 2).Select
    Range(ActiveCell, "C2").Value = ActiveSheet.Name

    ' Copy and consolidate the tables
    Sheets("January").Select
    Range("A1").CurrentRegion.Select
    Selection.Copy
    Sheets("Consolidate Tables").Select
    Range("A1").Select
    ActiveSheet.Paste
    Application.CutCopyMode = False

    Sheets("February").Select
    Range("A1").End(xlDown).Select
    ActiveCell.Offset(0, 2).Select
    Range(ActiveCell, "A2").Copy
    Sheets("Consolidate Tables").Select
    Range("A1").End(xlDown).Select
    ActiveCell.Offset(1, 0).Activate
    ActiveSheet.Paste
    Application.CutCopyMode = False
```

```
Sheets("March").Select
Range("A1").End(xlDown).Select
ActiveCell.Offset(0, 2).Select
Range(ActiveCell, "A2").Copy
Sheets("Consolidate Tables").Select
Range("A1").End(xlDown).Select
ActiveCell.Offset(1, 0).Activate
ActiveSheet.Paste
Application.CutCopyMode = False
```

```
End Sub
```

Stage 4: Finish and run

You have finished. Now run the macro one step at a time by using **F8**. You have fixed all the bugs. Now run the macro by inserting a button into the **Consolidate Data** sheet.

Reducing the lines of code

Exchanging repeated actions with loops

In the program that you ran, you typed extraneous lines of code. You pasted the name of the sheet in Column C in all three sheets, and you copied the data and pasted it three times.

Loop no. 1

In Column C, enter the name of the sheet.

Define a variable of the integer type. Call it i.

In the line of code Sheets(i), i is the number of the sheet. It is assumed that the sheet **January** is the first sheet in the workbook, the sheet **February** is the second, and so forth.

```
Dim i As Integer
For i = 1 To 3
    Sheets(i).Select
    Range(("A2"), Range("A2").End(xlDown)). _
        Offset(0, 2).Value = ActiveSheet.Name
Next i
```

Loop no. 2

Insert an additional loop to copy the data into the **Consolidate Data** sheet.

Before you run the loop, copy the header row to the **Consolidate Data** sheet. Then, the loop performs a circular action of copying the data to the **Consolidate Data** sheet.

```
Sheets("January").Select
Range("1:1").Copy
Sheets("Consolidate Tables").Select
Range("1:1").Select
ActiveSheet.Paste
Application.CutCopyMode = False
Range("A2").Activate
For i = 1 To 3
    Sheets(i).Select
    Range(("A2"), Range("A2").End(xlDown)).EntireRow.Copy
    Sheets("Consolidate Tables").Select
    ActiveSheet.Paste
    Application.CutCopyMode = False
    Range("A1").End(xlDown).Offset(1, 0).Activate
Next i
```

Making code more efficient

Do not select objects

Recorded macros are notorious for performing tasks inefficiently. The recorded macro will almost always select an object and then perform an action on the selected object, in two lines, as follows:

```
Range("1:1").Select
Selection.Copy
```

This is rarely necessary. Changing the selection takes precious time in the macro. You can usually specify the action directly to the range without selecting it. The following line is equivalent to the above lines:

```
Range("1:1").Copy
```

Do not select sheets

It is not necessary to select worksheets. If you want to perform actions on a sheet other than the ActiveSheet, you simply qualify each Range command with the name of the worksheet:

Before:

```
Sheets(i).Select
Range("A2").Copy
```

After:

```
Sheets(i).Range("A2").Copy
```

Combine copy and paste into a single statement

Immediately after you copy a range, you can add a parameter that tells Excel where to paste the results. The following five lines can be reduced to a single line:

Before:

```
Sheets("January").Select
Range("1:1").Select
Selection.Copy
Sheets("Consolidate Tables").Select
Range("1:1").Select
ActiveSheet.Paste
```

After:

```
Sheets("January").Range("1:1").Copy Destination:= _
    Sheets("Consolidate Tables").Range("1:1")
```

Eliminate redundant loops

Our program loops through the three sheets twice. With a little advanced planning, we should be able to fill in the month names and copy in the same loop. This will eliminate the need for the second loop. Also, there is no need to change the CutCopyMode to False until the end of the program.

Find the last used row using End ()

Excel worksheets offer 65,536 rows of data. The best way to find the last used row in column A is to start at cell A65536 and hit END up arrow. The code for this is as follows:

```
Range("A65536").End(xlUp)
```

The resulting macro contains just eight actual lines of code.

```
Sub ReallyShort()
 Dim i As Integer

'Copy the headings
 Sheets("January").Range("1:1").Copy Destination:= _
  Sheets("Consolidate Tables").Range("1:1")
 Sheets("Consolidate Tables").Range("C1").Value = "Month"

'Loop through the three worksheets
 For i = 1 To 3
  Sheets(i).Range("C1").Value = "Month"
  'Add Month Name to Column C
  Sheets(i).Range(Sheets(i).Range("C2"), Sheets(i).Range("A65536"). _
    End(xlUp).Offset(0, 2)).Value = Sheets(i).Name
  'Copy A2:C? to the next row on Consolidate Table sheet
  Sheets(i).Range(Sheets(i).Range("A2"), Sheets(i) _
    .Range("A2").End(xlDown)).EntireRow.Copy _
    Destination:=Sheets("Consolidate Tables") _
    .Range("A65536").End(xlUp).Offset(1, 0)
 Next i

Application.CutCopyMode = False

End Sub
```

Copying data from another workbook (opened or closed)

So far, the program you ran copied data from the active workbook. When you copy from another workbook, there are special considerations such as determining if the source workbook is open.

Switching between open workbooks

To move between workbooks, use either of these examples:

```
Windows("Book2").Activate or Workbooks("Book2").Activate
```

Note

Look at the lines of code. After the filename, there is no xls extension. Check the settings for displaying files in the window. If the files in the Window menu are displayed with the xls extension, add the extension to the file name.

```
Windows("Book2.xls").Activate
```

Switching to a closed workbook

To open a workbook:

```
Workbooks.Open Filename:="C:\My Documents\Book2.xls"
```

How can I tell if the workbook is open or closed?

If a macro is run and it contains lines of code that are supposed to copy data from an open or closed workbook, it is essential to first run a check to see whether the workbook containing the data is open. This check helps to avoid errors (it is possible that you forgot to open the workbook before you ran the macro). This check is performed through a function.

Add the check to the macro by using IF. The IF command sends a query to the function to calculate whether the workbook is open. If it is, the function returns TRUE.

```
Dim Ph As String
If Not Workbookopen("Book2.xls") Then
    Ph = Application.Workbooks("Book1.xls").Path
    Workbooks.Open Filename = Ph & "\Book2.xls", UpdateLinks:=0
Else
    Workbooks("Book2.xls").Activate
End If
```

Note

Notice the line of code for opening a workbook. At the end of the line, there is an addition:

```
UpdateLinks:=0
```

This addition prevents the **Update Links** message from being displayed.

The function:

```
Function Workbookopen(Book) As Boolean
    Dim Wk As String
    On Error GoTo Notopen
    Wk = Workbooks(Book).Name
    Workbookopen = True
    Exit Function
Notopen:
    Workbookopen = False
End Function
```

I copied the data and I want to close the workbook I opened

To save a workbook after updating it:

```
ActiveWorkbook.Save
```

To close a workbook:

```
ActiveWorkbook.Close
```

To close the workbook without saving it, while suppressing the warning that the workbook needs to be saved:

Option 1

```
Workbooks("Book2.xls").Close savechanges:=False
```

Option 2

We can fool Excel into thinking the workbook has already been saved and can therefore be closed.

```
Workbooks("Book2.xls").Saved = True
Workbooks("Book2.xls").Close
```

I want to save the data in a new sheet in the workbook

To insert a new sheet:

```
Sheets.Add
```

To insert and change the sheet's name:

```
Sheets.Add.Name = "Consolidate Data"
```

I want to save the data in a new workbook, change its name and save it in a folder

To add a new workbook:

```
Workbooks.Add
```

To save the workbook in the **My Documents** folder:

```
ActiveWorkbook.SaveAs Filename:="C:\My Documents\Book1.xls"
```

The data in the Consolidate Tables sheet is not formatted

The data you copied was pasted into the **Consolidate Data** sheet.

In the **Consolidate Data** sheet, the width of the columns is not uniform or does not automatically fit, according to the text/number in the cells. The numbers in the data columns are not formatted.

Automatically fitting the column width:

```
Columns("A:C").EntireColumn.AutoFit
```

Setting the column width:

```
Columns("A:C").ColumnWidth = 15
```

Formatting numbers in Column B:

```
Columns("B:B").NumberFormat = "#,##0;[Red]-#,##0"
```

Use **Paste Special** to copy formatting. Copy the formatting of Column A to Column C:

```
Columns("A:A").Copy
Columns("C:C").Select
Selection.PasteSpecial Paste:=xlPasteFormats, Operation:=xlNone, _
        SkipBlanks:=False, Transpose:=False
Application.CutCopyMode = False
```

I would like to define a name for a table to consolidate data

Select the data table and define a name for it.

```
Range("A1").CurrentRegion.Name = "Table"
```

Add a name to the data range

```
Range(Range("A1"), Range("A1").End(xlDown)).Name = "DataInAColumn"
```

Use this line of code to define a name for a cell, a row, a column, a sheet, or another cell range.

Now that you have finished, you will certainly want to print

Define the print area. For example, the current region will be printed.

```
ActiveSheet.PageSetup.PrintArea = Selection.CurrentRegion.Address
```

For printing, change the number of copies:

```
ActiveWindow.SelectedSheets.PrintOut Copies:=2
```

Chapter 28

Other VBA Techniques

Variables

When you run a macro, you will want to save textual data or the results of calculations for later use.

Variables are cells in the computer's memory that are opened with their definitions when the macro begins to run and erased from memory when the macro is finished. The types of variables are created to increase memory efficiency. To save whole numbers, less memory is required than to save character text of variable length.

Common variable types – examples

Range	Size in Memory	Name of Variable Type
From number -32767 to 32767	2 Bytes	Integer
-2 billion to 2 billion	4 Bytes	Long
-3.4 billion to 1.4 billion	4 Bytes	Single
Text with any number of characters		String
Date from 1/1/100 to 31/12/9999	8 Bytes	Date
Variable by data type		Variant
True or False	2 Bytes	Boolean

Variable Declaration

In order to force yourself to work with variables, insert the words Option Explicit into the top row of every module you open (highly recommended).

1. In VBE, select **Tools**, **Options**, **Editor**.

2. Select the **Require Variable Declaration** box, and click **OK**.

Insert the variable declaration at the beginning of the macro. Each variable should be defined with this syntax:

For example, save the name of the workbook as a variable. You can use all character components to save the variable. The variable name is actually an address in memory.

```
Option Explicit
```

```
Sub Macro1()
    Dim Wk As String
    Wk = ActiveWorkbook.Name
End Sub
```

Display a message to the user

Your program can communicate messages to the user. This communication is achieved through a Message box, also known as a **MsgBox**.

Displaying the results of calculations on variables in MsgBox

Example 1: Integer variables

Cells A1 and A2 contain whole numbers which, when multiplied, result in a product less than 32767.

The result of the calculation is displayed in **MsgBox**.

```
Sub Macro1()
    Dim A, B, Total As Integer
    A = Range("A1").Value
    B = Range("A2").Value
    Total = A * B
    MsgBox Total
End Sub
```

Example 2: String Variables

In **MsgBox**, display the file's name and path, and the address of a cell in the sheet.

In **MsgBox**, the letters vbCr insert a new line into the box, and the & symbol is used to concatenate parts of the message.

```
Sub Macro2()
    Dim Wk As String, Ph As String, AD As String
    AD = ActiveCell.Address
    Wk = ActiveWorkbook.Name
    Ph = ActiveWorkbook.Path
    MsgBox AD & vbCr & Wk & vbCr & Ph
End Sub
```

Example 3: Inserting text into MsgBox

```
Sub Macro3()
    Dim Wk As String
    Wk = ActiveWorkbook.Name
    MsgBox "ActiveWorkbook Name - " & " " " & Wk, , "Developer Message"
End Sub
```

To see the structure of the **MsgBox** syntax, select **MsgBox** in the module and press **F1**. See the examples in **Help**.

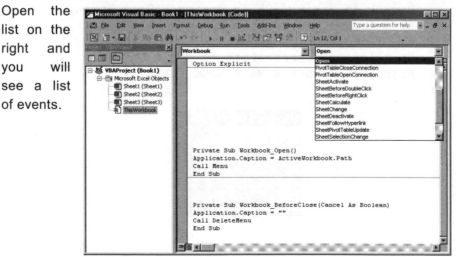

Events

In many events during your work, you will certainly want a macro to run automatically without your interference, such as a macro that is run when a workbook is opened or closed.

The sheet module **ThisWorkbook** should be used as storage for such events. Events that are stored in this sheet are loaded into Excel's memory when a workbook is opened, and they are run according to the type of event without your involvement while you work in the workbook.

Select the **ThisWorkbook** module. Above the module sheet, you will see two drop-down lists. Open the list on the left, and select **Workbook**.

Open the list on the right and you will see a list of events.

When an event from the list is selected, the event's framework is typed in the module.

The most common event is Workbook_Open. In the figure (see **Chapter 10, Information**), notice that Path has been inserted into Excel's title bar (the blue bar), and macro (menu) creates a menu and inserts it into Excel's menu.

Another very important event is Workbook_BeforeClose. While the workbook is being closed, this event automatically saves the workbook and deletes Path from the title bar.

You can use events for many other reasons. For example, an event called Workbook_BeforePrint inserts a line of code that handles the insertion of vital information into the top or bottom margins of every page that is printed in the workbook.

Conditional Statements – IF

The IF formula is one of the most useful formulas in Excel.

When you write a program in VBA, the use of IF is similar. The use of IF allows you to perform checks when you start a macro, continue running the program, or prevent the program from running until you have completed making the required corrections.

Syntax of IF statements

See the example below. The logical check line begins with IF and ends with THEN. If the result is positive, it is performed. If it is not, then Else. At the end, End If.

```
Dim A As String, B As String
A = Range("A1").Value
B = Range("A2").Value
If A > B Then
    MsgBox A
Else
    MsgBox
End If
```

Using IF to prevent a macro from running

Attach an icon to a macro. The macro should run commands for printing a report from a specific sheet.

In order to prevent printing from a sheet that is not specified, use IF to check whether the name of the active sheet is the sheet that will be printed; you do not want to print unnecessarily pages from another sheet.

Notice the words Exit Sub. Assuming there are no lines of code after IF, you can stop running the macro at that point if the name of the sheet is incorrect.

```
If ActiveSheet.Name = "January" Then
    ActiveWindow.SelectedSheets.PrintOut Copies = 1
Else
    MsgBox "Check the name of the sheet before running the macro"
    Exit Sub
End If
```

Loops

A large number of the tasks you can perform with a macro will be performed by loops.

Loops allow you to repeat the lines of code several times. The numbers of cycles are set at the entrance to the loop, whether by using a loop named Do While, or with a loop named For, in which you can set the number of times from the beginning.

Do While loop

Example: In the cells of Sheet 1, enter the list of sheets in the workbook.

```
Sub DoWhileLoop()
    Dim ShtsNumber, Sh As Integer
    ShtsNumber = Sheets.Count
    Range("A1").Activate
    Sh = 1
    Do While Sh <= ShtsNumber
    ActiveCell.Offset(Sh - 1, 0).Value = Sheets(Sh).Name
    Sh = Sh + 1
    Loop
End Sub
```

For loop

In this loop, the names of the sheets in the workbook are also entered into the cells of the sheet. In a loop of this type, you use less lines of code. It is also easy to use.

```
Sub ForLoop()
    Dim ShtsNumber, Sh As Integer
    ShtsNumber = Sheets.Count
    Range("A1").Activate
    For Sh = 1 To ShtsNumber
        ActiveCell.Offset(Sh - 1, 0).Value = Sheets(Sh).Name
    Next Sh
End Sub

For Sh = ShtsNumber To 1 Step -1
    ActiveCell.Offset(ShtsNumber - Sh, 0).Value = Sheets(Sh).Name
Next Sh
```

It is comfortable to use the For loop. You can run the loop forwards or backwards. To have the loop run backwards, add Step-1 and reverse the *from* and *to*.

```
For Sh = ShtsNumber To 1 Step -1
    ActiveCell.Offset(ShtsNumber - Sh, 0).Value = _
        Sheets(Sh).Name
Next Sh
```

For Each loop

As opposed to the first two loops, this loop searches a range of cells and performs whatever is required even when you do not have previous information about the number of events in which data will be changed or formatted.

In cells that are not empty, color the fonts within the cells red and make them bold.

```
Sub ColorEachCell()
    Dim C As Variant
    For Each C In Range("A1").CurrentRegion
        If C.Value <> "" Then
            With C
                .Font.ColorIndex = 3
                .Font.Bold = True
            End With
        End If
    Next C
End Sub
```

Planning Your Work Efficiently with Macros and Modules

Saving macros by subject in modules

If you save macros in various modules, you can maintain them and reduce the amount of examination required.

Do not use one module for a large number of macros and functions. Save a small number by subject. To jump from macro to macro, open the drop-down list on the right, above the module.

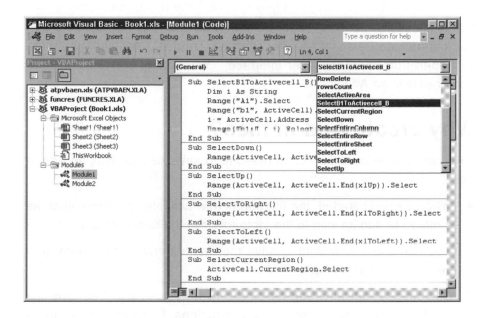

Your work in Excel includes a number of related workbooks

You increase the work for the users in your organization or another when data is retrieved from a number of workbooks. Concentrate all the macro commands in a single workbook, completely devoid of data. Maintaining macros and handling bugs is easier. If you discover a bug in one of the lines or you are required to make a change or an addition, your repair, change or addition will not lock out other users. You can easily change the workbook containing the macros without fear of corrupting the data.

It is recommended to save macros in xla type files.

Using xla Add-in files to store macros and functions

Excel uses a number of file types. One of them is the Add-in file, with an xla extension, as opposed to the xls extension used for regular Excel files.

Add-in files are hidden. They are different than the Personal.xls file. You can unhide Personal.xls with **Window**, **Unhide**. You cannot unhide an Add-in from the Excel user interface. You cannot select or activate worksheets in an Add-in file.

Why create Add-in files?

There are a number of important reasons to save xls type files as Add-in files.

▣ When Excel is started, the file opens and activates a macro, such as a macro to add an icon to the toolbars or to the Excel menus.

▣ You can use a password to save the macros and protect them from being viewed or changed.

▣ Customized functions can be stored in an Add-in file. You can use the Function wizard to activate the functions. Functions stored in an Add-in file are not prefixed with the name of the workbook.

▣ Saving macros in modules for performing complex tasks makes it easy to maintain them, update them, and add lines of code.

How do I create an Add-in file?

From the Excel menu, select **File, Save As**. In **Save As type**, select **Microsoft Excel Add-in**, and click **Save**

I created an Add-in file, and I want to convert it to a regular xls file

Select **ThisWorkbook** module.

Click the **Properties** icon.

Change **IsAddIn** to **False**.

See figure.

How do I hide the modules of an Add-in file and protect them?

1. In VBE, from **Tools**, select **VBA Project**, **Properties**.

2. Select the **Protection** tab.

3. Select the box **Lock project for viewing**.

4. Type a password in the first box, and then in the second one to confirm it.

5. Click **OK**.

6. Save the file.

How do I install an Add-in file in the Add-in list?

The Add-in list is actually a list of shortcuts.

You add an Add-in file just like you add a shortcut, with the path of the file on the hard disk or the network.

1. From **Tools**, select **Add-ins.**

2. Click **Browse**.

3. In the **Browse** dialog box, locate and select the Add-in in the folder in which the file is saved.

4. Click **OK**.

5. Select the box next to the name of the Add-in.

6. Click **OK**.

Tips, Useful Commands and Answers to Commonly Asked Questions

How do I insert the SUM formula?

A seemingly simple problem is summing data. The problem is how to insert a SUM formula with a relative or absolute reference to sum numeric data in a data range.

Summing with an absolute reference

Define two variables and insert them into the first and last cell address in the cell range being summed. Use the & sign to concatenate the formula text with the cell addresses you saved as variables.

```
Sub SumFunction()
    Dim Ad1, Ad2 As String
    Ad1 = ActiveCell.Address
    ActiveCell.End(xlDown).Activate
    Ad2 = ActiveCell.Address
    ActiveCell.Offset(1, 0).Activate
    ActiveCell.Value = "=Sum(" & Ad1 & ":" & Ad2 & ")"
End Sub
```

Alternatively, you can reduce saving the sum address to a single variable by using the word Address.

```
Dim AD As String
Range(ActiveCell, ActiveCell.End(xlDown)).Select
AD = ActiveWindow.RangeSelection.Address
ActiveCell.End(xlDown).Offset(1, 0).Activate
ActiveCell.Value = "=Sum(" & AD & ")"
```

Summing with a relative reference

Insert the lines of code to delete the & sign from the above macro.

```
ActiveCell.Replace What:="$", Replacement:=""
```

How do I prevent the Workbook_Open macro from running?

Press **Shift** while the workbook is open.

How do I freeze the window and sheets and keep them from jumping all over the place when the macro is running?

At the beginning of the macro, insert the line:

```
Application.ScreenUpdating = False
```

At the end, before End Sub, unfreeze the screen:

```
Application.ScreenUpdating = True
```

Using this technique will speed up your macros dramatically.

How do I prevent Excel alerts from being displayed?

At the beginning of the macro, insert the line:

```
Application.DisplayAlerts = False
```

How do I run a macro on a protected sheet?

In a protected sheet, changes are not allowed. This includes changing the formatting and/or pasting data. Assuming the sheet is not password-protected, run a command to clear the password:

```
ActiveSheet.Unprotect
```

To restore protection to the sheet:

```
ActiveSheet.Protect
```

You can run a macro on a protected sheet. Running the following command protects the cells of the sheet and their formatting from being changed by the user, but allows the macro to run without the need to remove the protection.

```
ActiveSheet.Protect UserInterfaceOnly:=True
```

This setting is not saved with the workbook. You must add user interface only protection for each Excel session.

When inserting the macro into the module, I have a problem with lines of code being split up, so the macro does not work

Use an underscore to split long lines of code and create continuity. Be sure to type a space before the underscore.

How can I run a macro on a specific date or time?

To run a macro 5 minutes from now:

```
Application.OnTime Now + TimeValue("00:05:00"), "MyMacro"
```

To run a macro at a preset time:

```
Application.OnTime TimeValue("17:00:00"), "MyMacro"
```

How do I prevent the Update Links message from being displayed?

At the end of the line of code that opens the Excel workbook, enter UpdateLinks:=0.

```
Dim Ph As String
Ph = Application.ActiveWorkbook.Path
Workbooks.Open Filename:=Ph & "\AAA.xls", UpdateLinks:=0
```

How do I paste a number format from an Excel sheet directly into the lines of code?

Type `Selection.NumberFormat = ""`

From the **Format Cells** dialog box, choose **Number**, **Custom**. From the **Type** box, copy the format you created by using **Ctrl+C**, and press **Ctrl+V** between the quotation marks in the lines of code.

Result:

```
Selection.NumberFormat = "#,##0.00 ;[Red}(#,##0.00);-    ;@"
```

Index

Function Reference

* = Included in Analysis ToolPak

Database functions

DAVERAGE(database,field,criteria)

Averages the values in a column in a list or database that match conditions that you specify.

DCOUNT(database,field,criteria)

Counts the cells that contain numbers in a column in a list or database that match conditions that you specify.

DCOUNTA(database,field,criteria)

Counts all of the nonblank cells in a column in a list or database that match conditions that you specify.

DGET(database,field,criteria)

Extracts a single value from a column in a list or database that matches conditions you specify.

DMAX(database,field,criteria)

Returns the largest number in a column in a list or database that matches conditions you specify.

DMIN(database,field,criteria)

Returns the smallest number in a column in a list or database that matches conditions you specify.

DPRODUCT(database,field,criteria)

Multiplies the values in a column in a list or database that match conditions that you specify.

DSUM(database,field,criteria)

Adds the numbers in a column in a list or database that match conditions that you specify.

GETPIVOTDATA(pivot_table,name)

Returns data stored in a PivotTable report. You can use GETPIVOTDATA to retrieve summary data from a PivotTable report, provided the summary data is visible in the report.

Date and time functions

DATE(year,month,day)

Returns the serial number that represents a particular date.

DATEDIF(start_date,end_date,unit)

Calculates the number of days, months, or years between two dates. This function is provided for compatibility with Lotus 1-2-3.

DATEVALUE(date_text)

Returns the serial number of the date represented by date_text. Use DATEVALUE to convert a date represented by text to a serial number.

DAY(serial_number)

Returns the day of a date, represented by a serial number. The day is given as an integer ranging from 1 to 31.

DAYS360(start_date,end_date,method)

Returns the number of days between two dates based on a 360-day year (twelve 30-day months), which is used in some accounting calculations. Use this function to help compute payments if your accounting system is based on twelve 30-day months.

EDATE(start_date,months)*

Returns the serial number that represents the date that is the indicated number of months before or after a specified date (the start_date). Use EDATE to calculate maturity dates or due dates that fall on the same day of the month as the date of issue.

EOMONTH(start_date,months)*

Returns the serial number for the last day of the month that is the indicated number of months before or after start_date. Use EOMONTH to calculate maturity dates or due dates that fall on the last day of the month.

HOUR(serial_number)

Returns the hour of a time value. The hour is given as an integer, ranging from 0 (12:00 A.M.) to 23 (11:00 P.M.).

MINUTE(serial_number)

Returns the minutes of a time value. The minute is given as an integer, ranging from 0 to 59.

MONTH(serial_number)

Returns the month of a date represented by a serial number. The month is given as an integer, ranging from 1 (January) to 12 (December).

NETWORKDAYS(start_date,end_date,holidays)*

Returns the number of whole working days between start_date and end_date. Working days exclude weekends and any dates identified in holidays. Use NETWORKDAYS to calculate employee benefits that accrue based on the number of days worked during a specific term.

NOW( )

Returns the serial number of the current date and time.

SECOND(serial_number)

Returns the seconds of a time value. The second is given as an integer in the range 0 (zero) to 59.

TIME(hour,minute,second)

Returns the decimal number for a particular time. The decimal number returned by TIME is a value ranging from 0 to 0.99999999, representing the times from 0:00:00 (12:00:00 A.M.) to 23:59:59 (11:59:59 P.M.).

TIMEVALUE(time_text)

Returns the decimal number of the time represented by a text string. The decimal number is a value ranging from 0 (zero) to 0.99999999, representing the times from 0:00:00 (12:00:00 A.M.) to 23:59:59 (11:59:59 P.M.).

TODAY( )

Returns the serial number of the current date. The serial number is the date-time code used by Microsoft Excel for date and time calculations.

WEEKDAY(serial_number,return_type)

Returns the day of the week corresponding to a date. The day is given as an integer, ranging from 1 (Sunday) to 7 (Saturday), by default.

WEEKNUM(serial_num,return_type)*

Returns a number that indicates where the week falls numerically within a year.

WORKDAY(start_date,days,holidays)*

Returns a number that represents a date that is the indicated number of working days before or after a date (the starting date). Working days exclude weekends and any dates identified as holidays. Use WORKDAY to exclude weekends or holidays when you calculate invoice due dates, expected delivery times, or the number of days of work performed. To view the number as a date, click Cells on the Format menu, click Date in the Category box, and then click a date format in the Type box.

YEAR(serial_number)

Returns the year corresponding to a date. The year is returned as an integer in the range 1900-9999.

YEARFRAC(start_date,end_date,basis)*

Calculates the fraction of the year represented by the number of whole days between two dates (the start_date and the end_date). Use the YEARFRAC worksheet function to identify the proportion of a whole year's benefits or obligations to assign to a specific term.

Engineering functions

BIN2DEC(number)*

Converts a binary number to decimal.

BIN2HEX(number,places)*

Converts a binary number to hexadecimal.

BIN2OCT(number,places)*

Converts a binary number to octal.

CONVERT(number,from_unit,to_unit)*

Converts a number from one measurement system to another. For example, CONVERT can translate a table of distances in miles to a table of distances in kilometers.

DEC2BIN(number,places)*

Converts a decimal number to binary.

DEC2HEX(number,places)*

Converts a decimal number to hexadecimal.

DEC2OCT(number,places)*

Converts a decimal number to octal.

HEX2BIN(number,places)*

Converts a hexadecimal number to binary.

HEX2DEC(number)*

Converts a hexadecimal number to decimal.

Financial functions

ACCRINT(issue,first_interest,settlement,rate,par,frequency,basis)*

Returns the accrued interest for a security that pays periodic interest.

ACCRINTM(issue,maturity,rate,par,basis)*

Returns the accrued interest for a security that pays interest at maturity

AMORDEGRC(cost,date_purchased,first_period,salvage,period,rate,basis)*

Returns the depreciation for each accounting period. This function is provide for the French accounting system. If an asset is purchased in the middle of the accounting period, the prorated depreciation is taken into account. The function is similar to AMORLINC, except that a depreciation coefficient is applied in the calculation depending on the life of the assets.

AMORLINC(cost,date_purchased,first_period,salvage,period,rate,basis)

Returns the depreciation for each accounting period. This function is provided for the French accounting system. If an asset is purchased in the middle of the accounting period, the prorated depreciation is taken into account.

COUPDAYBS(settlement,maturity,frequency,basis)*

Returns the number of days from the beginning of the coupon period to the settlement date.

COUPDAYS(settlement,maturity,frequency,basis)*

Returns the number of days in the coupon period that contains the settlement date.

COUPDAYSNC(settlement,maturity,frequency,basis)*

Returns the number of days from the settlement date to the next coupon date.

COUPNCD(settlement,maturity,frequency,basis)*

Returns a number that represents the next coupon date after the settlement date. To view the number as a date, click Cells on the Format menu, click Date in the Category box, and then click a date format in the Type box.

COUPNUM(settlement,maturity,frequency,basis)*

Returns the number of coupons payable between the settlement date and maturity date, rounded up to the nearest whole coupon.

COUPPCD(settlement,maturity,frequency,basis)*

Returns a number that represents the previous coupon date before the settlement date. To view the number as a date, click Cells on the Format menu, click Date in the Category box, and then click a date format in the Type box.

CUMIPMT(rate,nper,pv,start_period,end_period,type)*

Returns the cumulative interest paid on a loan between start_period and end_period.

CUMPRINC(rate,nper,pv,start_period,end_period,type)*

Returns the cumulative principal paid on a loan between start_period and end_period.

DB(cost,salvage,life,period,month)

Returns the depreciation of an asset for a specified period using the fixed-declining balance method.

DDB(cost,salvage,life,period,factor)

Returns the depreciation of an asset for a specified period using the double-declining balance method or some other method you specify.

DISC(settlement,maturity,pr,redemption,basis)*

Returns the discount rate for a security.

DOLLARDE(fractional_dollar,fraction)*

Converts a dollar price expressed as a fraction into a dollar price expressed as a decimal number. Use DOLLARDE to convert fractional dollar numbers, such as securities prices, to decimal numbers.

DOLLARFR(decimal_dollar,fraction)*

Converts a dollar price expressed as a decimal number into a dollar price expressed as a fraction. Use DOLLARFR to convert decimal numbers to fractional dollar numbers, such as securities prices.

DURATION(settlement,maturity,coupon yld,frequency,basis)*

Returns the Macauley duration for an assumed par value of $100. Duration is defined as the weighted average of the present value of the cash flows and is used as a measure of a bond price's response to changes in yield.

EFFECT(nominal_rate,npery)*

Returns the effective annual interest rate, given the nominal annual interest rate and the number of compounding periods per year.

FV(rate,nper,pmt,pv,type)

Returns the future value of an investment based on periodic, constant payments and a constant interest rate.

FVSCHEDULE(principal,schedule)*

Returns the future value of an initial principal after applying a series of compound interest rates. Use FVSCHEDULE to calculate future value of an investment with a variable or adjustable rate.

INTRATE(settlement,maturity,investment,redemption,basis)*

Returns the interest rate for a fully invested security.

IPMT(rate,per,nper,pv,fv,type)

Returns the interest payment for a given period for an investment based on periodic, constant payments and a constant interest rate. For a more complete description of the arguments in IPMT and for more information about annuity functions, see PV.

IRR(values,guess)

Returns the internal rate of return for a series of cash flows represented by the numbers in values. These cash flows do not have to be even, as they would be for an annuity. However, the cash flows must occur at regular intervals, such as monthly or annually. The internal rate of return is the interest rate received for an investment consisting of payments (negative values) and income (positive values) that occur at regular periods.

ISPMT(rate,per,nper,pv)

Calculates the interest paid during a specific period of an investment. This function is provided for compatibility with Lotus 1-2-3.

MDURATION(settlement,maturity,coupon,yld,frequency,basis)*

Returns the modified duration for a security with an assumed par value of $100.

MIRR(values,finance_rate,reinvest_rate)

Returns the modified internal rate of return for a series of periodic cash flows. MIRR considers both the cost of the investment and the interest received on reinvestment of cash.

NOMINAL(effect_rate,npery)*

Returns the nominal annual interest rate, given the effective rate and the number of compounding periods per year.

NPER(rate, pmt, pv, fv, type)

Returns the number of periods for an investment based on periodic, constant payments and a constant interest rate.

NPV(rate,value1,value2, ...)

Calculates the net present value of an investment by using a discount rate and a series of future payments (negative values) and income (positive values).

ODDFPRICE(settlement,maturity,issue,first_coupon,rate,yld,redemption ,frequency,basis)*

Returns the price per $100 face value of a security having an odd (short or long) first period.

ODDFYIELD(settlement,maturity,issue,first_coupon,rate,pr,redemption,f requency,basis)*

Returns the yield of a security that has an odd (short or long) first period.

ODDLPRICE(settlement,maturity,last_interest,rate,yld,redemption,frequ ency,basis)*

Returns the price per $100 face value of a security having an odd (short or long) last coupon period.

ODDLYIELD(settlement,maturity,last_interest,rate,pr,redemption,frequency,basis)*

Returns the yield of a security that has an odd (short or long) last period.

PMT(rate,nper,pv,fv,type)

Calculates the payment for a loan based on constant payments and a constant interest rate.

PPMT(rate,per,nper,pv,fv,type)

Returns the payment on the principal for a given period for an investment based on periodic, constant payments and a constant interest rate.

PRICE(settlement,maturity,rate,yld,redemption,frequency,basis)*

Returns the price per $100 face value of a security that pays periodic interest.

PRICEDISC(settlement,maturity,discount,redemption,basis)*

Returns the price per $100 face value of a discounted security.

PRICEMAT(settlement,maturity,issue,rate,yld,basis)*

Returns the price per $100 face value of a security that pays interest at maturity.

PV(rate,nper,pmt,fv,type)

Returns the present value of an investment. The present value is the total amount that a series of future payments is worth now. For example, when you borrow money, the loan amount is the present value to the lender.

RATE(nper,pmt,pv,fv,type,guess)

Returns the interest rate per period of an annuity. RATE is calculated by iteration and can have zero or more solutions. If the successive results of RATE do not converge to within 0.0000001 after 20 iterations, RATE returns the #NUM! error value.

RECEIVED(settlement,maturity,investment,discount,basis)*

Returns the amount received at maturity for a fully invested security.

SLN(cost,salvage,life)

Returns the straight-line depreciation of an asset for one period.

SYD(cost,salvage,life,per)

Returns the sum-of-years' digits depreciation of an asset for a specified period.

TBILLEQ(settlement,maturity,discount)*

Returns the bond-equivalent yield for a Treasury bill.

TBILLPRICE(settlement,maturity,discount)*

Returns the price per $100 face value for a Treasury bill.

TBILLYIELD(settlement,maturity,pr)*

Returns the yield for a Treasury bill.

VDB(cost,salvage,life,start_period,end_period,factor,no_switch)

Returns the depreciation of an asset for any period you specify, including partial periods, using the double-declining balance method or some other method you specify. VDB stands for variable declining balance.

XIRR(values,dates,guess)*

Returns the internal rate of return for a schedule of cash flows that is not necessarily periodic. To calculate the internal rate of return for a series of periodic cash flows, use the IRR function.

XNPV(rate,values,dates)*

Returns the net present value for a schedule of cash flows that is not necessarily periodic. To calculate the net present value for a series of cash flows that is periodic, use the NPV function.

YIELD(settlement,maturity,rate,pr,redemption,frequency,basis)*

Returns the yield on a security that pays periodic interest. Use YIELD to calculate bond yield.

YIELDDISC(settlement,maturity,pr,redemption,basis)*

Returns the annual yield for a discounted security.

YIELDMAT(settlement,maturity,issue,rate,pr,basis)*

Returns the annual yield of a security that pays interest at maturity.

Information functions

CELL(info_type,reference)

Returns information about the formatting, location, or contents of the upper-left cell in a reference.

COUNTBLANK(range)

Counts empty cells in a specified range of cells.

INFO(type_text)

Returns information about the current operating environment.

ISBLANK(value)

Returns TRUE if Value refers to an empty cell.

ISERROR(value)

Returns TRUE if Value refers to any error value (#N/A, #VALUE!, #REF!, #DIV/0!, #NUM!, #NAME?, or #NULL!).

ISERR(value)

Returns TRUE if Value refers to any error value except #N/A.

ISEVEN(number)*

Returns TRUE if number is even, or FALSE if number is odd.

ISLOGICAL(value)

Returns TRUE if Value refers to a logical value.

ISNA(value)

Returns TRUE if Value refers to the #N/A (value not available) error value.

ISNONTEXT(value)

Returns TRUE if Value refers to any item that is not text. (Note that this function returns TRUE if value refers to a blank cell.)

ISNUMBER(value)

Returns TRUE if Value refers to a number.

ISODD(number)*

Returns TRUE if number is odd, or FALSE if number is even.

ISREF(value)

Returns TRUE if Value refers to a reference.

ISTEXT(value)

Returns TRUE if Value refers to text.

N(value)

Returns a value converted to a number.

NA( )

Returns the error value #N/A. #N/A is the error value that means "no value is available." Use NA to mark empty cells. By entering #N/A in cells where you are missing information, you can avoid the problem of unintentionally including empty cells in your calculations. (When a formula refers to a cell containing #N/A, the formula returns the #N/A error value.)

Logical functions

AND(logical1,logical2, ...)

Returns TRUE if all its arguments are TRUE; returns FALSE if one or more arguments is FALSE.

FALSE( )

Returns the logical value FALSE.

IF(logical_test,value_if_true,value_if_false)

Returns one value if a condition you specify evaluates to TRUE and another value if it evaluates to FALSE.

NOT(logical)

Reverses the value of its argument. Use NOT when you want to make sure a value is not equal to one particular value.

OR(logical1,logical2,...)

Returns TRUE if any argument is TRUE; returns FALSE if all arguments are FALSE.

TRUE( )

Returns the logical value TRUE.

Lookup functions

ADDRESS(row_num,column_num,abs_num,a1,sheet_text)

Creates a cell address as text, given specified row and column numbers.

AREAS(reference)

Returns the number of areas in a reference. An area is a range of contiguous cells or a single cell.

CHOOSE(index_num,value1,value2,...)

Uses index_num to return a value from the list of value arguments. Use CHOOSE to select one of up to 29 values based on the index number. For example, if value1 through value7 are the days of the week, CHOOSE returns one of the days when a number between 1 and 7 is used as index_num.

COLUMN(reference)

Returns the column number of the given reference.

COLUMNS(array)

Returns the number of columns in an array or reference.

HLOOKUP(lookup_value,table_array,row_index_num,range_lookup)

Searches for a value in the top row of a table or an array of values, and then returns a value in the same column from a row you specify in the table or array. Use HLOOKUP when your comparison values are located in a row across the top of a table of data, and you want to look down a specified number of rows. Use VLOOKUP when your comparison values are located in a column to the left of the data you want to find.

HYPERLINK(link_location,friendly_name)

Creates a shortcut or jump that opens a document stored on a network server, an intranet, or the Internet. When you click the cell that contains the HYPERLINK function, Microsoft Excel opens the file stored at link_location.

INDEX(array,row_num,column_num)

Returns the value of a specified cell or array of cells within array.

INDEX(reference,row_num,column_num,area_num)

Returns a reference to a specified cell or cells within reference.

INDIRECT(ref_text,a1)

Returns the reference specified by a text string. References are immediately evaluated to display their contents. Use INDIRECT when you want to change the reference to a cell within a formula without changing the formula itself.

LOOKUP(lookup_value,lookup_vector,result_vector)

Returns a value either from a one-row or one-column range. This vector form of LOOKUP looks in a one-row or one-column range (known as a vector) for a value and returns a value from the same position in a second one-row or one-column range. Included for compatibility with other worksheets. Use VLOOKUP instead.

LOOKUP(lookup_value,array)

Returns a value from an array. The array form of LOOKUP looks in the first row or column of an array for the specified value and returns a value from the same position in the last row or column of the array. Included for compatibility with other spreadsheet programs. Use VLOOKUP instead.

MATCH(lookup_value,lookup_array,match_type)

Returns the relative position of an item in an array that matches a specified value in a specified order. Use MATCH instead of one of the LOOKUP functions when you need the position of an item in a range instead of the item itself.

OFFSET(reference,rows,cols,height,width)

Returns a reference to a range that is a specified number of rows and columns from a cell or range of cells. The reference that is returned can be a single cell or a range of cells. You can specify the number of rows and the number of columns to be returned.

ROW(reference)

Returns the row number of a reference.

ROWS(array)

Returns the number of rows in a reference or array.

RTD(ProgID,Server,Topic,[Topic2],...)

New in Excel XP – Retrieves real-time data from a program that supports COM automation.

TRANSPOSE(array)

Returns a vertical range of cells as a horizontal range, or vice versa. TRANSPOSE must be entered as an array formula in a range that has the same number of rows and columns, respectively, as array has columns and rows. Use TRANSPOSE to shift the vertical and horizontal orientation of an array on a worksheet. For example, some functions, such as LINEST, return horizontal arrays. LINEST returns a horizontal array of the slope and Y-intercept for a line.

VLOOKUP(lookup_value,table_array,col_index_num,range_lookup)

Searches for a value in the leftmost column of a table, and then returns a value in the same row from a column you specify in the table. Use VLOOKUP instead of HLOOKUP when your comparison values are located in a column to the left of the data you want to find.

Math functions

ABS(number)

Returns the absolute value of a number. The absolute value of a number is the number without its sign.

CEILING(number,significance)

Returns number rounded up, away from zero, to the nearest multiple of significance. For example, if you want to avoid using pennies in your prices and your product is priced at $4.42, use the formula =CEILING(4.42,0.05) to round prices up to the nearest nickel.

COMBIN(number,number_chosen)

Returns the number of combinations for a given number of items. Use COMBIN to determine the total possible number of groups for a given number of items.

COUNTIF(range,criteria)

Counts the number of cells within a range that meet the given criteria.

EVEN(number)

Returns number rounded up to the nearest even integer. You can use this function for processing items that come in twos. For example, a packing crate accepts rows of one or two items. The crate is full when the number of items, rounded up to the nearest two, matches the crate's capacity.

EXP(number)

Returns e raised to the power of number. The constant e equals 2.71828182845904, the base of the natural logarithm.

FACT(number)

Returns the factorial of a number. The factorial of a number is equal to 1*2*3*...* number.

FLOOR(number,significance)

Rounds number down, toward zero, to the nearest multiple of significance.

GCD(number1,number2, ...)*

Returns the greatest common divisor of two or more integers. The greatest common divisor is the largest integer that divides both number1 and number2 without a remainder.

INT(number)

Rounds a number down to the nearest integer.

LCM(number1,number2, ...)*

Returns the least common multiple of integers. The least common multiple is the smallest positive integer that is a multiple of all integer arguments number1, number2, and so on. Use LCM to add fractions with different denominators.

MOD(number,divisor)

Returns the remainder after number is divided by divisor. The result has the same sign as divisor.

MROUND(number,multiple)*

Returns a number rounded to the desired multiple.

ODD(number)

Returns number rounded up to the nearest odd integer.

PI( )

Returns the number 3.14159265358979, the mathematical constant pi, accurate to 15 digits.

POWER(number,power)

Returns the result of a number raised to a power.

PRODUCT(number1,number2, ...)

Multiplies all the numbers given as arguments and returns the product.

QUOTIENT(numerator,denominator)*

Returns the integer portion of a division. Use this function when you want to discard the remainder of a division.

RAND( )

Returns an evenly distributed random number greater than or equal to 0 and less than 1. A new random number is returned every time the worksheet is calculated.

RANDBETWEEN(bottom,top)*

Returns a random number between the numbers you specify. A new random number is returned every time the worksheet is calculated.

ROMAN(number,form)

Converts an arabic numeral to roman, as text.

ROUND(number,num_digits)

Rounds a number to a specified number of digits.

ROUNDDOWN(number,num_digits)

Rounds a number down, toward zero.

ROUNDUP(number,num_digits)

Rounds a number up, away from 0 (zero).

SIGN(number)

Determines the sign of a number. Returns 1 if the number is positive, zero (0) if the number is 0, and -1 if the number is negative.

SQRT(number)

Returns a positive square root.

SUBTOTAL(function_num,ref1,ref2,...)

Returns a subtotal in a list or database. It is generally easier to create a list with subtotals using the Subtotals command (Data menu). Once the subtotal list is created, you can modify it by editing the SUBTOTAL function.

SUM(number1,number2, ...)

Adds all the numbers in a range of cells.

SUMIF(range,criteria,sum_range)

Adds the cells specified by a given criteria.

SUMPRODUCT(array1,array2,array3, ...)

Multiplies corresponding components in the given arrays, and returns the sum of those products.

TRUNC(number,num_digits)

Truncates a number to an integer by removing the fractional part of the number.

Statistical functions

AVEDEV(number1,number2, ...)

Returns the average of the absolute deviations of data points from their mean. AVEDEV is a measure of the variability in a data set.

AVERAGE(number1,number2, ...)

Returns the average (arithmetic mean) of the arguments.

AVERAGEA(value1,value2,...)

Calculates the average (arithmetic mean) of the values in the list of arguments. In addition to numbers, text and logical values such as TRUE and FALSE are included in the calculation.

CORREL(array1,array2)

Returns the correlation coefficient of the array1 and array2 cell ranges. Use the correlation coefficient to determine the relationship between two properties. For example, you can examine the relationship between a location's average temperature and the use of air conditioners.

COUNT(value1,value2, ...)

Counts the number of cells that contain numbers and numbers within the list of arguments. Use COUNT to get the number of entries in a number field in a range or array of numbers.

COUNTA(value1,value2, ...)

Counts the number of cells that are not empty and the values within the list of arguments. Use COUNTA to count the number of cells that contain data in a range or array.

FORECAST(x,known_y's,known_x's)

Calculates, or predicts, a future value by using existing values. The predicted value is a y-value for a given x-value. The known values are existing x-values and y-values, and the new value is predicted by using linear regression. You can use this function to predict future sales, inventory requirements, or consumer trends.

FREQUENCY(data_array,bins_array)

Calculates how often values occur within a range of values, and then returns a vertical array of numbers. For example, use FREQUENCY to count the number of test scores that fall within ranges of scores. Because FREQUENCY returns an array, it must be entered as an array formula.

GEOMEAN(number1,number2, ...)

Returns the geometric mean of an array or range of positive data. For example, you can use GEOMEAN to calculate average growth rate given compound interest with variable rates.

GROWTH(known_y's,known_x's,new_x's,const)

Calculates predicted exponential growth by using existing data. GROWTH returns the y-values for a series of new x-values that you specify by using existing x-values and y-values. You can also use the GROWTH worksheet function to fit an exponential curve to existing x-values and y-values.

INTERCEPT(known_y's,known_x's)

Calculates the point at which a line will intersect the y-axis by using existing x-values and y-values. The intercept point is based on a best-fit regression line plotted through the known x-values and known y-values. Use the intercept when you want to determine the value of the dependent variable when the independent variable is 0 (zero). For example, you can use the INTERCEPT function to predict a metal's electrical resistance at 0°C when your data points were taken at room temperature and higher.

LARGE(array,k)

Returns the k-th largest value in a data set. You can use this function to select a value based on its relative standing. For example, you can use LARGE to return the highest, runner-up, or third-place score.

LINEST(known_y's,known_x's,const,stats)

Calculates the statistics for a line by using the "least squares" method to calculate a straight line that best fits your data, and returns an array that describes the line. Because this function returns an array of values, it must be entered as an array formula.

LOGEST(known_y's,known_x's,const,stats)

In regression analysis, calculates an exponential curve that fits your data and returns an array of values that describes the curve. Because this function returns an array of values, it must be entered as an array formula.

MAX(number1,number2,...)

Returns the largest value in a set of values.

MAXA(value1,value2,...)

Returns the largest value in a list of arguments. Text and logical values such as TRUE and FALSE are compared as well as numbers.

MEDIAN(number1,number2, ...)

Returns the median of the given numbers. The median is the number in the middle of a set of numbers; that is, half the numbers have values that are greater than the median, and half have values that are less.

MIN(number1,number2, ...)

Returns the smallest number in a set of values.

MINA(value1,value2,...)

Returns the smallest value in the list of arguments. Text and logical values such as TRUE and FALSE are compared as well as numbers.

MODE(number1,number2, ...)

Returns the most frequently occurring, or repetitive, value in an array or range of data. Like MEDIAN, MODE is a location measure.

NORMDIST(x,mean,standard_dev,cumulative)

Returns the normal cumulative distribution for the specified mean and standard deviation. This function has a very wide range of applications in statistics, including hypothesis testing.

PERCENTILE(array,k)

Returns the k-th percentile of values in a range. You can use this function to establish a threshold of acceptance. For example, you can decide to examine candidates who score above the 90th percentile.

PERCENTRANK(array,x,significance)

Returns the rank of a value in a data set as a percentage of the data set. This function can be used to evaluate the relative standing of a value within a data set. For example, you can use PERCENTRANK to evaluate the standing of an aptitude test score among all scores for the test.

PERMUT(number,number_chosen)

Returns the number of permutations for a given number of objects that can be selected from number objects. A permutation is any set or subset of objects or events where internal order is significant. Permutations are different from combinations, for which the internal order is not significant. Use this function for lottery-style probability calculations.

PROB(x_range,prob_range,lower_limit,upper_limit)

Returns the probability that values in a range are between two limits. If upper_limit is not supplied, returns the probability that values in x_range are equal to lower_limit.

QUARTILE(array,quart)

Returns the quartile of a data set. Quartiles often are used in sales and survey data to divide populations into groups. For example, you can use QUARTILE to find the top 25 percent of incomes in a population.

RANK(number,ref,order)

Returns the rank of a number in a list of numbers. The rank of a number is its size relative to other values in a list. (If you were to sort the list, the rank of the number would be its position.)

SLOPE(known_y's,known_x's)

Returns the slope of the linear regression line through data points in known_y's and known_x's. The slope is the vertical distance divided by the horizontal distance between any two points on the line, which is the rate of change along the regression line.

SMALL(array,k)

Returns the k-th smallest value in a data set. Use this function to return values with a particular relative standing in a data set.

STDEV(number1,number2,...)

Estimates standard deviation based on a sample. The standard deviation is a measure of how widely values are dispersed from the average value (the mean).

TREND(known_y's,known_x's,new_x's,const)

Returns values along a linear trend. Fits a straight line (using the method of least squares) to the arrays known_y's and known_x's. Returns the y-values along that line for the array of new_x's that you specify.

TRIMMEAN(array,percent)

Returns the mean of the interior of a data set. TRIMMEAN calculates the mean taken by excluding a percentage of data points from the top and bottom tails of a data set. You can use this function when you wish to exclude outlying data from your analysis.

VAR(number1,number2,...)

Estimates variance based on a sample.

Text and data functions

ASC(text)

Changes full-width (double-byte) English letters or katakana within a character string to half-width (single-byte) characters.

CHAR(number)

Returns the character specified by a number. Use CHAR to translate code page numbers you might get from files on other types of computers into characters.

CLEAN(text)

Removes all nonprintable characters from text. Use CLEAN on text imported from other applications that contains characters that may not print with your operating system. For example, you can use CLEAN to remove some low-level computer code that is frequently at the beginning and end of data files and cannot be printed.

CODE(text)

Returns a numeric code for the first character in a text string. The returned code corresponds to the character set used by your computer.

CONCATENATE(text1,text2,...)

Joins several text strings into one text string.

DOLLAR(number,decimals)

Converts a number to text using currency format, with the decimals rounded to the specified place. The format used is $#,##0.00_);($#,##0.00).

EXACT(text1,text2)

Compares two text strings and returns TRUE if they are exactly the same, FALSE otherwise. EXACT is case-sensitive but ignores formatting differences. Use EXACT to test text being entered into a document.

FIND(find_text,within_text,start_num)

FIND finds one text string (find_text) within another text string (within_text), and returns the number of the starting position of find_text, from the first character of within_text. You can also use SEARCH to find one text string within another, but unlike SEARCH, FIND is case sensitive and doesn't allow wildcard characters.

FIXED(number,decimals,no_commas)

Rounds a number to the specified number of decimals, formats the number in decimal format using a period and commas, and returns the result as text.

LEFT(text,num_chars)

LEFT returns the first character or characters in a text string, based on the number of characters you specify.

LEN(text)

LEN returns the number of characters in a text string.

LOWER(text)

Converts all uppercase letters in a text string to lowercase.

MID(text,start_num,num_chars)

MID returns a specific number of characters from a text string, starting at the position you specify, based on the number of characters you specify.

PROPER(text)

Capitalizes the first letter in a text string and any other letters in text that follow any character other than a letter. Converts all other letters to lowercase letters.

REPLACE(old_text,start_num,num_chars,new_text)

REPLACE replaces part of a text string, based on the number of characters you specify, with a different text string.

REPT(text,number_times)

Repeats text a given number of times. Use REPT to fill a cell with a number of instances of a text string.

RIGHT(text,num_chars)

RIGHT returns the last character or characters in a text string, based on the number of characters you specify.

SEARCH(find_text,within_text,start_num)

SEARCH returns the number of the character at which a specific character or text string is first found, beginning with start_num. Use SEARCH to determine the location of a character or text string within another text string so that you can use the MID or REPLACE functions to change the text.

SUBSTITUTE(text,old_text,new_text,instance_num)

Substitutes new_text for old_text in a text string. Use SUBSTITUTE when you want to replace specific text in a text string; use REPLACE when you want to replace any text that occurs in a specific location in a text string.

T(value)

Returns the text referred to by value.

TEXT(value,format_text)

Converts a value to text in a specific number format.

TRIM(text)

Removes all spaces from text except for single spaces between words. Use TRIM on text that you have received from another application that may have irregular spacing.

UPPER(text)

Converts text to uppercase.

VALUE(text)

Converts a text string that represents a number to a number.

Quick Order Form

Fax orders: 702-220-4510. Send this form.

Email orders: orders@MaxVol.com

Mail orders: Holy Maurici, 12380 Aud, Uniontown OH 44685

Web orders: www.MaxVol.com

Please send the following books:

Name

Address

Telephone

Email

Sales Tax: Please add 5.75% for products shipped to Ohio.

Payment: ___ Check ___ Mastercard ___ Visa ___ Amex

Card Number:

Name on Card: ___ Exp. ___

Quick Order Form

Fax orders: 707-220-4510. Send this form.

E-mail orders: orders@MrExcel.com

Mail orders: Holy Macro!, 13386 Judy, Uniontown OH 44685

Web orders: www.MrExcel.com

Please send the following books:

_____

_____

Name: _____

Address: _____

Telephone: _____

E-Mail: _____

Sales Tax: Please add 5.25% for products shipped to Ohio.

Payment: ___ Check ___ Mastercard ___ Visa ___ AmEx

Card Number: _____

Name on Card: _____**Exp:** _____